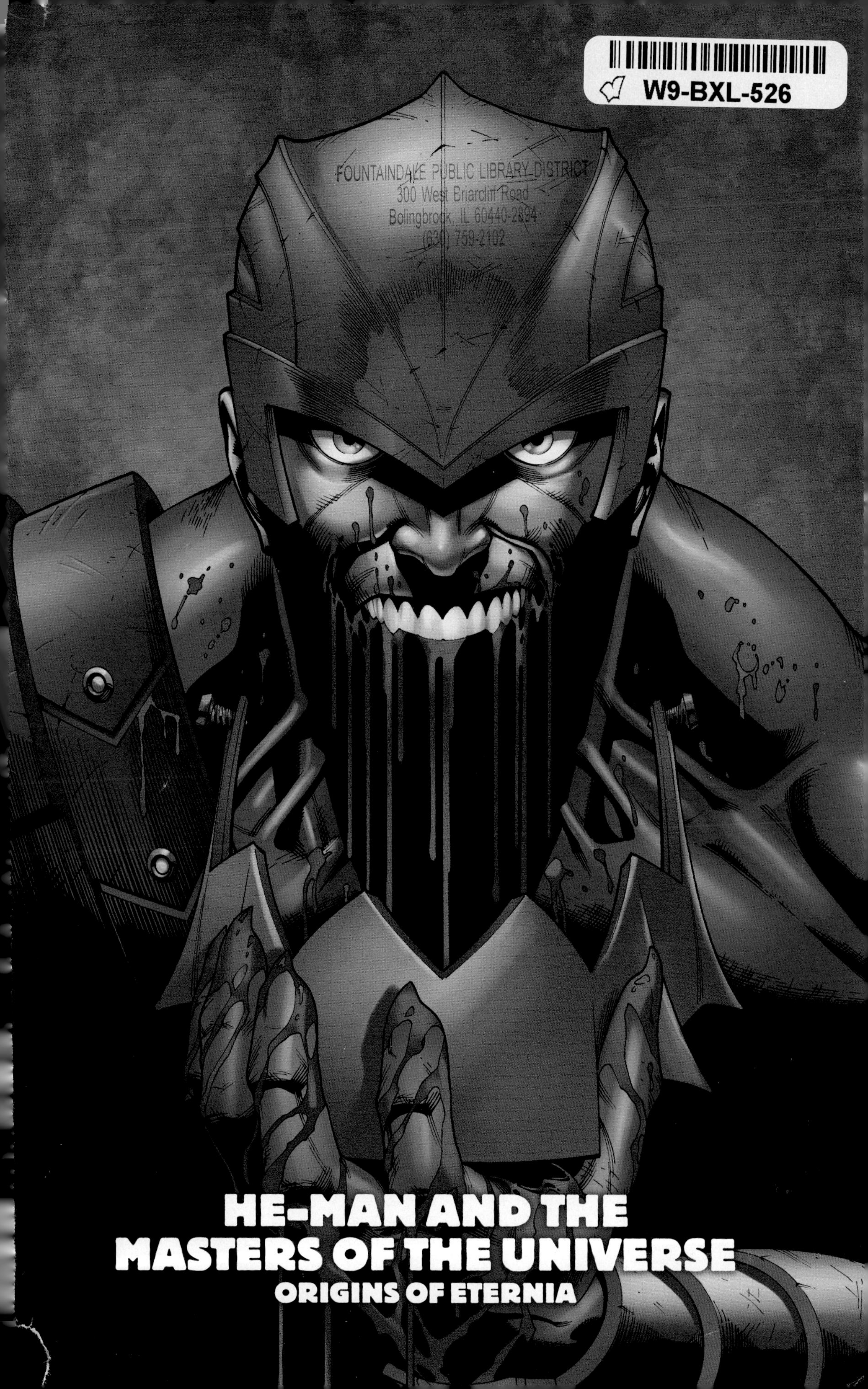

FOUNTAINDALE PUBLIC LIBRARY DISTRICT
300 West Briarcliff Road
Bolingbrook, IL 60440-2894
(630) 759-2102
HE-MAN AND THE
MASTERS OF THE UNIVERSE
ORIGINS OF ETERNIA

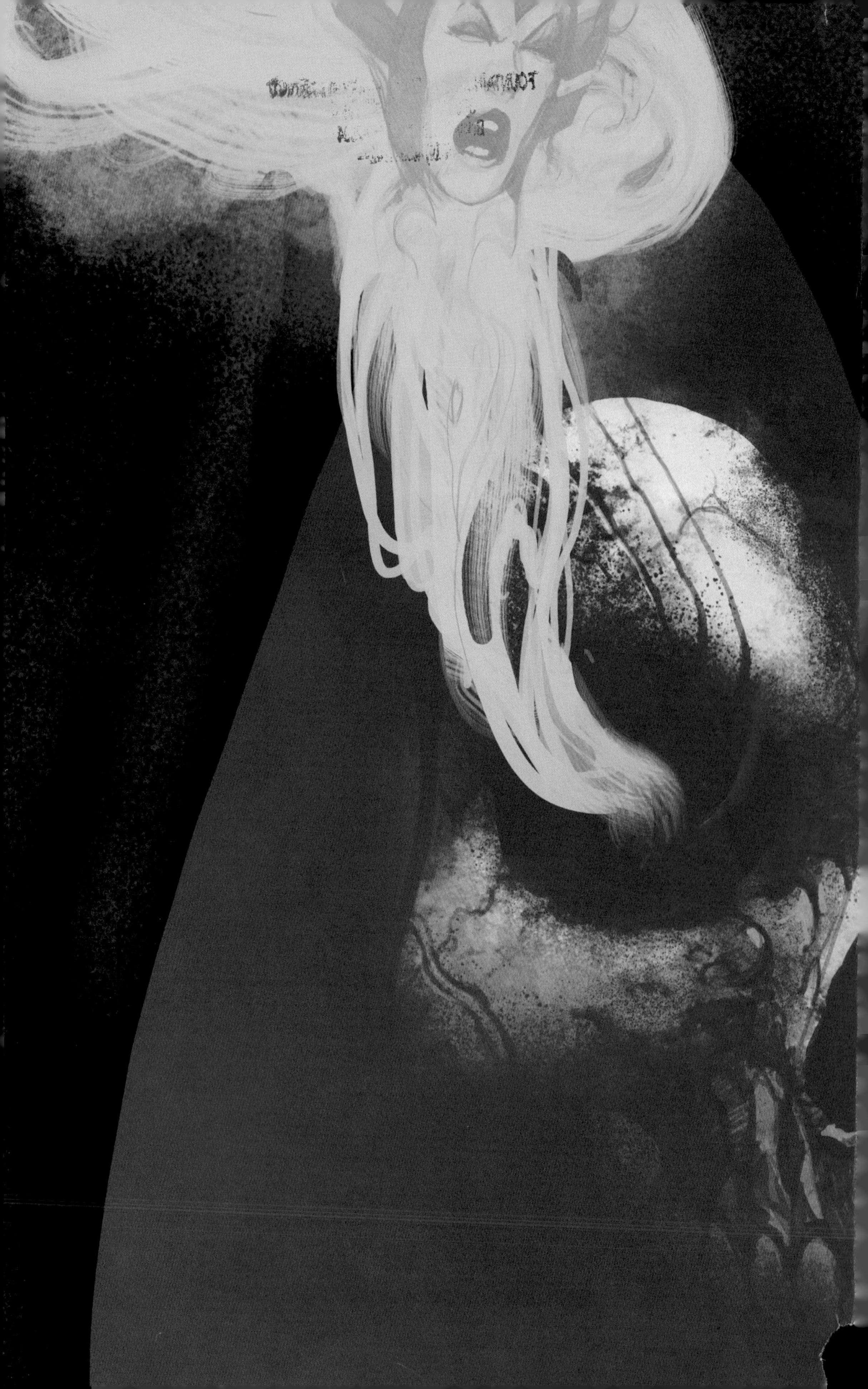

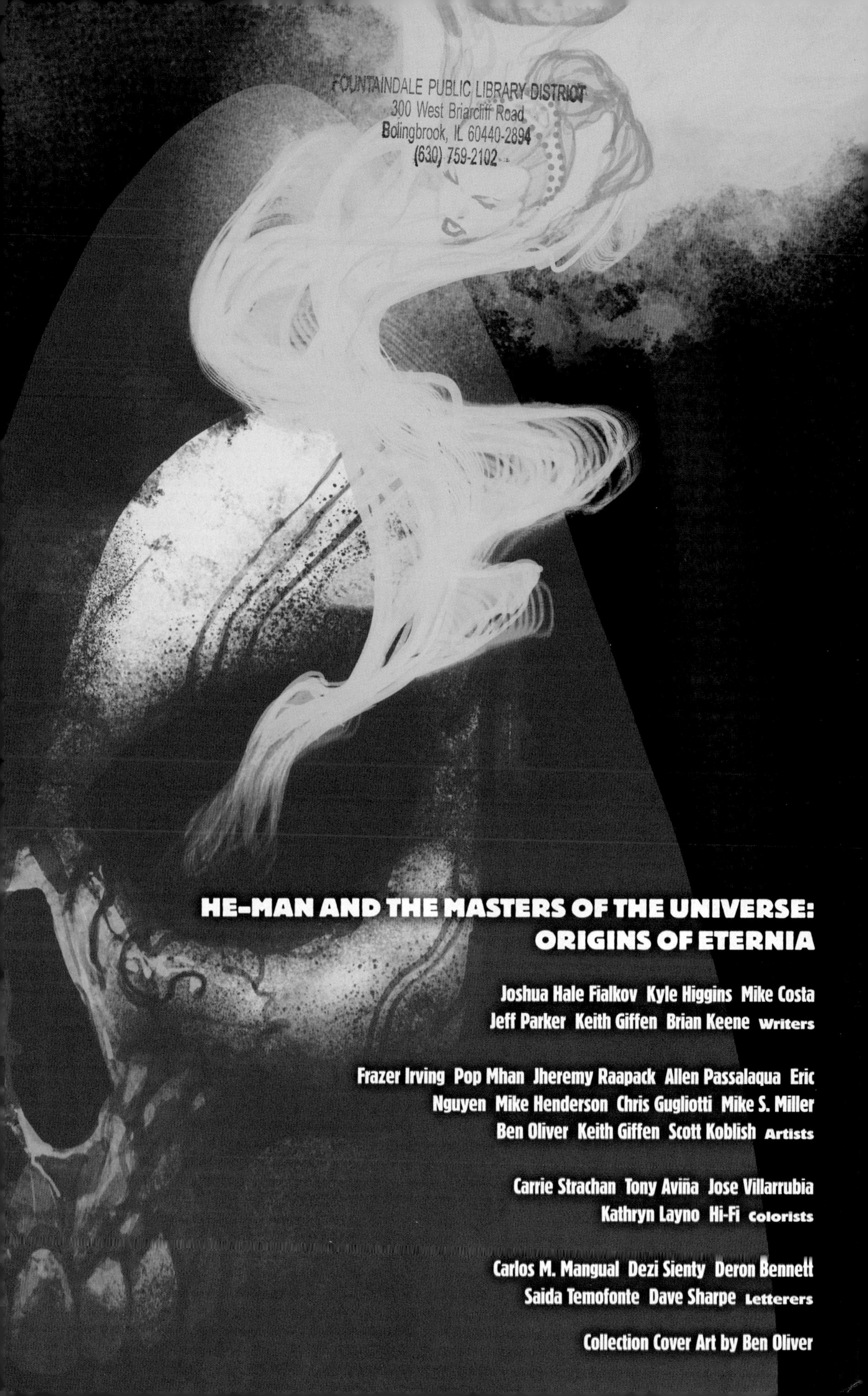

HE-MAN AND THE MASTERS OF THE UNIVERSE: ORIGINS OF ETERNIA

Joshua Hale Fialkov Kyle Higgins Mike Costa
Jeff Parker Keith Giffen Brian Keene **Writers**

Frazer Irving Pop Mhan Jheremy Raapack Allen Passalaqua Eric Nguyen Mike Henderson Chris Gugliotti Mike S. Miller Ben Oliver Keith Giffen Scott Koblish **Artists**

Carrie Strachan Tony Aviña Jose Villarrubia
Kathryn Layno Hi-Fi **Colorists**

Carlos M. Mangual Dezi Sienty Deron Bennett
Saida Temofonte Dave Sharpe **Letterers**

Collection Cover Art by Ben Oliver

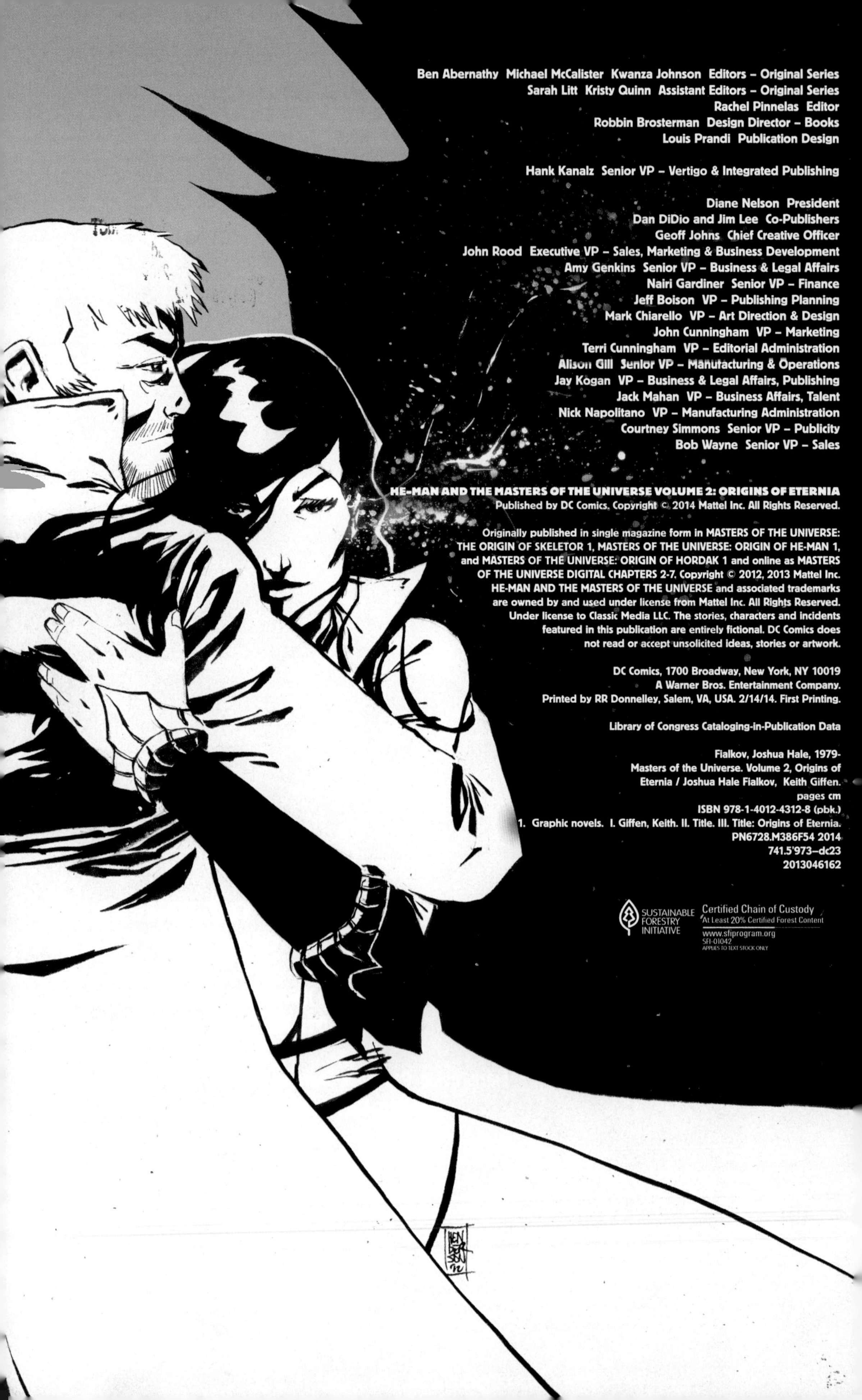

Ben Abernathy Michael McCalister Kwanza Johnson Editors – Original Series
Sarah Litt Kristy Quinn Assistant Editors – Original Series
Rachel Pinnelas Editor
Robbin Brosterman Design Director – Books
Louis Prandi Publication Design

Hank Kanalz Senior VP – Vertigo & Integrated Publishing

Diane Nelson President
Dan DiDio and Jim Lee Co-Publishers
Geoff Johns Chief Creative Officer
John Rood Executive VP – Sales, Marketing & Business Development
Amy Genkins Senior VP – Business & Legal Affairs
Nairi Gardiner Senior VP – Finance
Jeff Boison VP – Publishing Planning
Mark Chiarello VP – Art Direction & Design
John Cunningham VP – Marketing
Terri Cunningham VP – Editorial Administration
Alison Gill Senior VP – Manufacturing & Operations
Jay Kogan VP – Business & Legal Affairs, Publishing
Jack Mahan VP – Business Affairs, Talent
Nick Napolitano VP – Manufacturing Administration
Courtney Simmons Senior VP – Publicity
Bob Wayne Senior VP – Sales

HE-MAN AND THE MASTERS OF THE UNIVERSE VOLUME 2: ORIGINS OF ETERNIA

DC Comics, 1700 Broadway, New York, NY 10019
A Warner Bros. Entertainment Company.
Printed by RR Donnelley, Salem, VA, USA. 2/14/14. First Printing.

Library of Congress Cataloging-in-Publication Data

Fialkov, Joshua Hale, 1979-
Masters of the Universe. Volume 2, Origins of Eternia / Joshua Hale Fialkov, Keith Giffen.
pages cm
ISBN 978-1-4012-4312-8 (pbk.)
1. Graphic novels. I. Giffen, Keith. II. Title. III. Title: Origins of Eternia.
PN6728.M386F54 2014
741.5'973–dc23
2013046162

SUSTAINABLE FORESTRY INITIATIVE
Certified Chain of Custody
At Least 20% Certified Forest Content
www.sfiprogram.org
SFI-01042
APPLIES TO TEXT STOCK ONLY

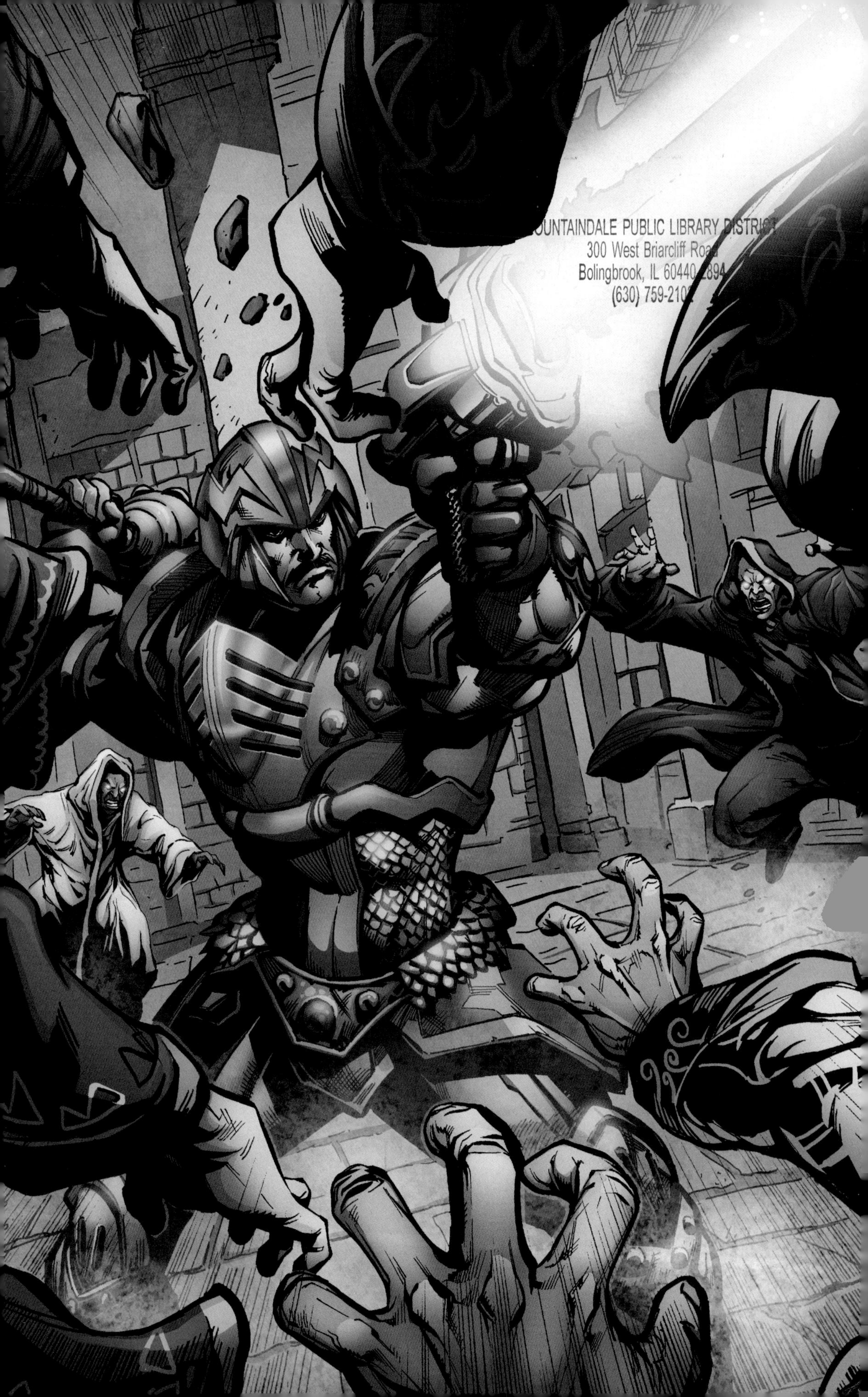

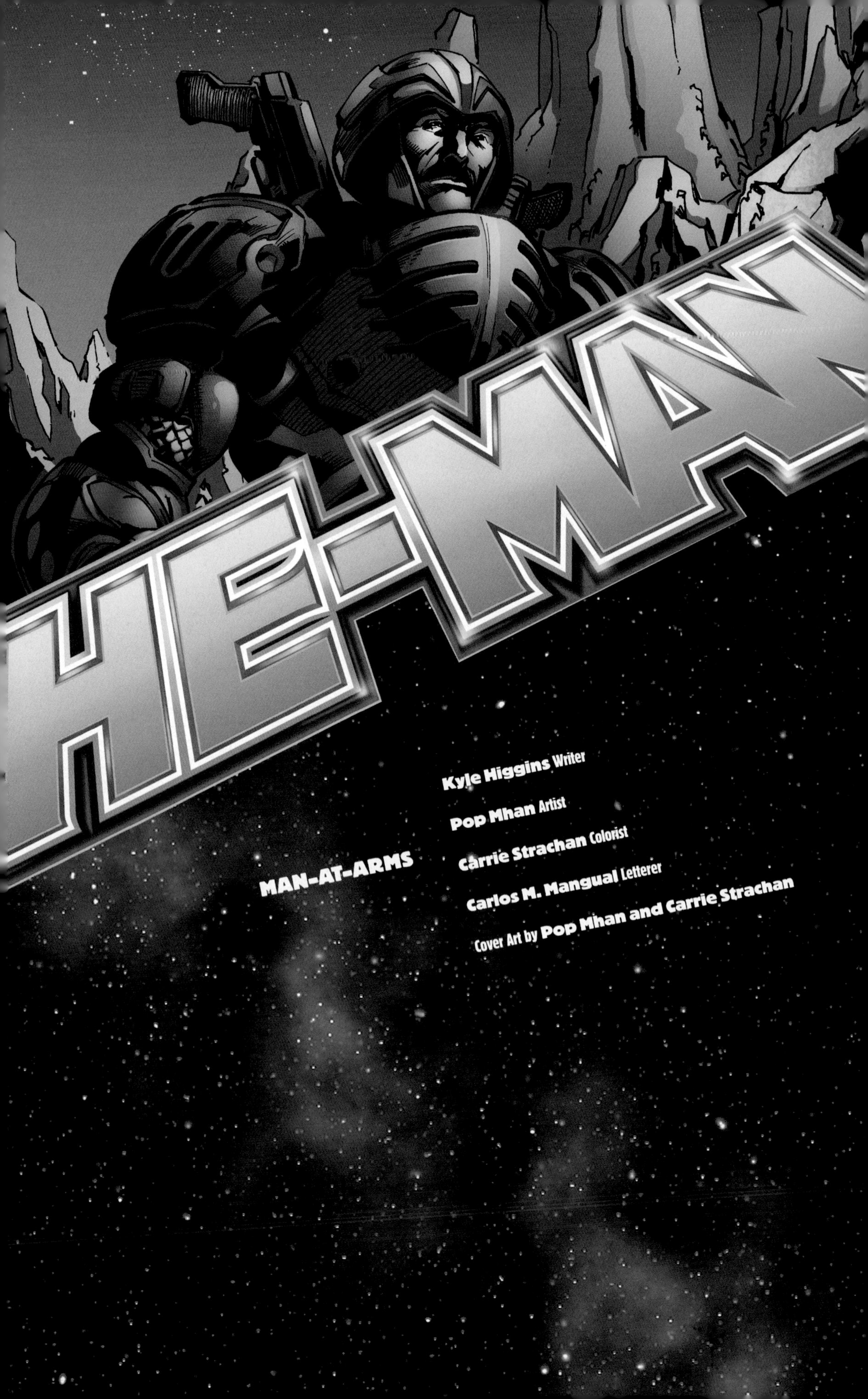
HE-MAN
MAN-AT-ARMS
Kyle Higgins Writer
Pop Mhan Artist
Carrie Strachan Colorist
Carlos M. Mangual Letterer
Cover Art by Pop Mhan and Carrie Strachan

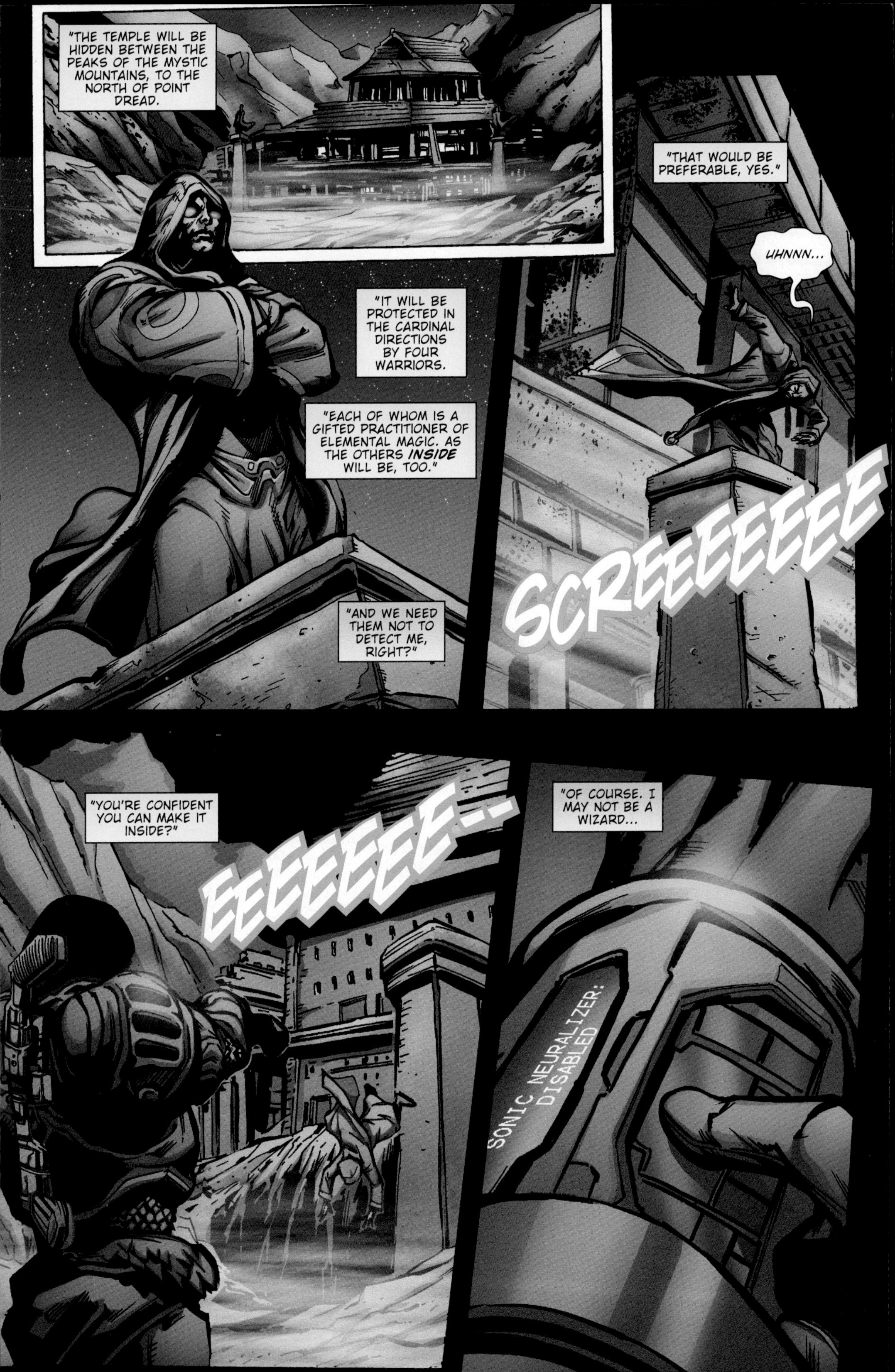
"THE TEMPLE WILL BE HIDDEN BETWEEN THE PEAKS OF THE MYSTIC MOUNTAINS, TO THE NORTH OF POINT DREAD.
"IT WILL BE PROTECTED IN THE CARDINAL DIRECTIONS BY FOUR WARRIORS.
"EACH OF WHOM IS A GIFTED PRACTITIONER OF ELEMENTAL MAGIC. AS THE OTHERS INSIDE WILL BE, TOO."
"AND WE NEED THEM NOT TO DETECT ME, RIGHT?"
"THAT WOULD BE PREFERABLE, YES."
UHNNN...
SCREEEEEEEE
"YOU'RE CONFIDENT YOU CAN MAKE IT INSIDE?"
EEEEEEEE--
"OF COURSE. I MAY NOT BE A WIZARD...
SONIC NEURALIZER: DISABLED

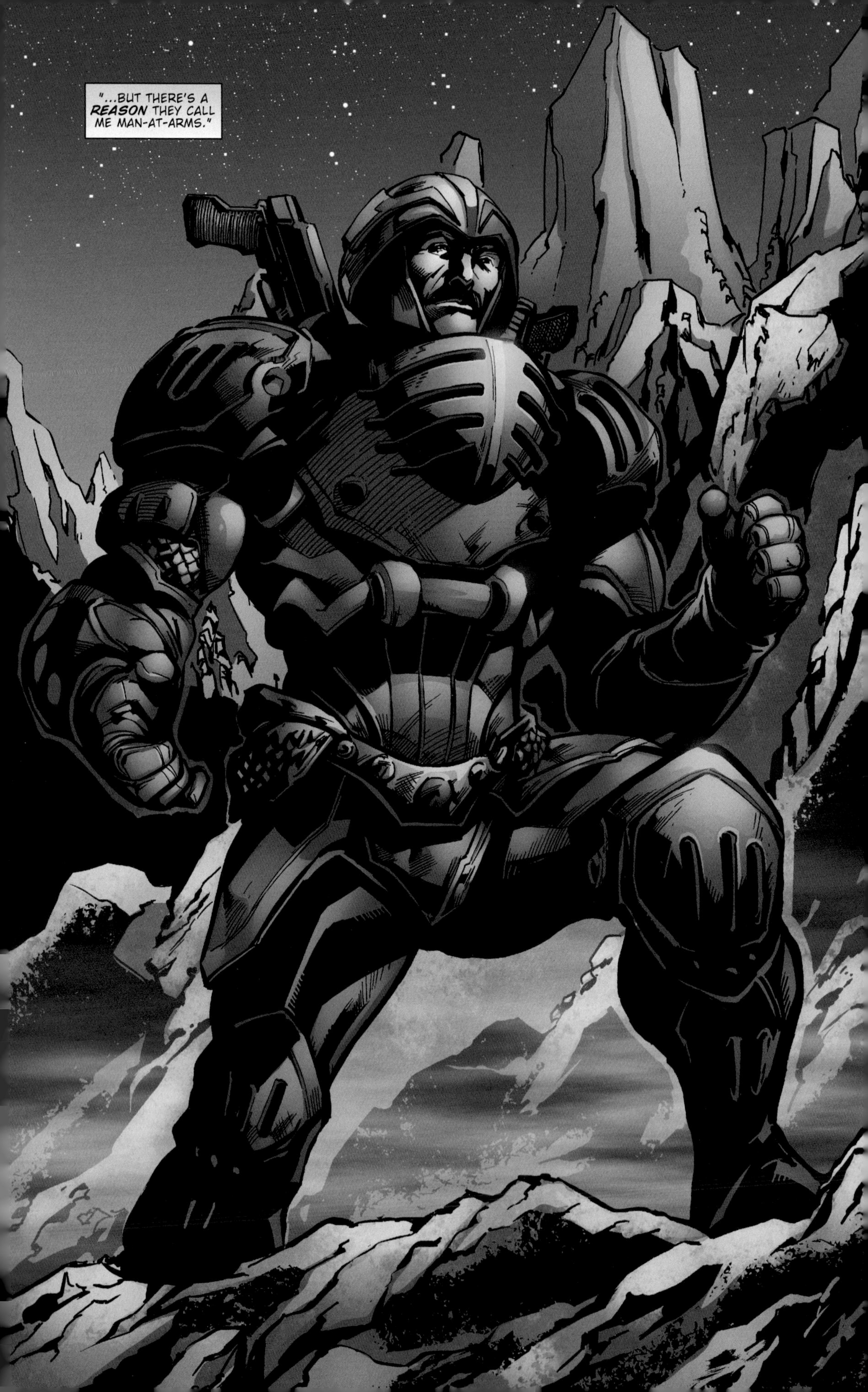
"...BUT THERE'S A REASON THEY CALL ME MAN-AT-ARMS."

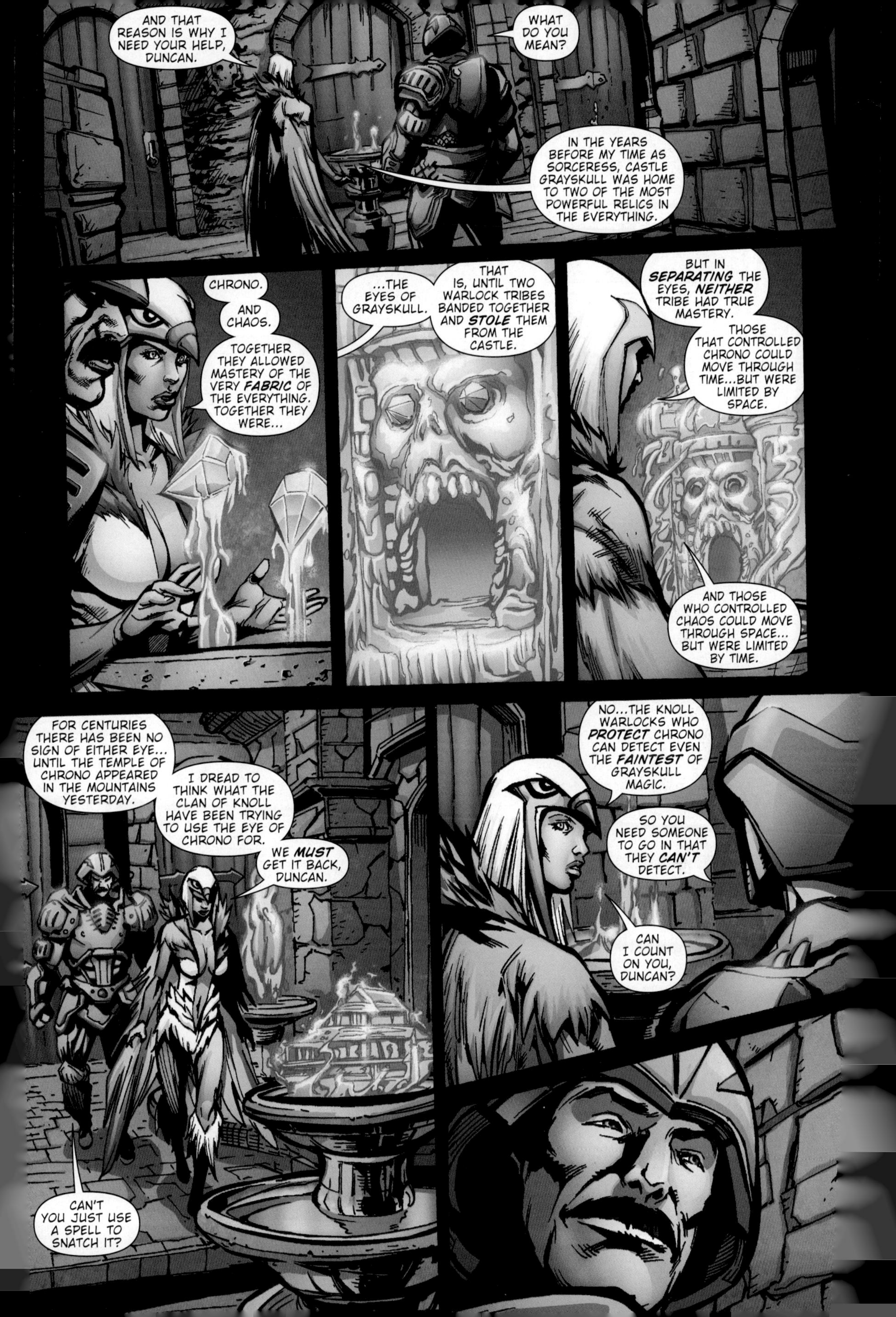
AND THAT REASON IS WHY I NEED YOUR HELP, DUNCAN.
WHAT DO YOU MEAN?
IN THE YEARS BEFORE MY TIME AS SORCERESS, CASTLE GRAYSKULL WAS HOME TO TWO OF THE MOST POWERFUL RELICS IN THE EVERYTHING.
CHRONO.
AND CHAOS.
TOGETHER THEY ALLOWED MASTERY OF THE VERY FABRIC OF THE EVERYTHING. TOGETHER THEY WERE...
...THE EYES OF GRAYSKULL.
THAT IS, UNTIL TWO WARLOCK TRIBES BANDED TOGETHER AND STOLE THEM FROM THE CASTLE.
BUT IN SEPARATING THE EYES, NEITHER TRIBE HAD TRUE MASTERY.
THOSE THAT CONTROLLED CHRONO COULD MOVE THROUGH TIME...BUT WERE LIMITED BY SPACE.
AND THOSE WHO CONTROLLED CHAOS COULD MOVE THROUGH SPACE... BUT WERE LIMITED BY TIME.
FOR CENTURIES THERE HAS BEEN NO SIGN OF EITHER EYE... UNTIL THE TEMPLE OF CHRONO APPEARED IN THE MOUNTAINS YESTERDAY.
I DREAD TO THINK WHAT THE CLAN OF KNOLL HAVE BEEN TRYING TO USE THE EYE OF CHRONO FOR.
WE MUST GET IT BACK, DUNCAN.
CAN'T YOU JUST USE A SPELL TO SNATCH IT?
NO...THE KNOLL WARLOCKS WHO PROTECT CHRONO CAN DETECT EVEN THE FAINTEST OF GRAYSKULL MAGIC.
SO YOU NEED SOMEONE TO GO IN THAT THEY CAN'T DETECT.
CAN I COUNT ON YOU, DUNCAN?

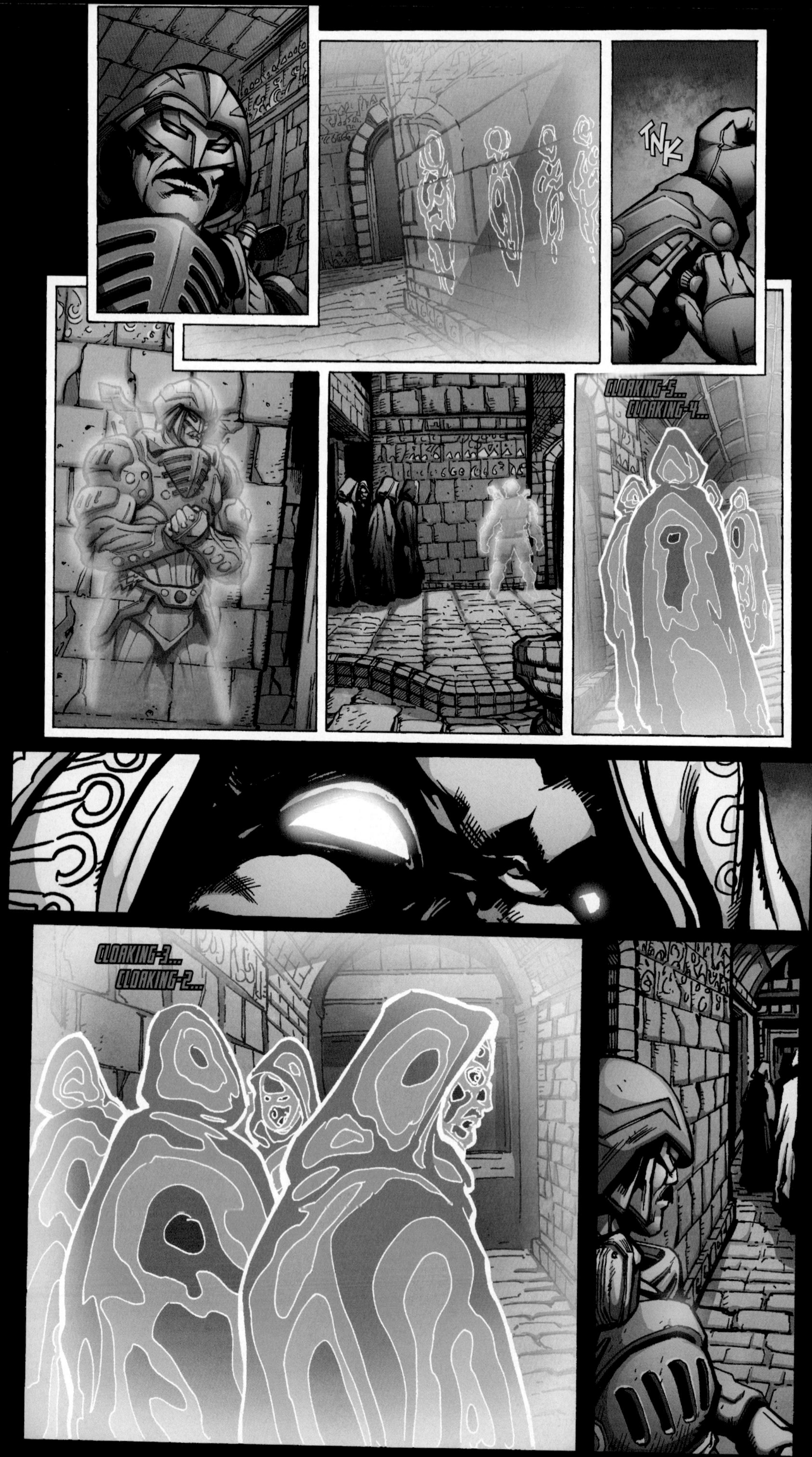
TNK
CLOAKING-5...
CLOAKING-4...
CLOAKING-3...
CLOAKING-2...

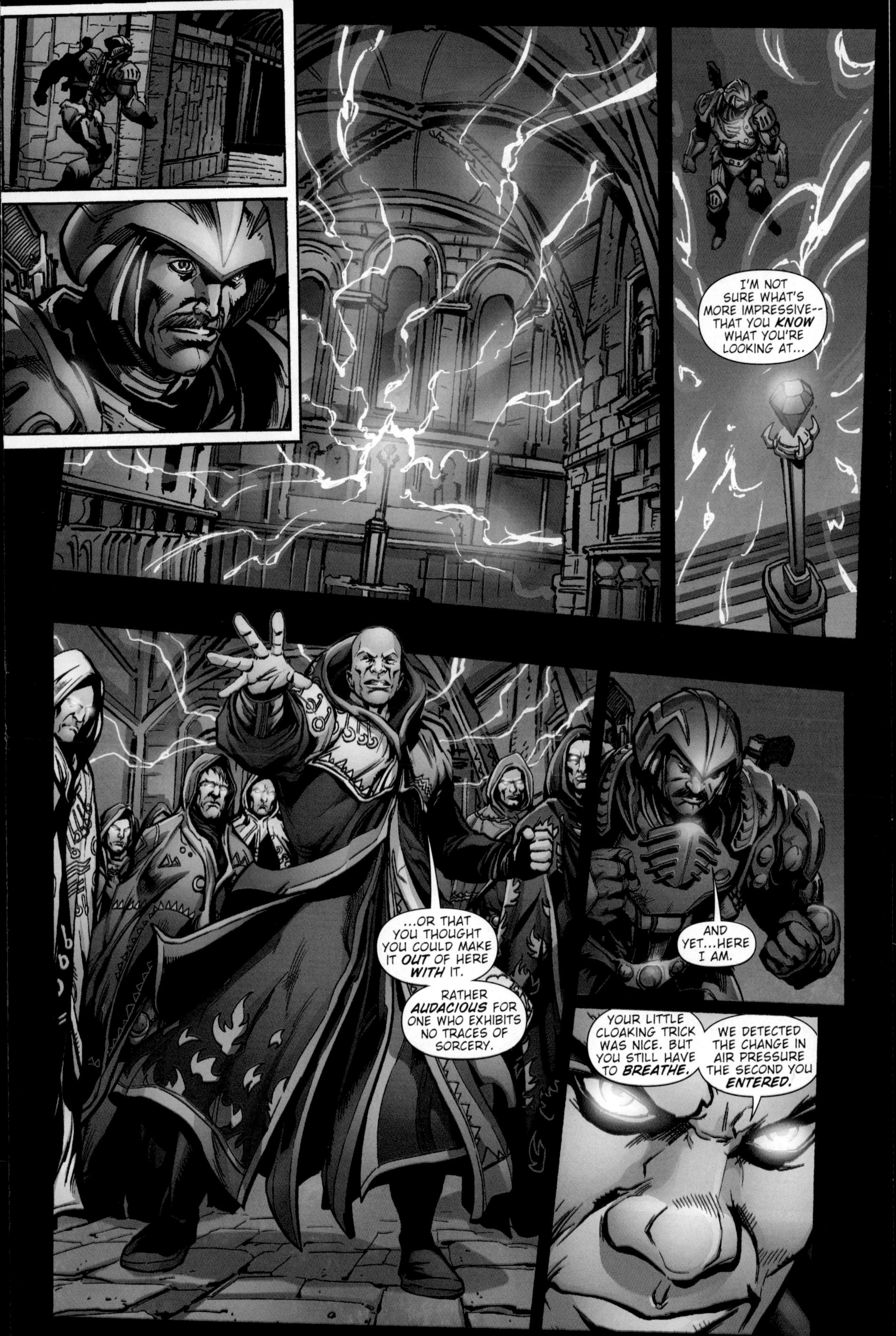

I'M NOT SURE WHAT'S MORE IMPRESSIVE-- THAT YOU KNOW WHAT YOU'RE LOOKING AT...
...OR THAT YOU THOUGHT YOU COULD MAKE IT OUT OF HERE WITH IT.
RATHER AUDACIOUS FOR ONE WHO EXHIBITS NO TRACES OF SORCERY.
AND YET...HERE I AM.
YOUR LITTLE CLOAKING TRICK WAS NICE. BUT YOU STILL HAVE TO BREATHE.
WE DETECTED THE CHANGE IN AIR PRESSURE THE SECOND YOU ENTERED.

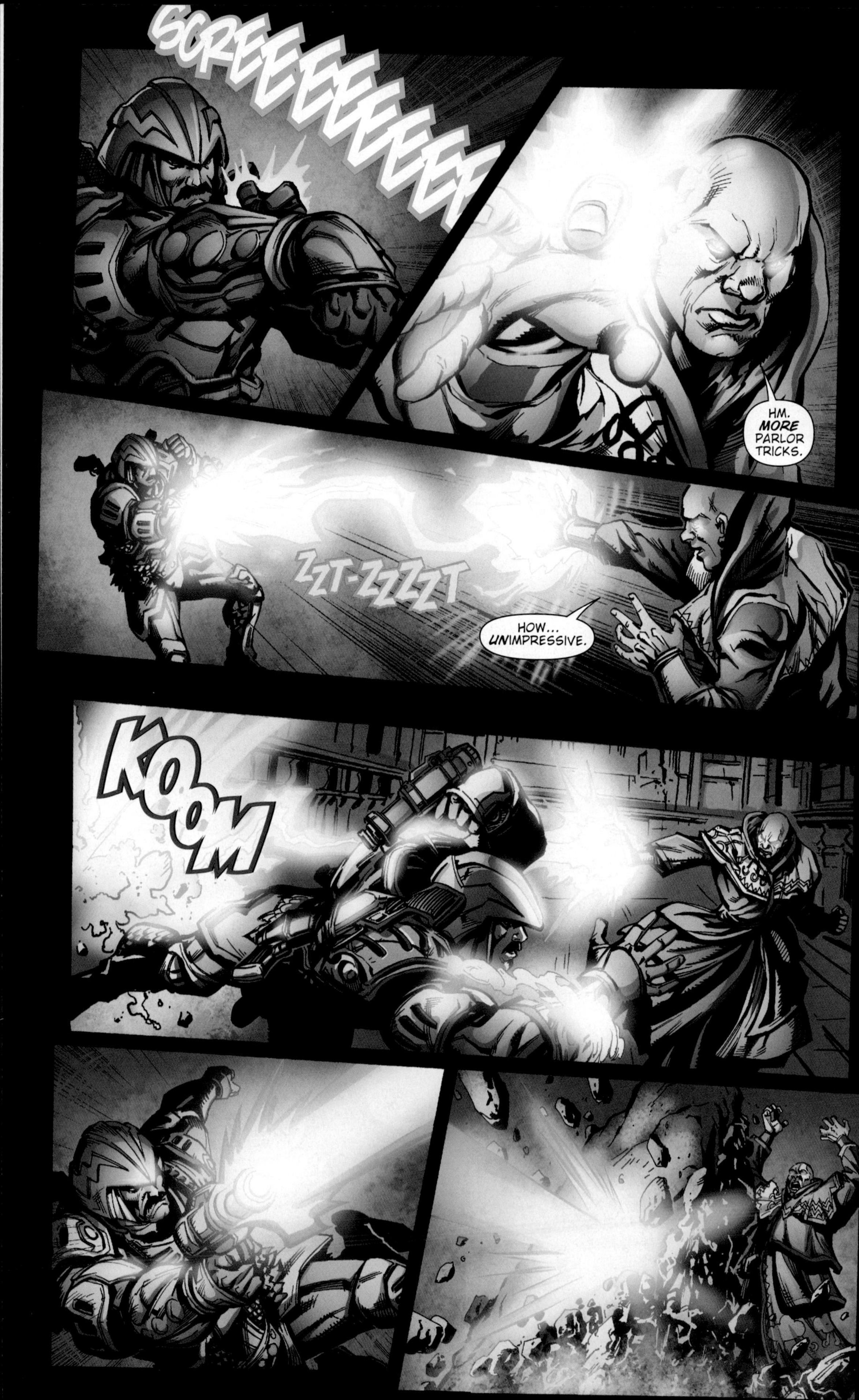
SCREEEEEEEEEP
HM. MORE PARLOR TRICKS.
ZZT-ZZZZZT
HOW... UNIMPRESSIVE.
KOOOM

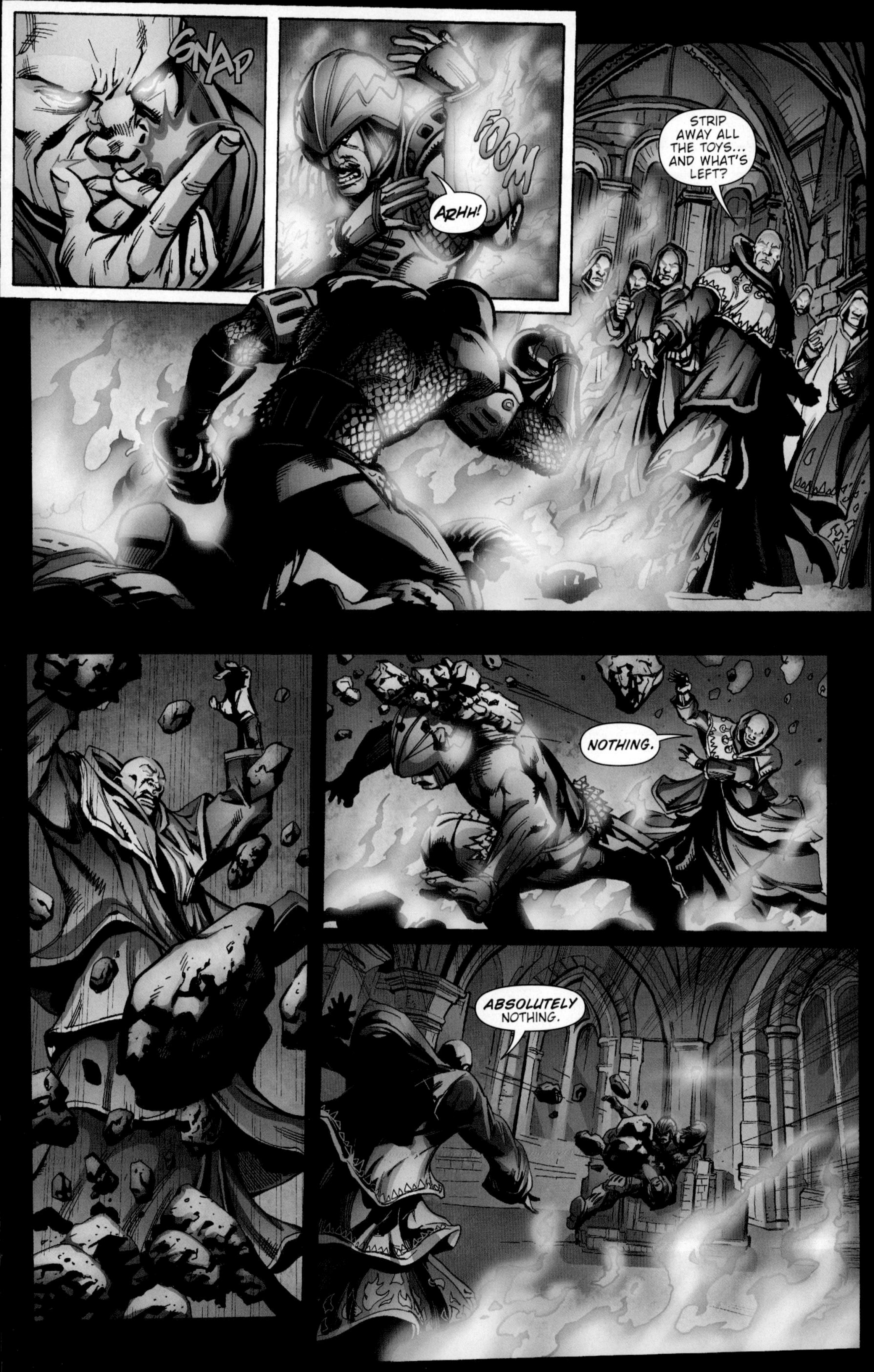
SNAP
FOOM
ARHH!
STRIP AWAY ALL THE TOYS... AND WHAT'S LEFT?
NOTHING.
ABSOLUTELY NOTHING.

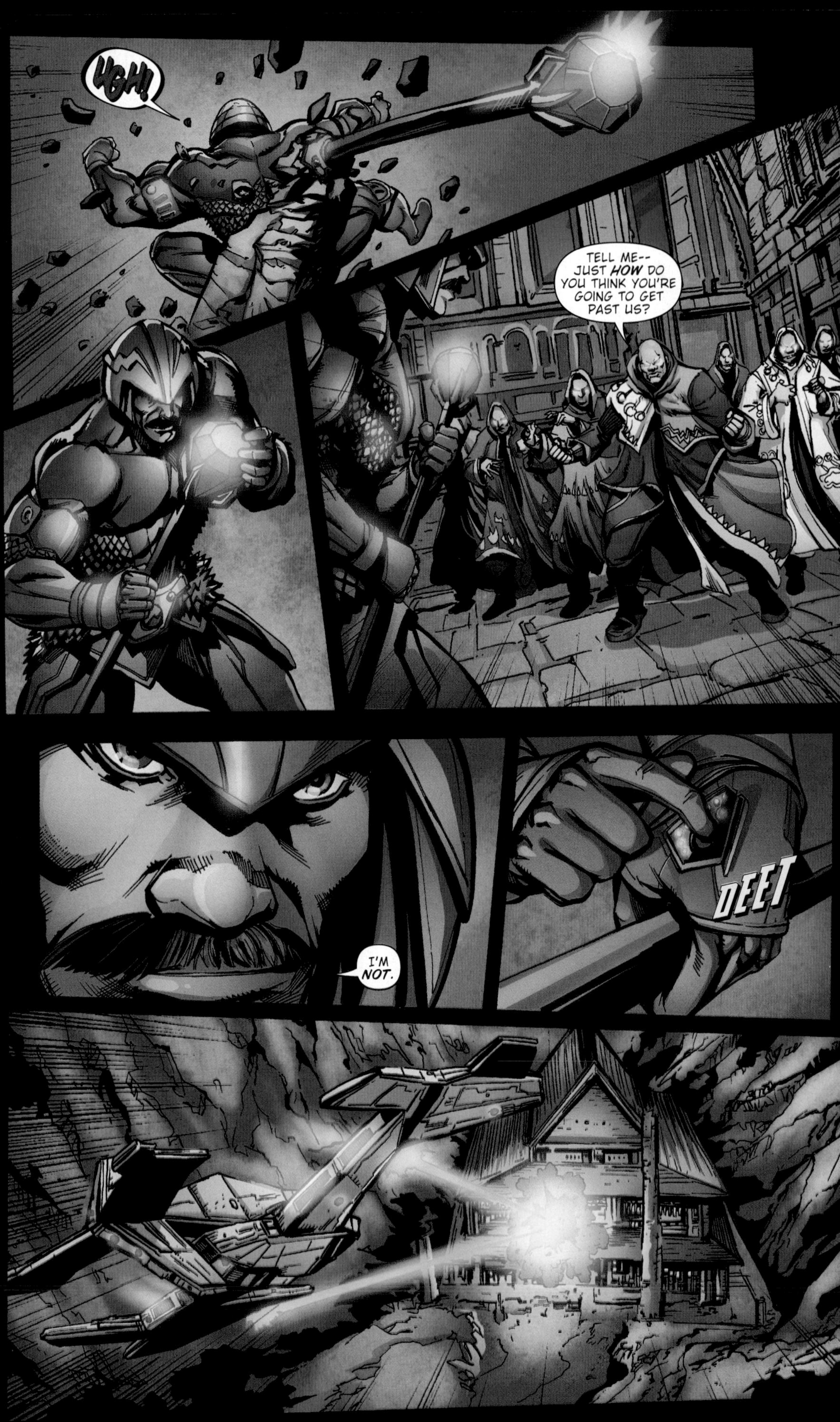

UGH!
TELL ME-- JUST HOW DO YOU THINK YOU'RE GOING TO GET PAST US?
I'M NOT.
DEET

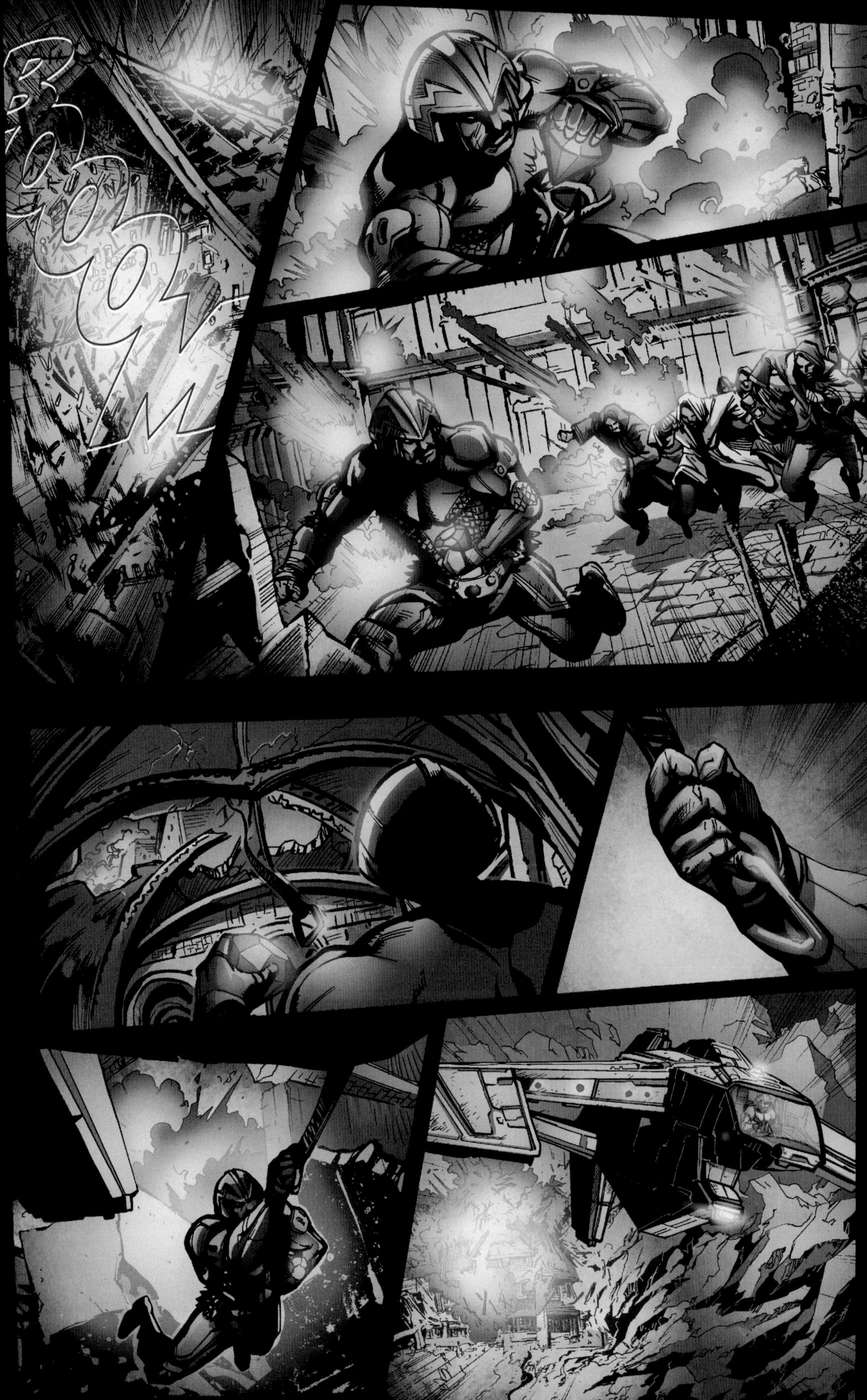
BROOOM

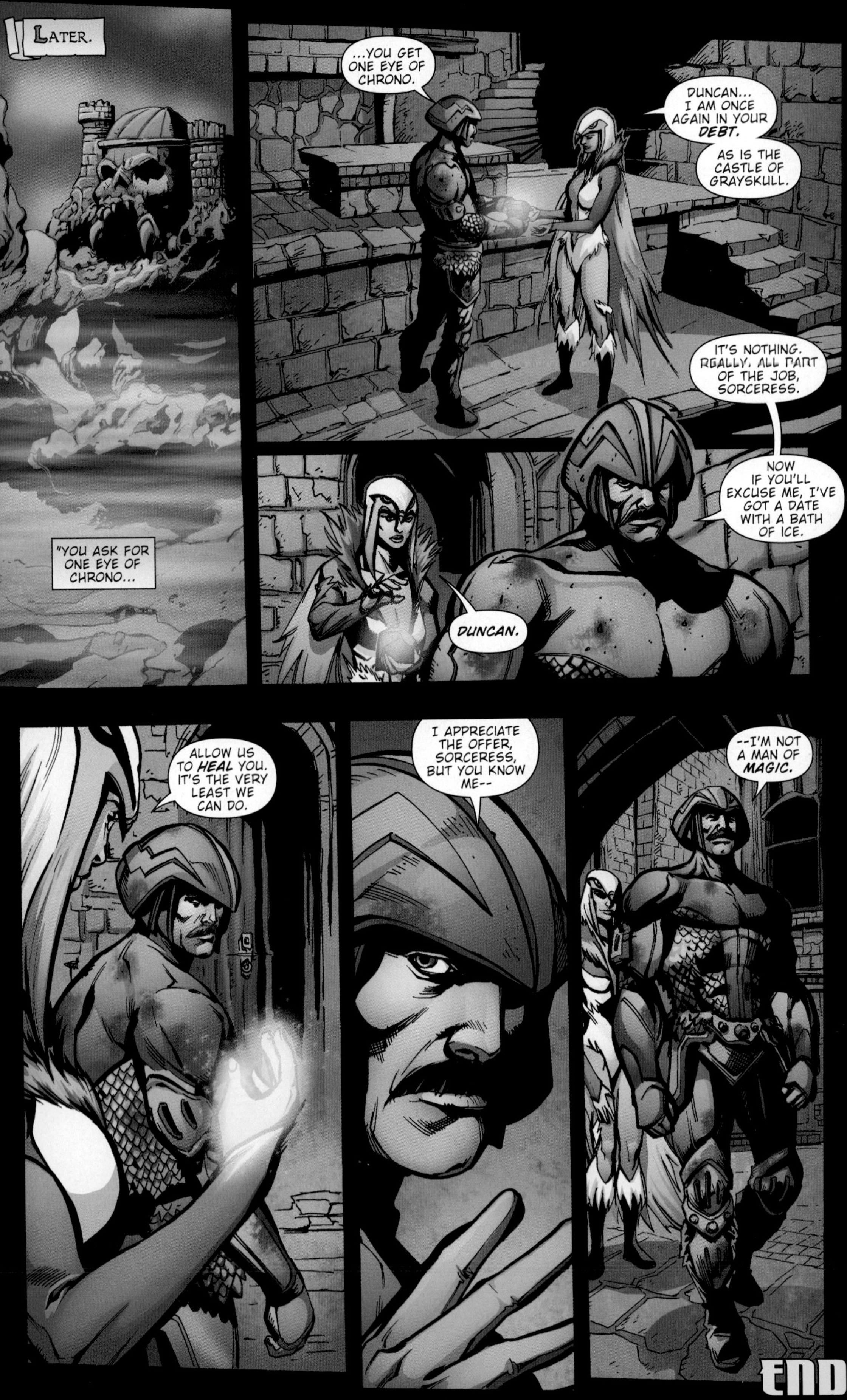
LATER.
"YOU ASK FOR ONE EYE OF CHRONO...
...YOU GET ONE EYE OF CHRONO.
DUNCAN... I AM ONCE AGAIN IN YOUR DEBT.
AS IS THE CASTLE OF GRAYSKULL.
IT'S NOTHING. REALLY. ALL PART OF THE JOB, SORCERESS.
NOW IF YOU'LL EXCUSE ME, I'VE GOT A DATE WITH A BATH OF ICE.
DUNCAN.
ALLOW US TO HEAL YOU. IT'S THE VERY LEAST WE CAN DO.
I APPRECIATE THE OFFER, SORCERESS, BUT YOU KNOW ME--
--I'M NOT A MAN OF MAGIC.
END

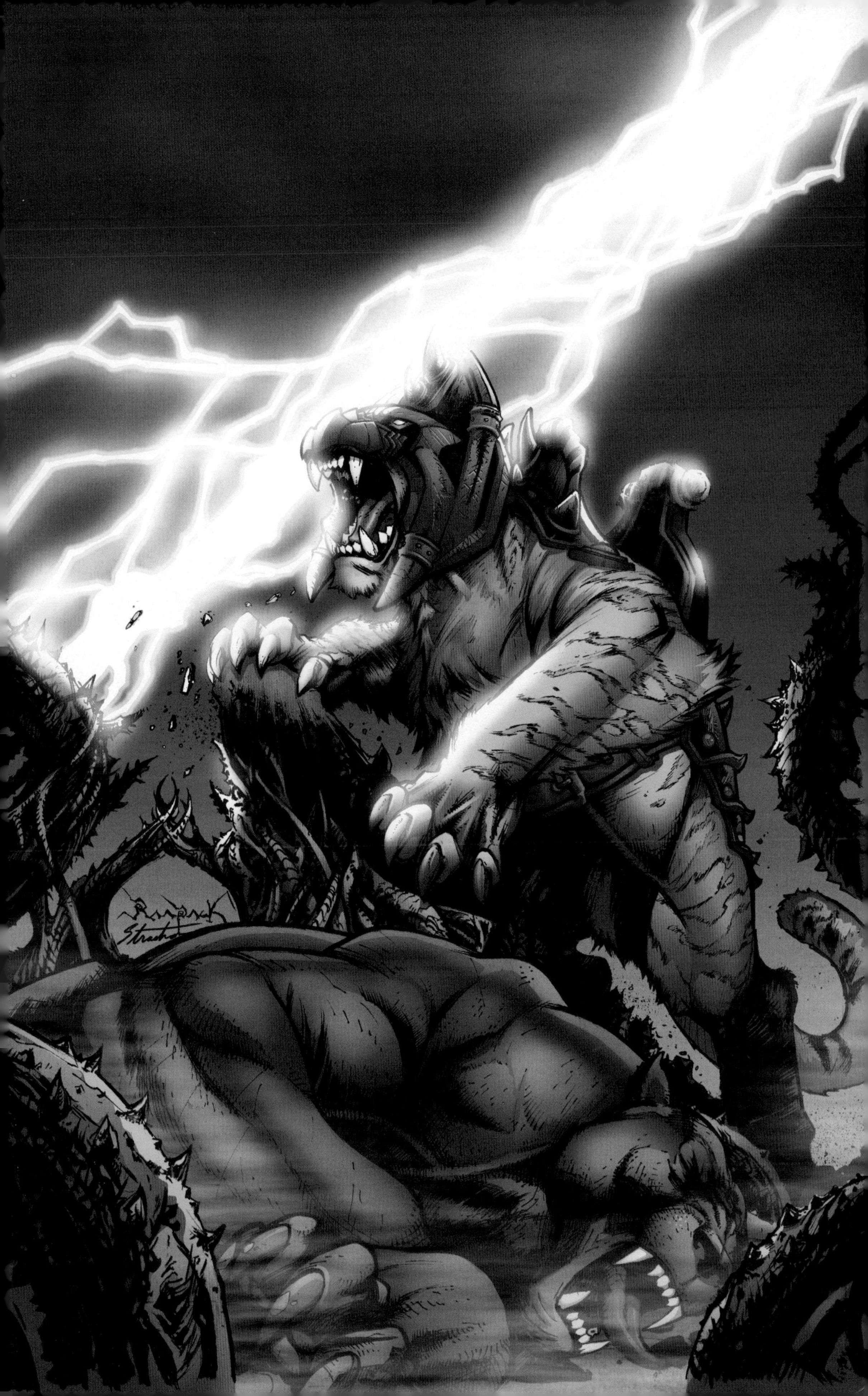

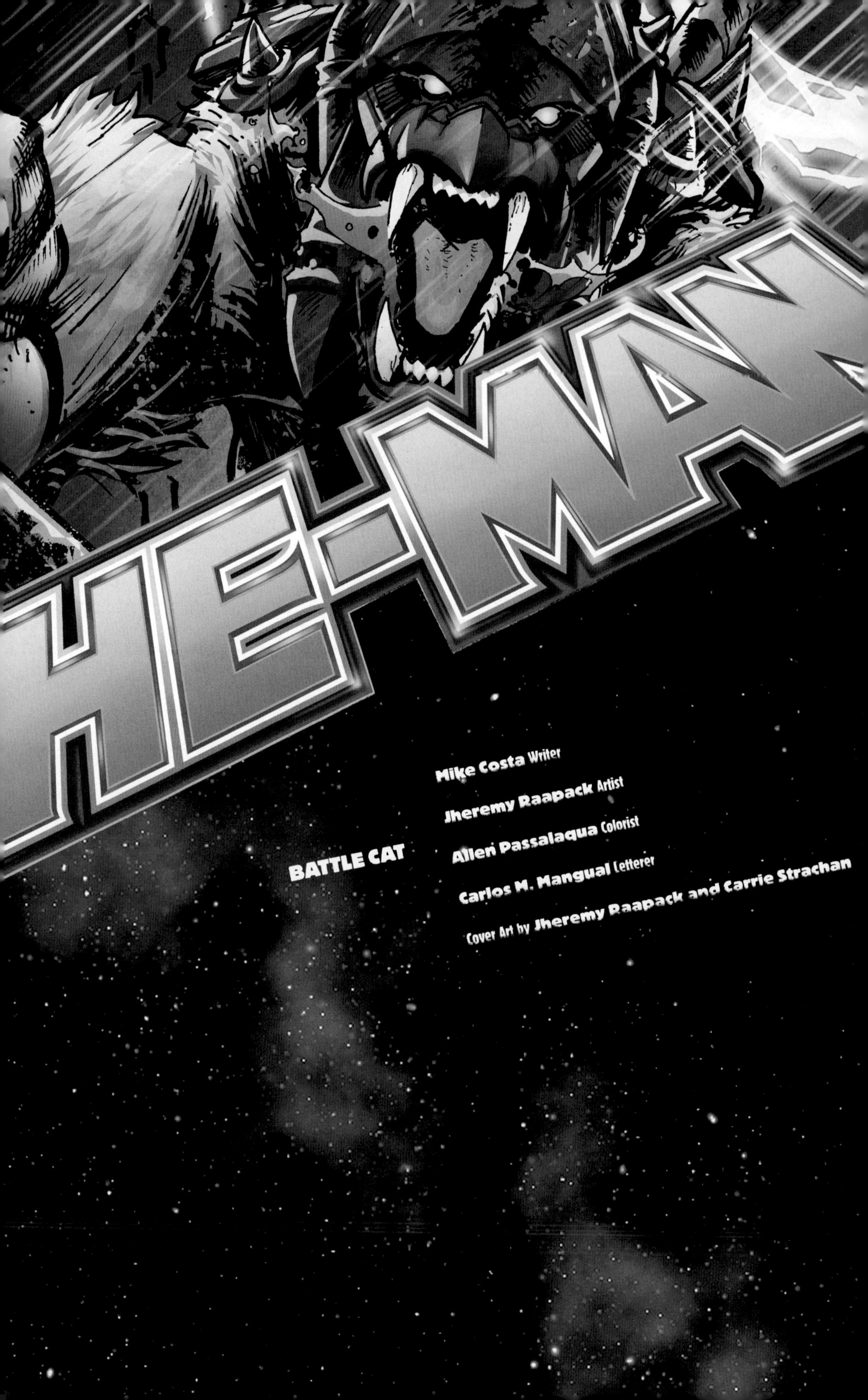

BATTLE CAT

Mike Costa Writer

Jheremy Raapack Artist

Allen Passalaqua Colorist

Carlos M. Mangual Letterer

Cover Art by **Jheremy Raapack and Carrie Strachan**

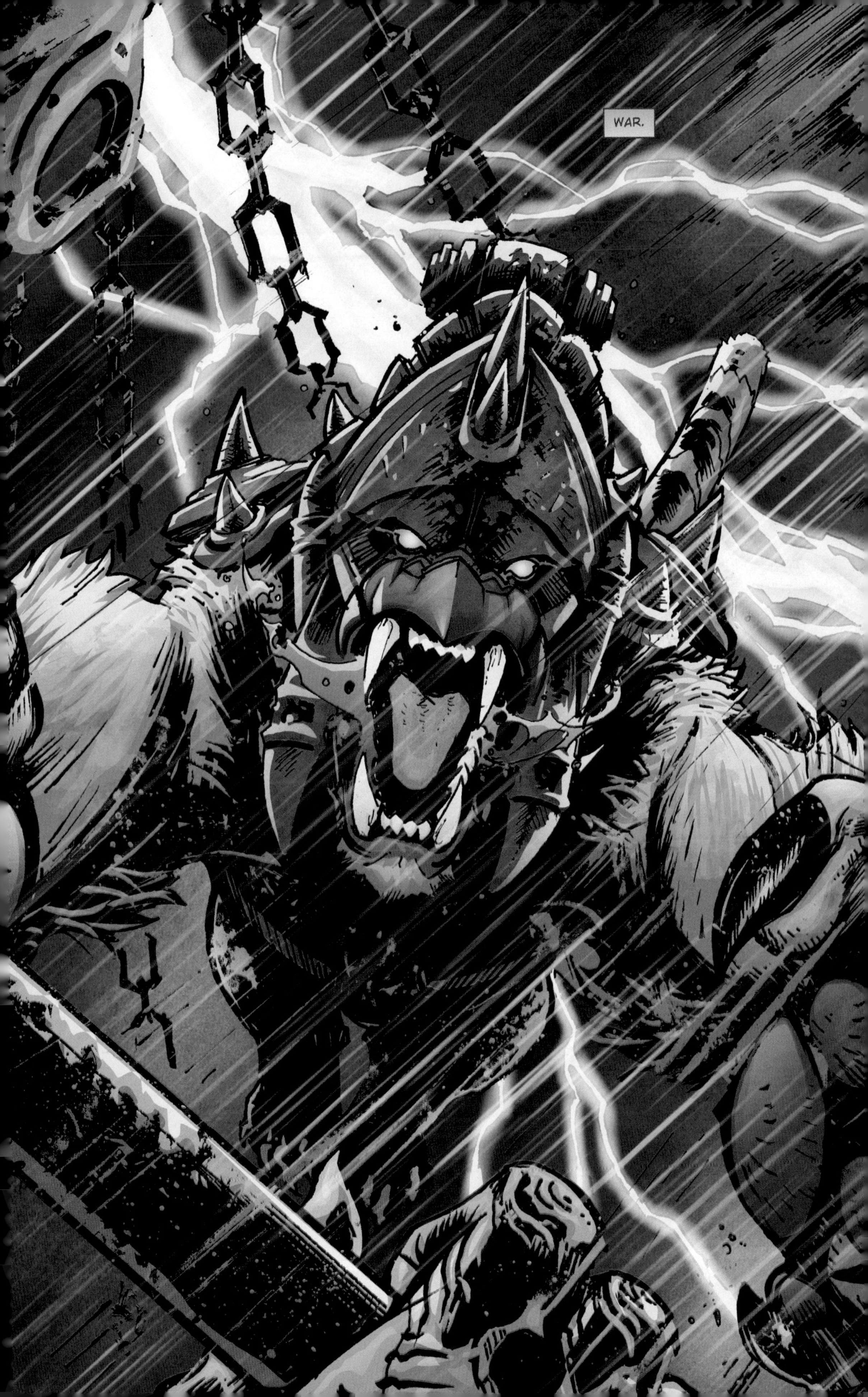
WAR.

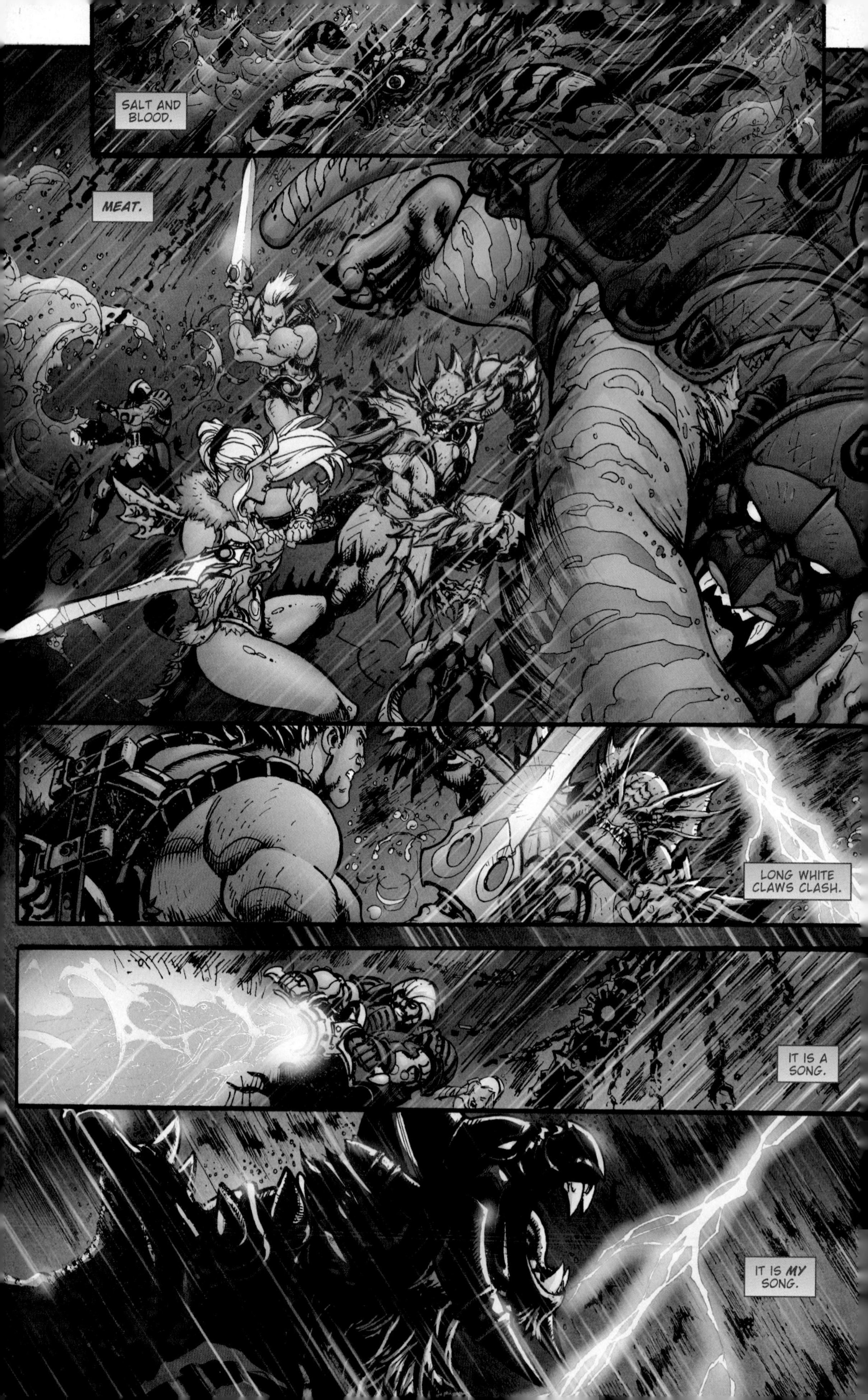
SALT AND BLOOD.
MEAT.
LONG WHITE CLAWS CLASH.
IT IS A SONG.
IT IS MY SONG.

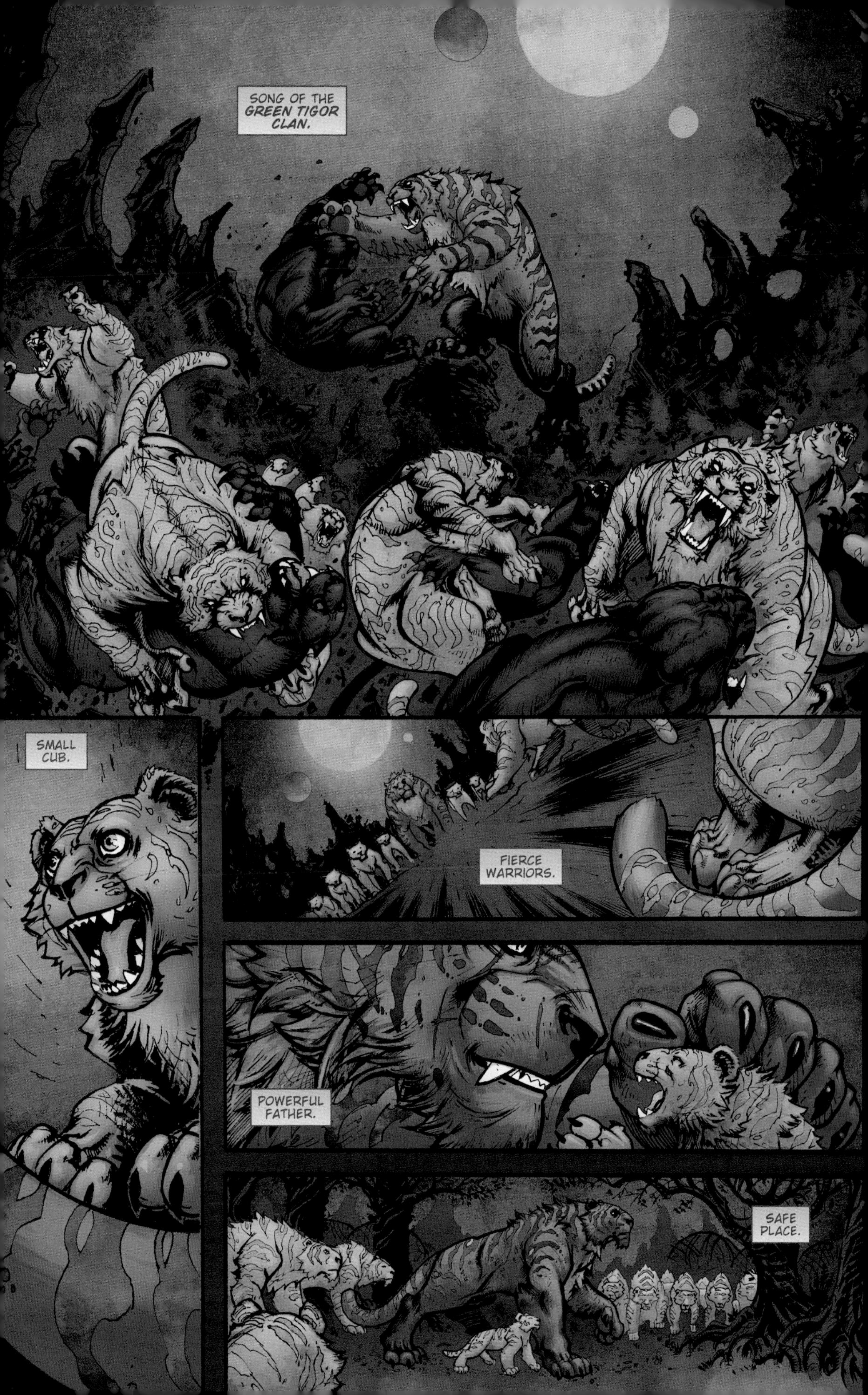
SONG OF THE GREEN TIGOR CLAN.
SMALL CUB.
FIERCE WARRIORS.
POWERFUL FATHER.
SAFE PLACE.

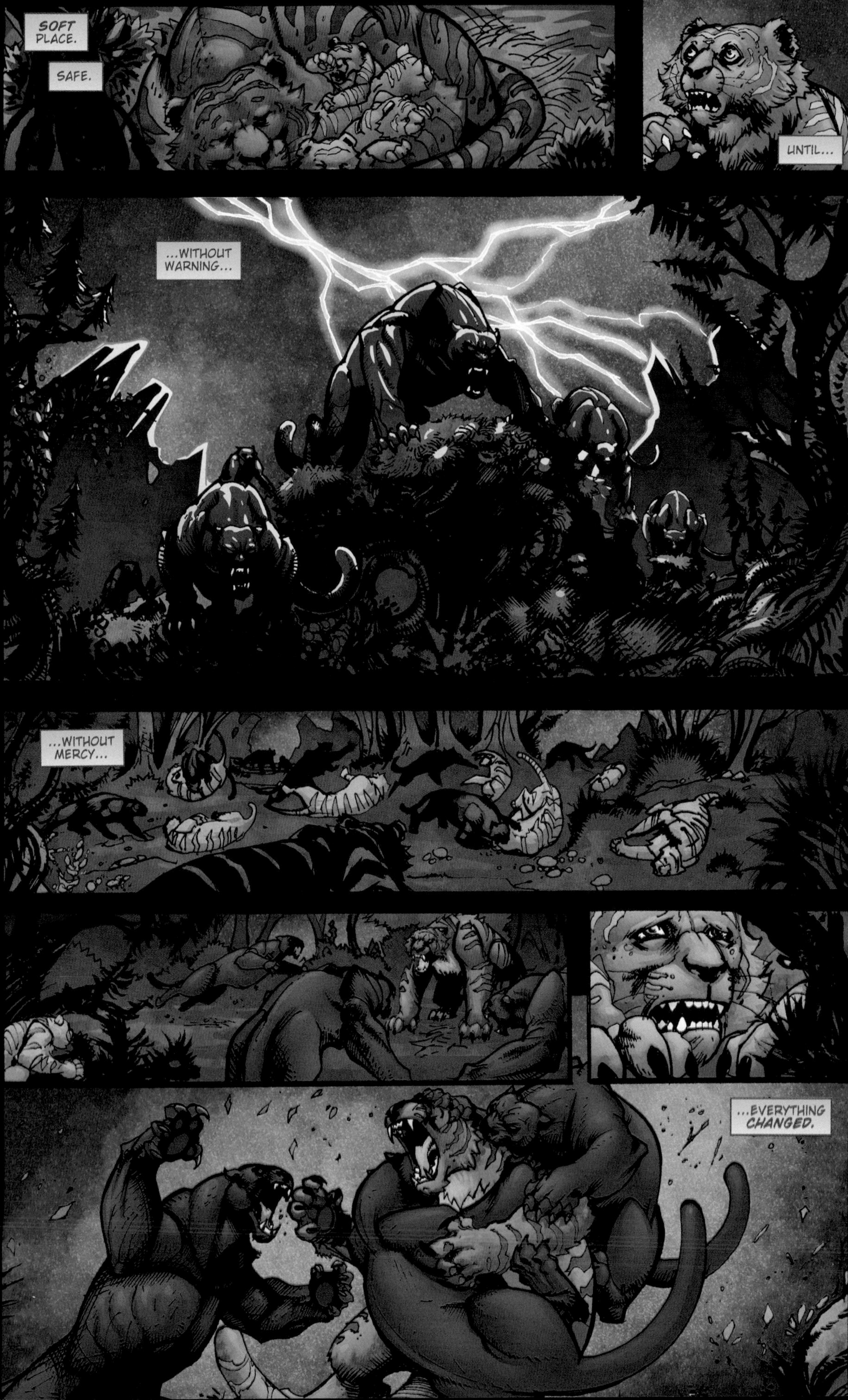
SOFT PLACE.
SAFE.
UNTIL...
...WITHOUT WARNING...
...WITHOUT MERCY...
...EVERYTHING CHANGED.

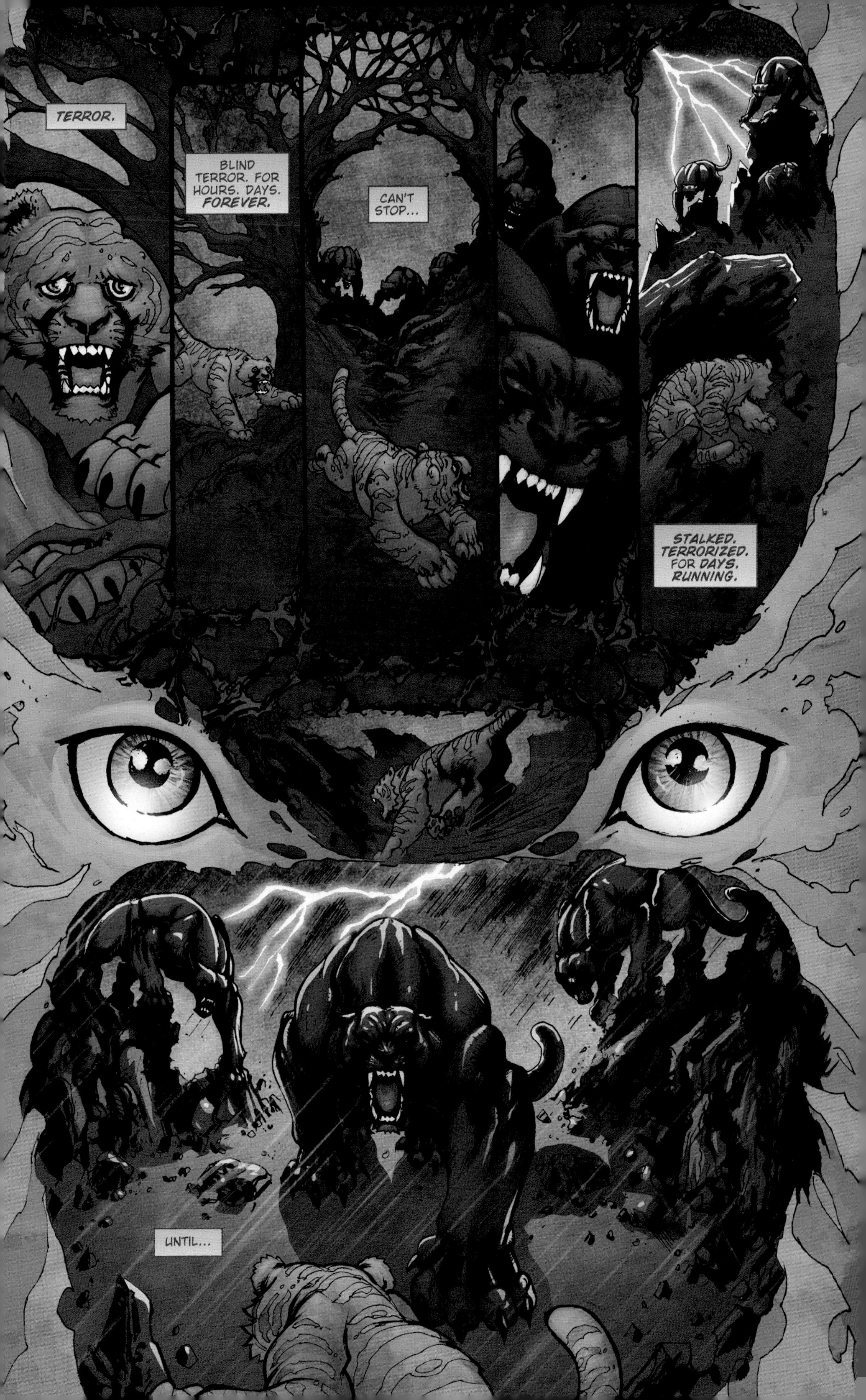
TERROR.
BLIND TERROR. FOR HOURS. DAYS. FOREVER.
CAN'T STOP...
STALKED. TERRORIZED. FOR DAYS. RUNNING.
UNTIL...

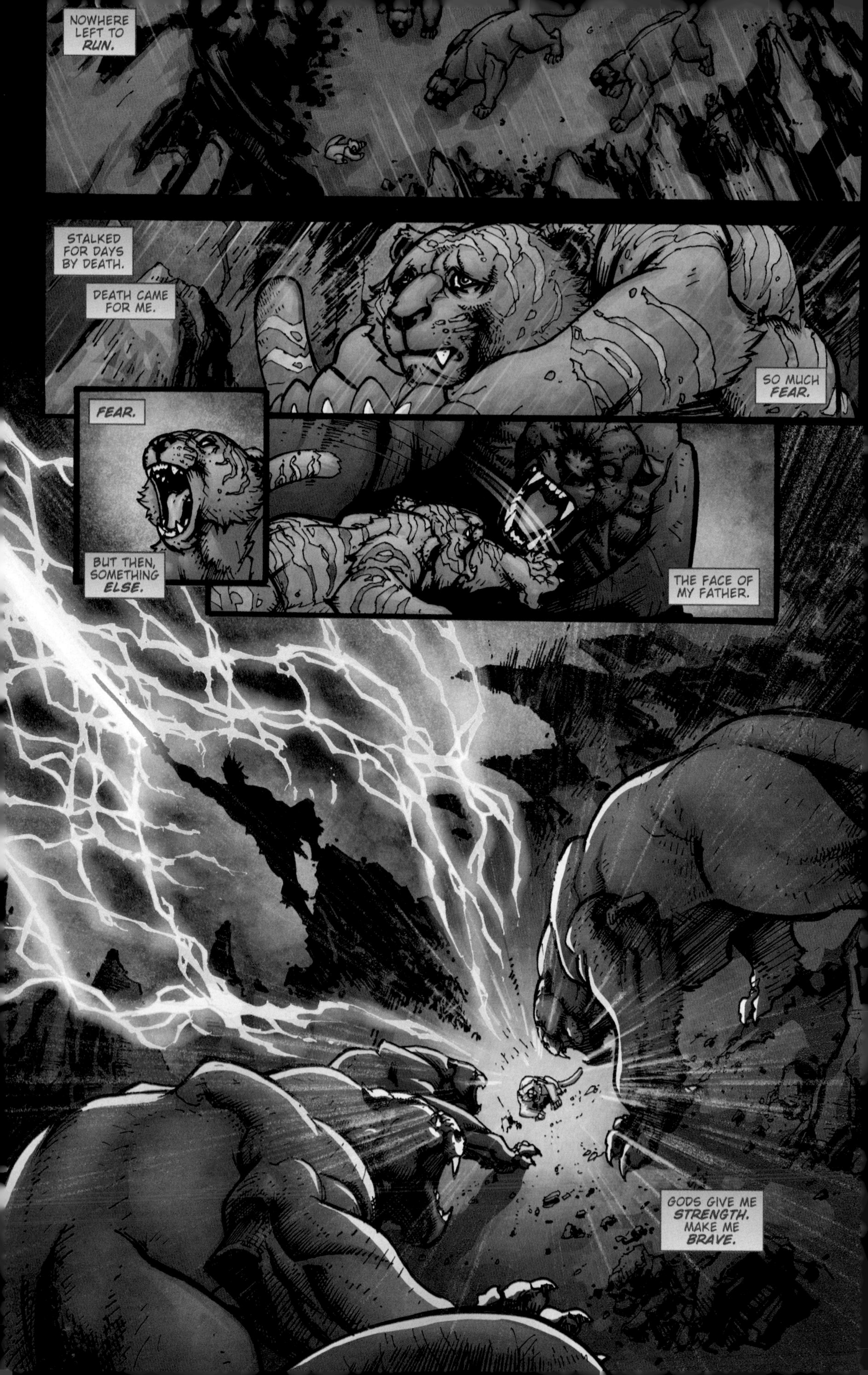
NOWHERE LEFT TO RUN.
STALKED FOR DAYS BY DEATH.
DEATH CAME FOR ME.
SO MUCH FEAR.
FEAR.
BUT THEN, SOMETHING ELSE.
THE FACE OF MY FATHER.
GODS GIVE ME STRENGTH. MAKE ME BRAVE.

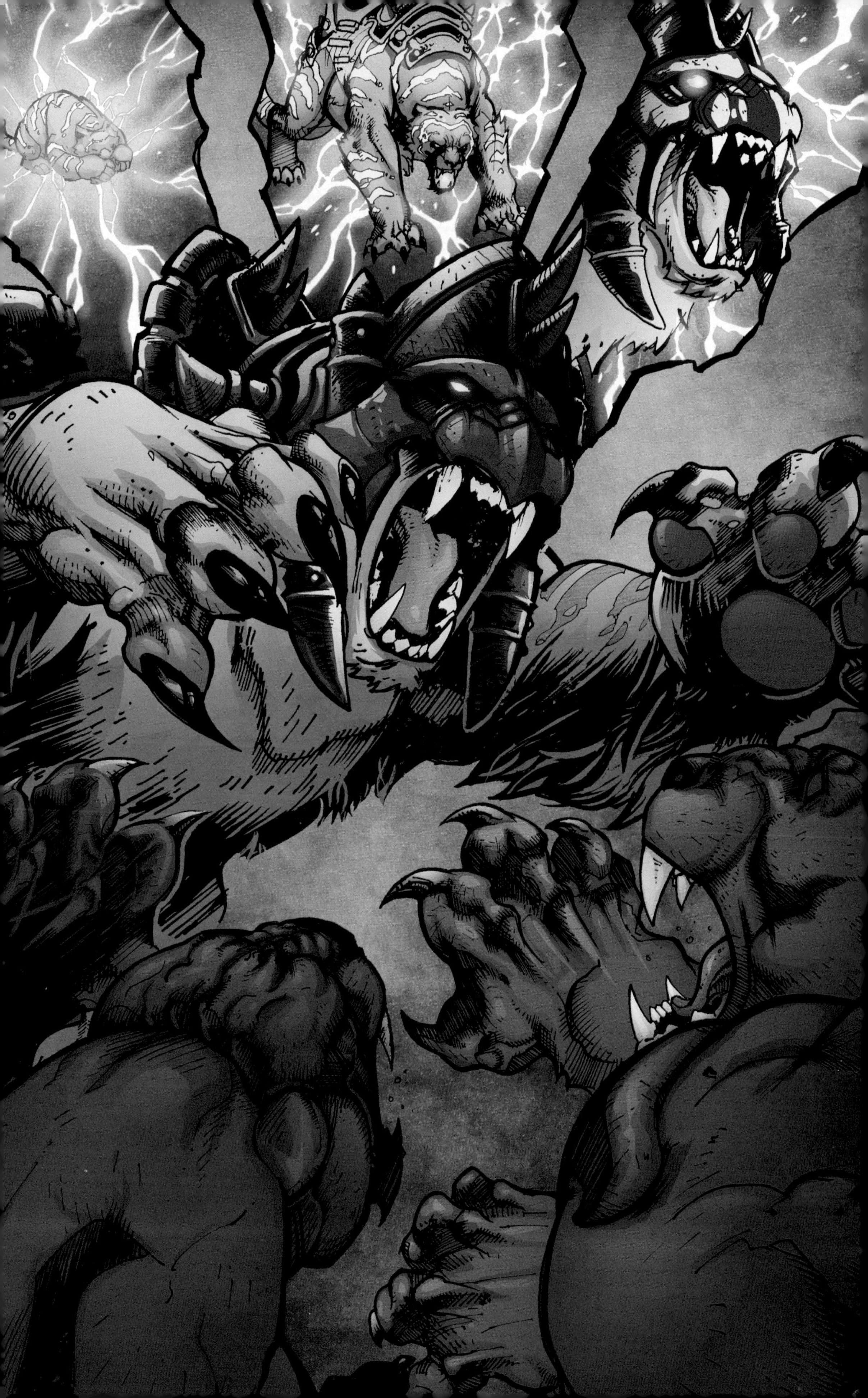

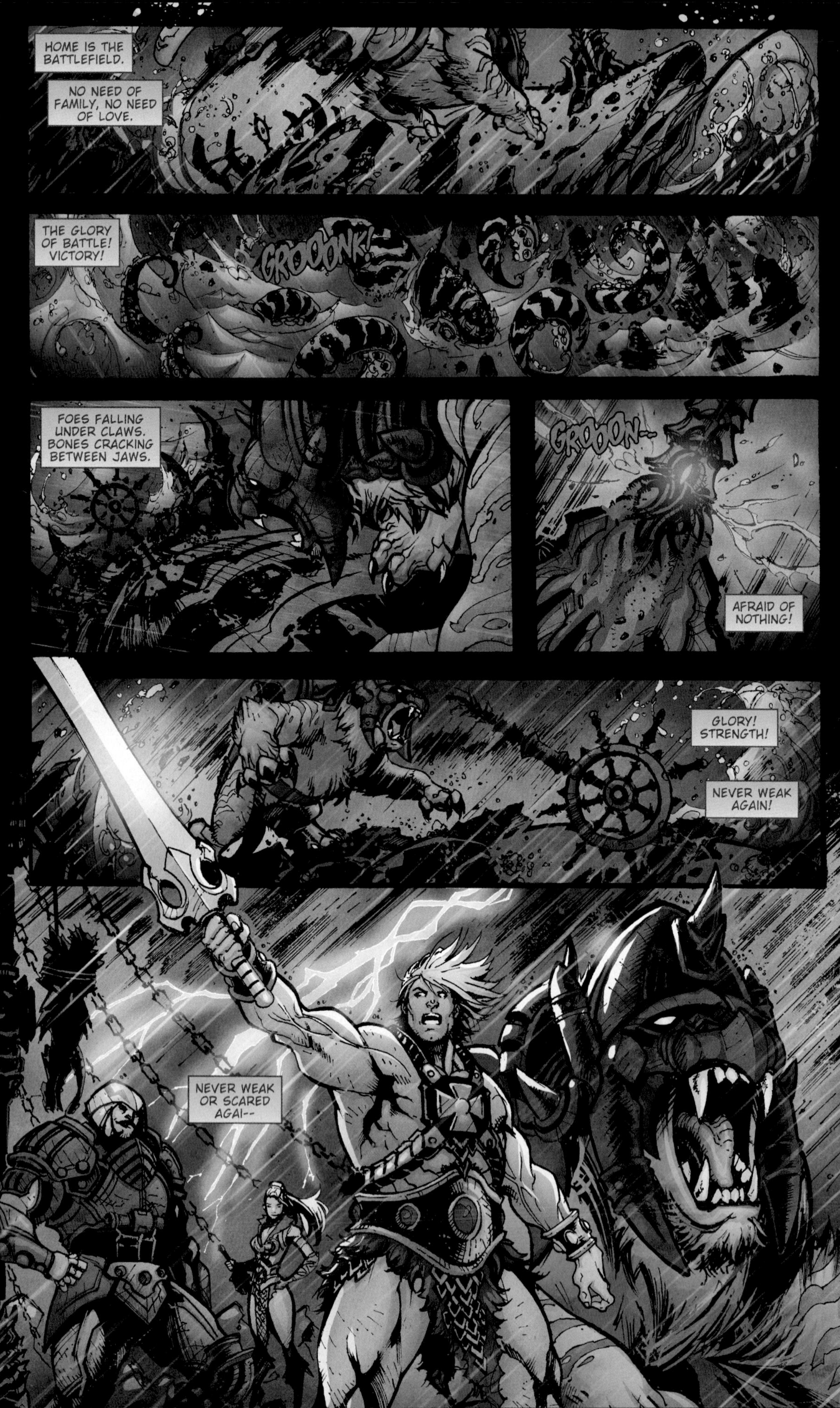

HOME IS THE BATTLEFIELD.
NO NEED OF FAMILY, NO NEED OF LOVE.
THE GLORY OF BATTLE! VICTORY!
GROOONK!
FOES FALLING UNDER CLAWS. BONES CRACKING BETWEEN JAWS.
GROOON--
AFRAID OF NOTHING!
GLORY! STRENGTH!
NEVER WEAK AGAIN!
NEVER WEAK OR SCARED AGAI--

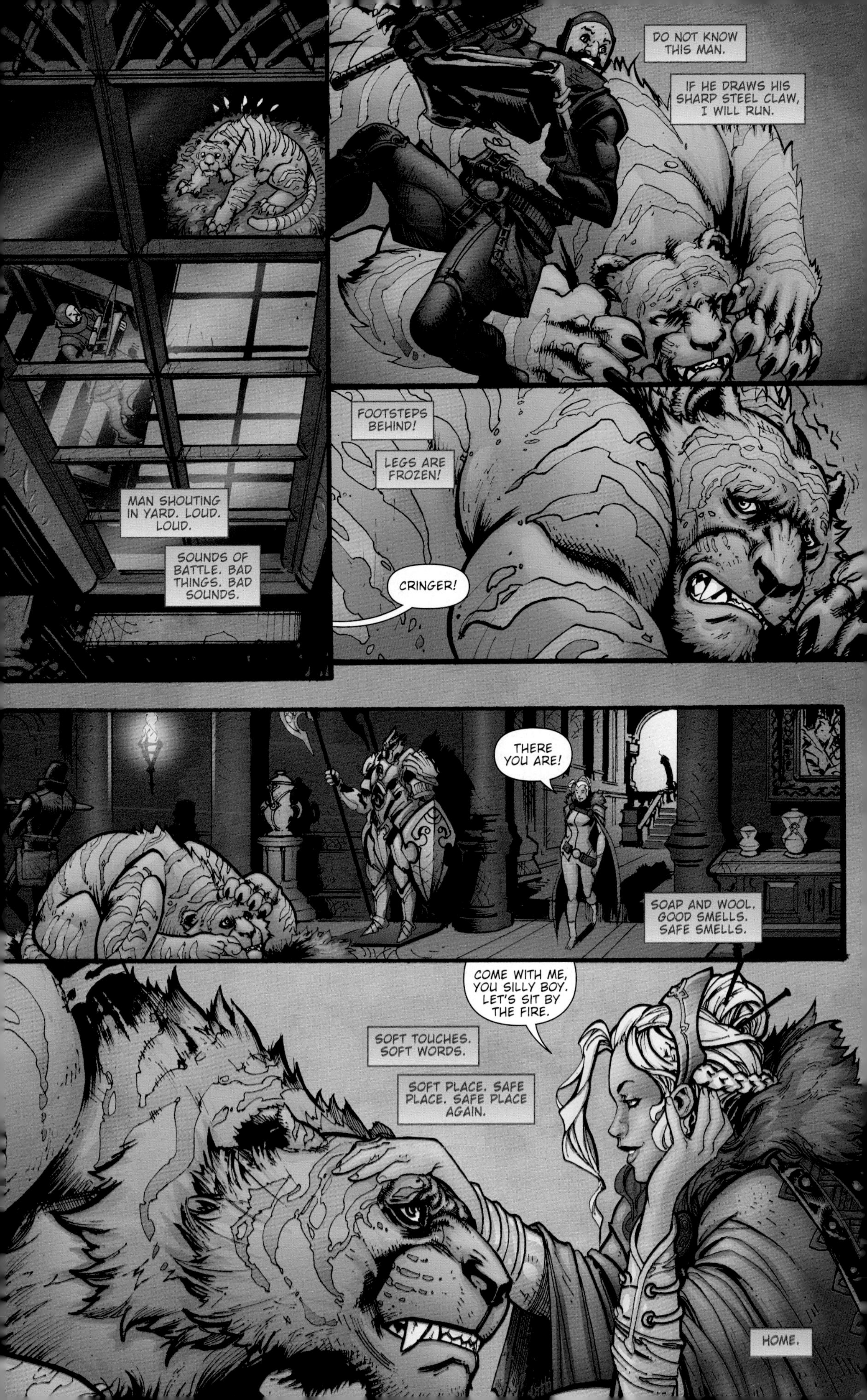
MAN SHOUTING IN YARD. LOUD. LOUD.
SOUNDS OF BATTLE. BAD THINGS. BAD SOUNDS.
DO NOT KNOW THIS MAN.
IF HE DRAWS HIS SHARP STEEL CLAW, I WILL RUN.
FOOTSTEPS BEHIND!
LEGS ARE FROZEN!
CRINGER!
THERE YOU ARE!
SOAP AND WOOL. GOOD SMELLS. SAFE SMELLS.
COME WITH ME, YOU SILLY BOY. LET'S SIT BY THE FIRE.
SOFT TOUCHES. SOFT WORDS.
SOFT PLACE. SAFE PLACE. SAFE PLACE AGAIN.
HOME.

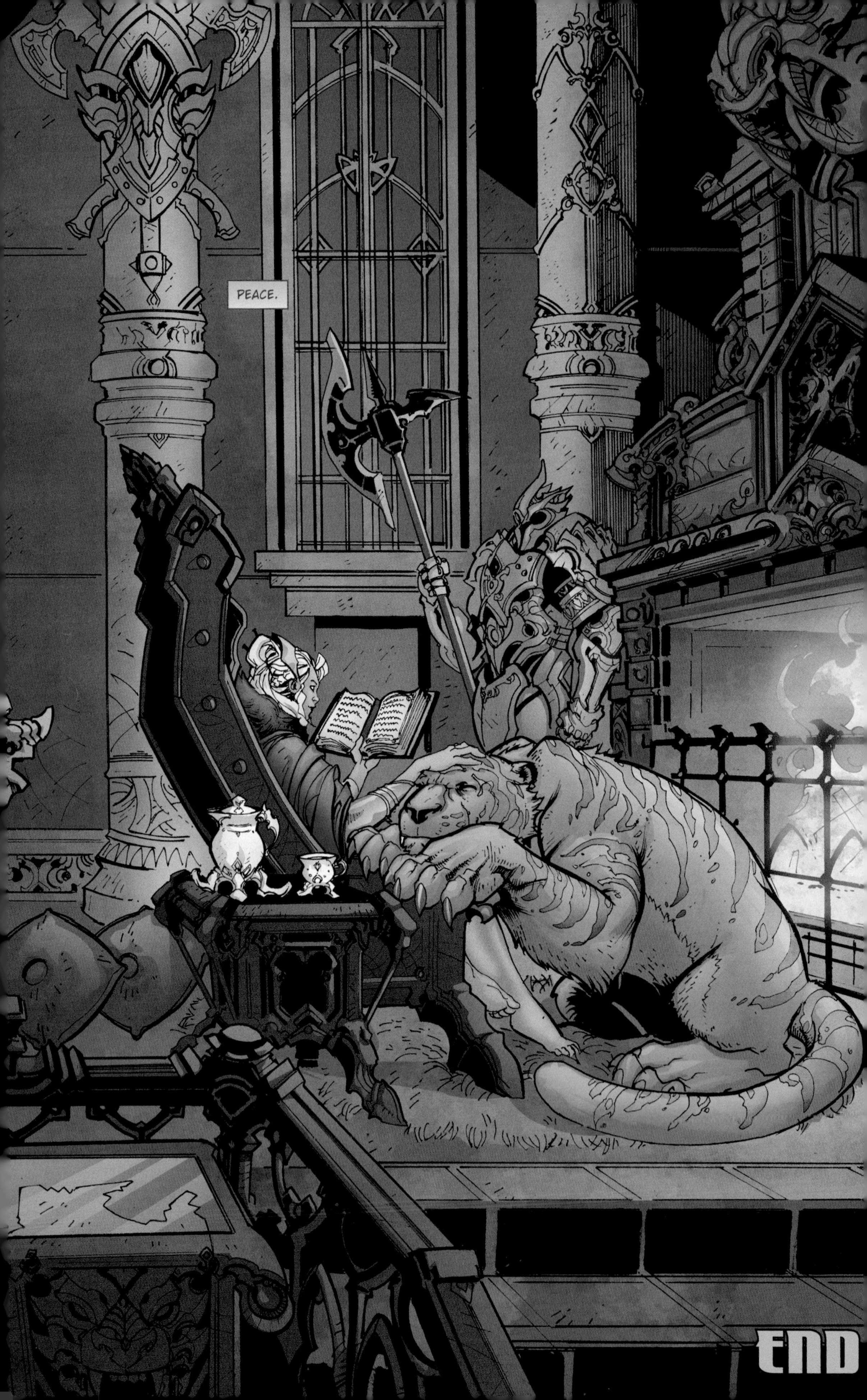
PEACE.
END

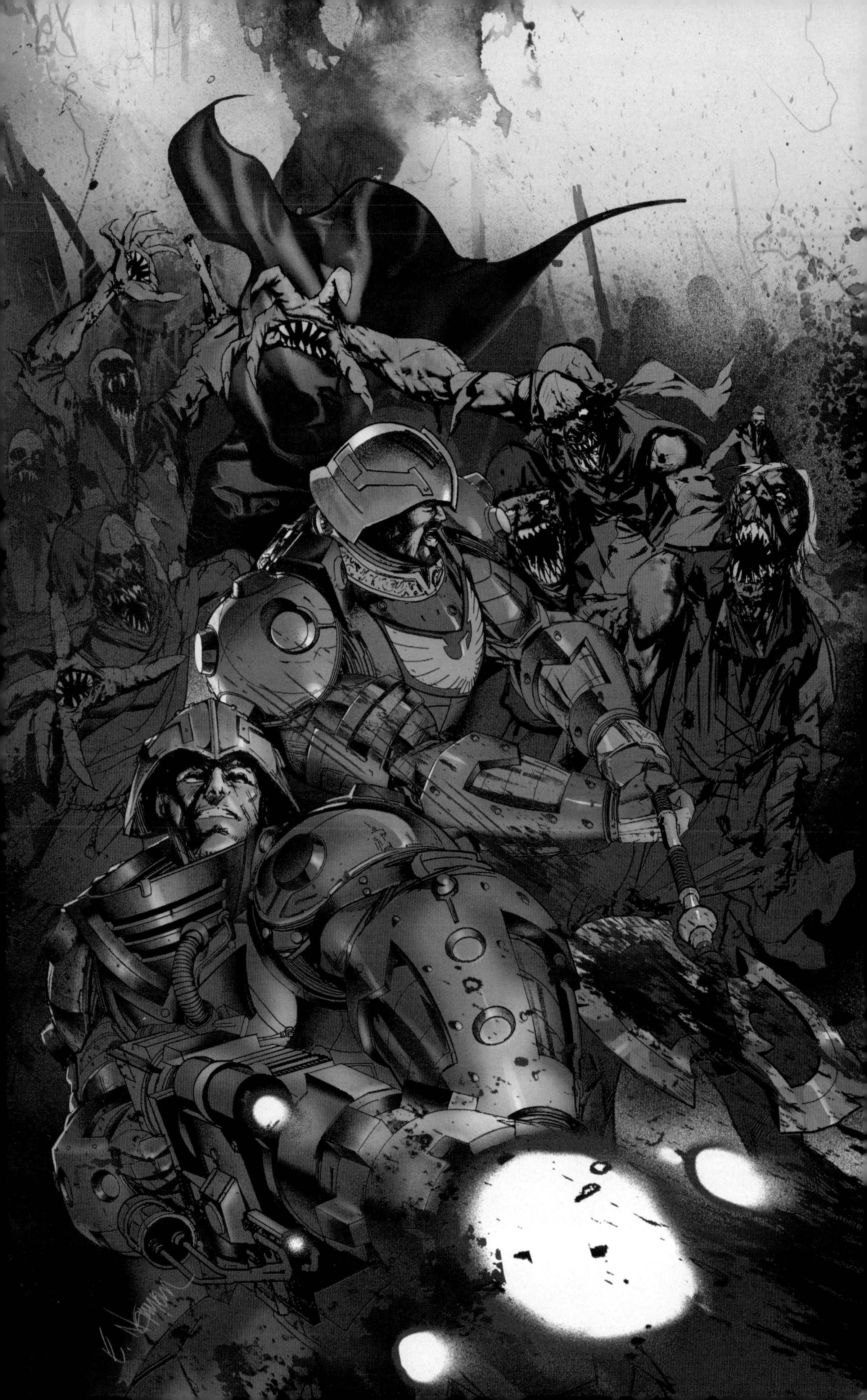

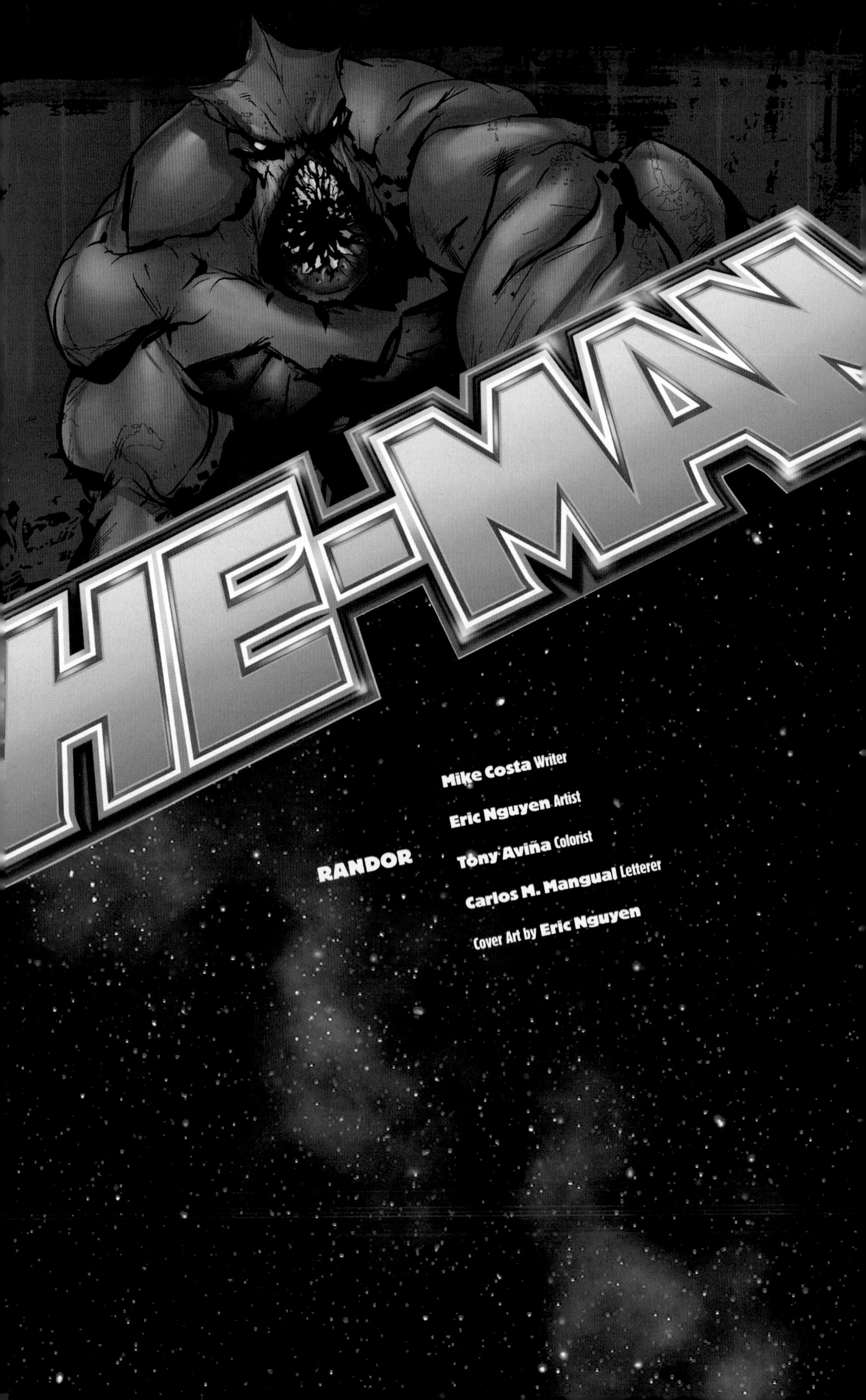
HE-MAN
RANDOR
Mike Costa Writer
Eric Nguyen Artist
Tony Aviña Colorist
Carlos M. Mangual Letterer
Cover Art by Eric Nguyen

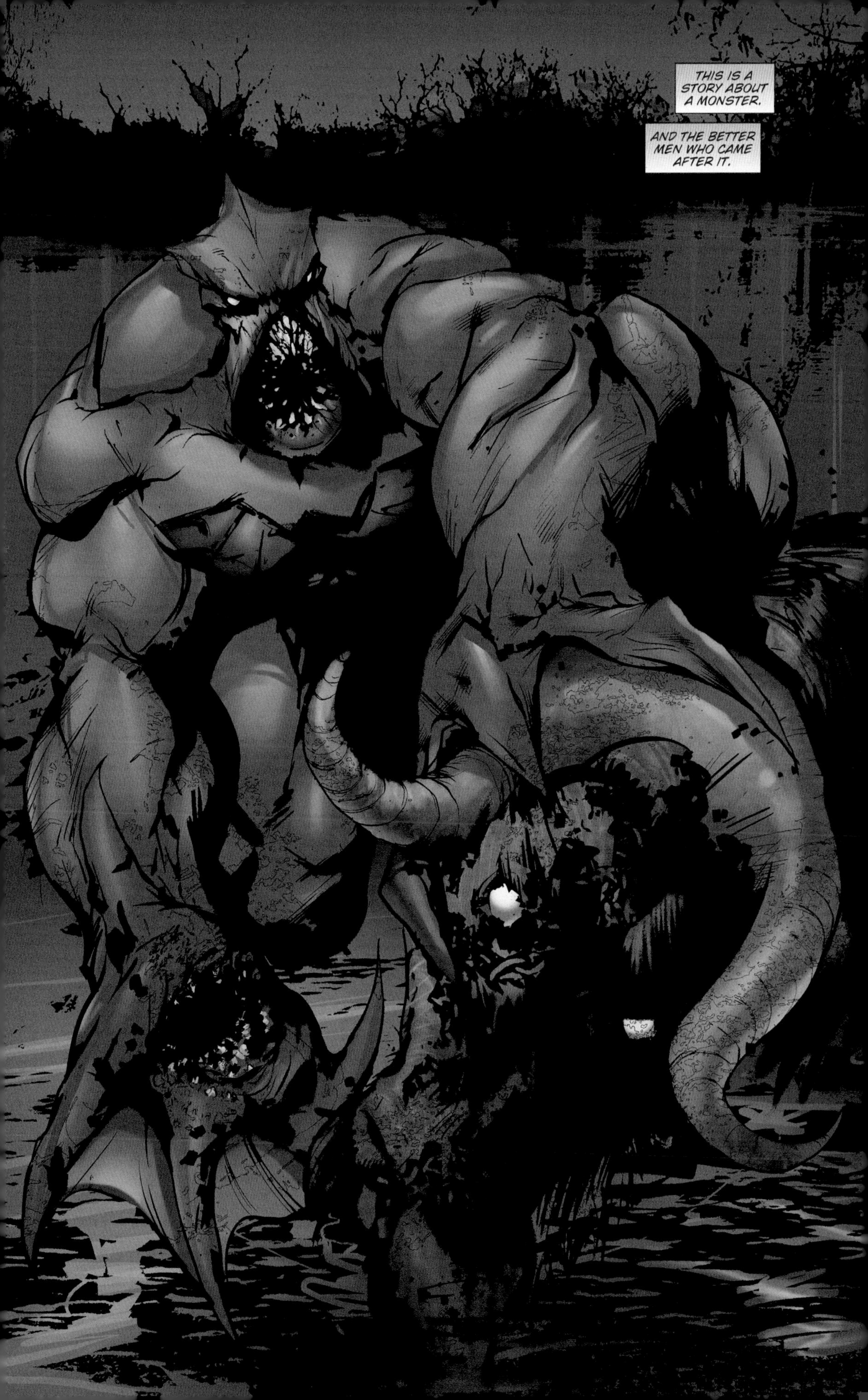
THIS IS A STORY ABOUT A MONSTER.
AND THE BETTER MEN WHO CAME AFTER IT.

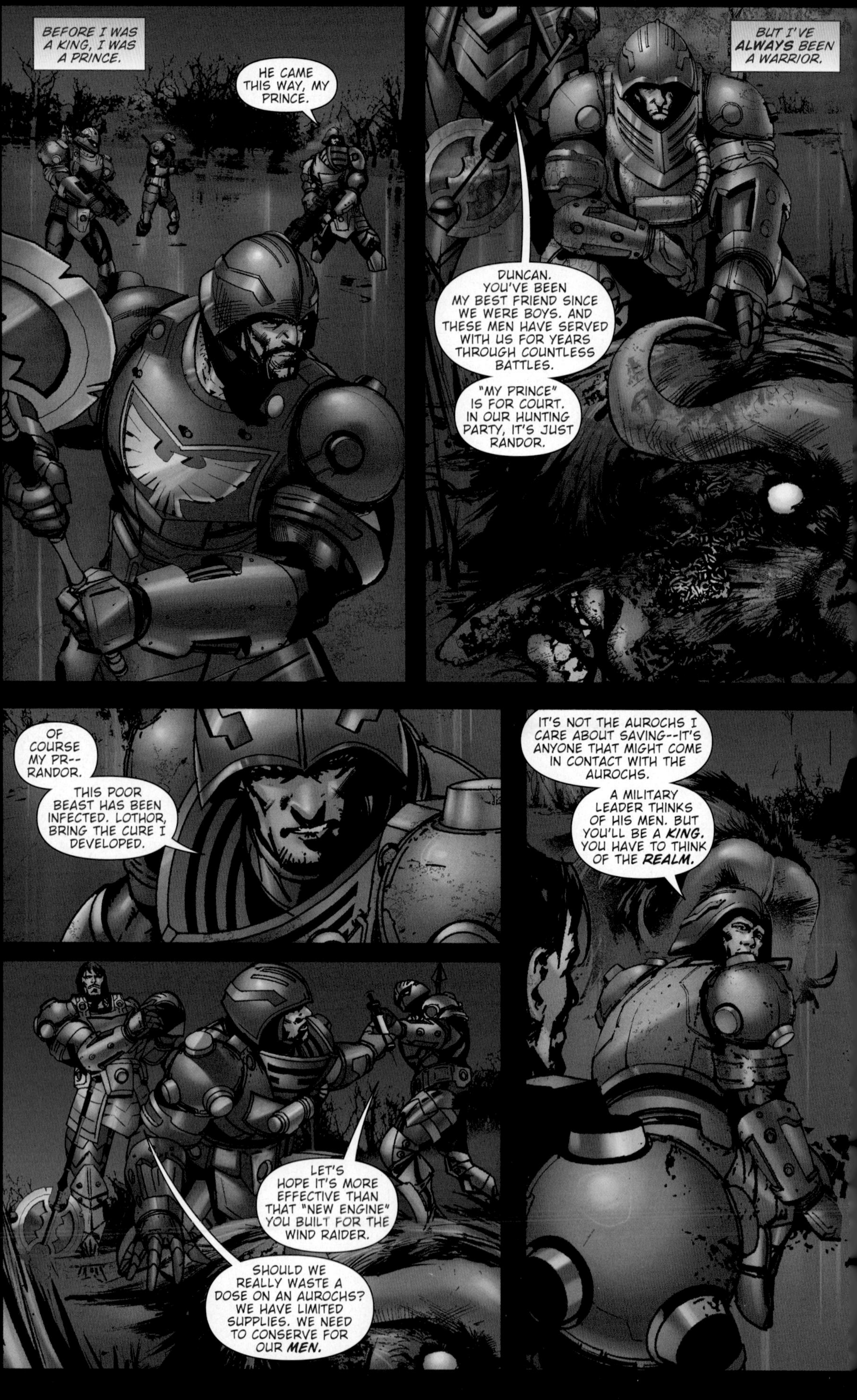
BEFORE I WAS A KING, I WAS A PRINCE.
HE CAME THIS WAY, MY PRINCE.
BUT I'VE **ALWAYS** BEEN A WARRIOR.
DUNCAN. YOU'VE BEEN MY BEST FRIEND SINCE WE WERE BOYS. AND THESE MEN HAVE SERVED WITH US FOR YEARS THROUGH COUNTLESS BATTLES.
"MY PRINCE" IS FOR COURT. IN OUR HUNTING PARTY, IT'S JUST RANDOR.
OF COURSE MY PR-- RANDOR.
THIS POOR BEAST HAS BEEN INFECTED. LOTHOR, BRING THE CURE I DEVELOPED.
LET'S HOPE IT'S MORE EFFECTIVE THAN THAT "NEW ENGINE" YOU BUILT FOR THE WIND RAIDER.
SHOULD WE REALLY WASTE A DOSE ON AN AUROCHS? WE HAVE LIMITED SUPPLIES. WE NEED TO CONSERVE FOR OUR ***MEN.***
IT'S NOT THE AUROCHS I CARE ABOUT SAVING--IT'S ANYONE THAT MIGHT COME IN CONTACT WITH THE AUROCHS.
A MILITARY LEADER THINKS OF HIS MEN. BUT YOU'LL BE A ***KING.*** YOU HAVE TO THINK OF THE ***REALM.***

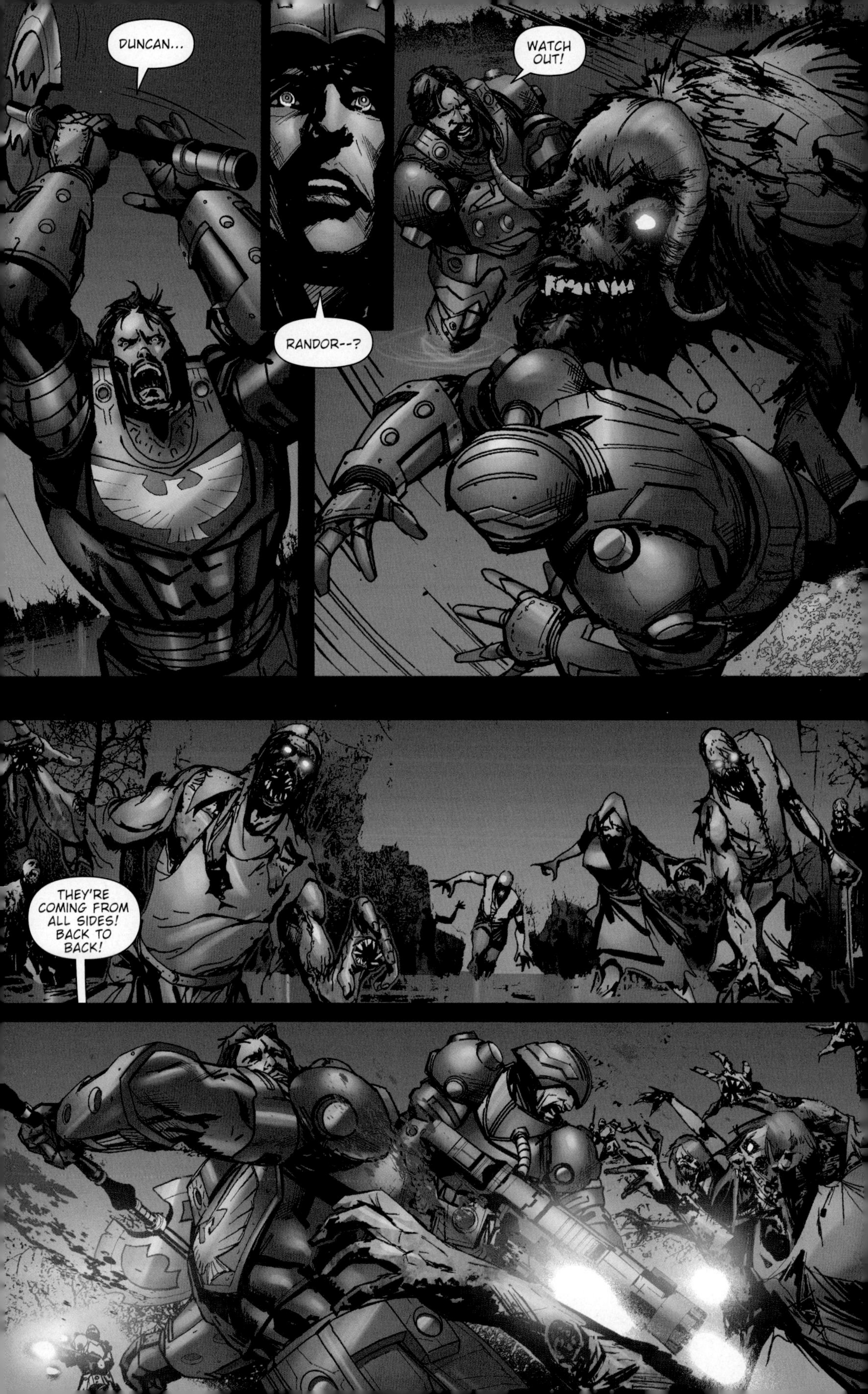
DUNCAN...
RANDOR--?
WATCH OUT!
THEY'RE COMING FROM ALL SIDES! BACK TO BACK!

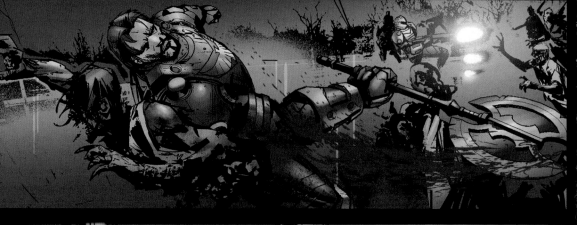

I LEARNED MANY THINGS THAT DAY.

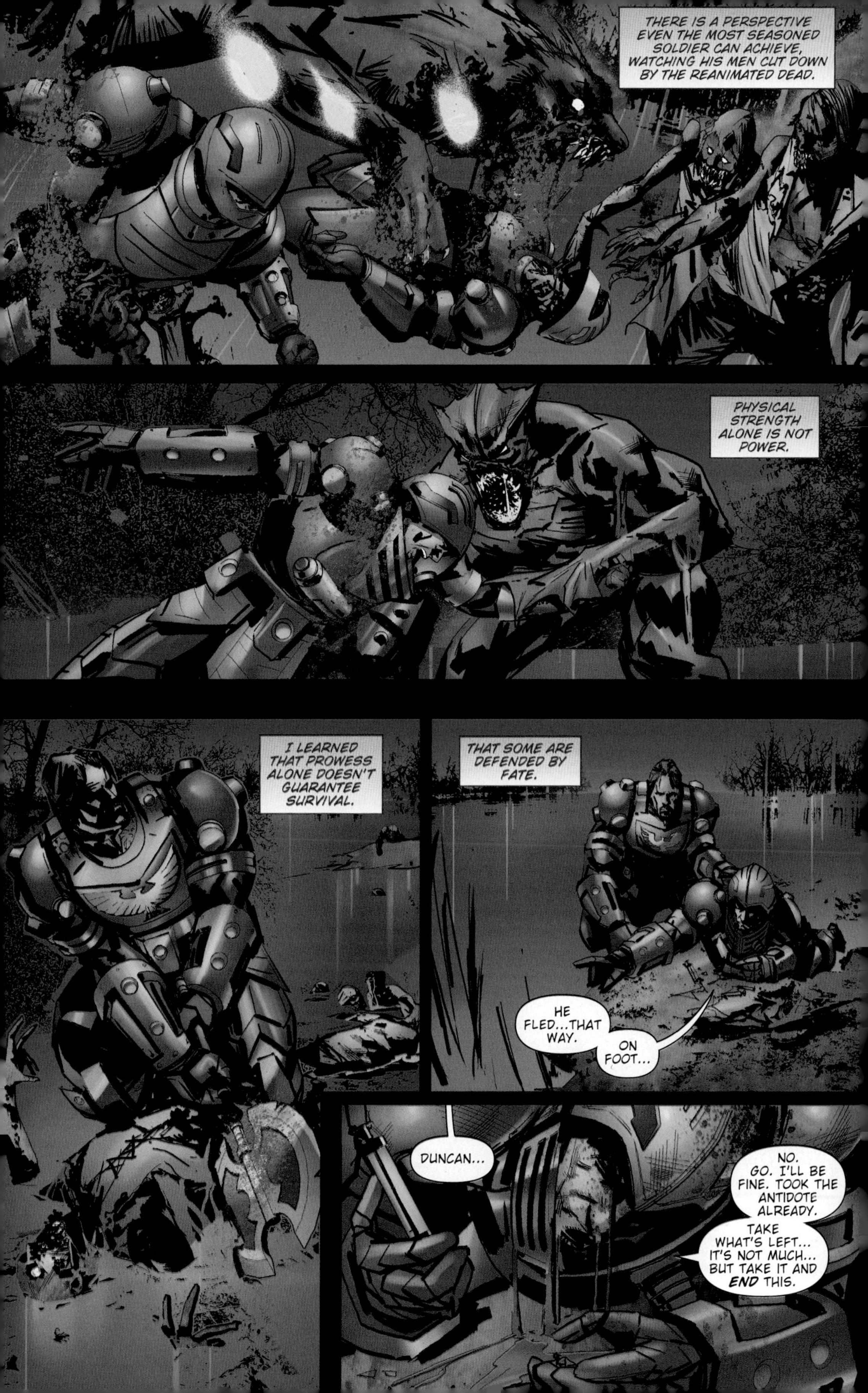
THERE IS A PERSPECTIVE EVEN THE MOST SEASONED SOLDIER CAN ACHIEVE, WATCHING HIS MEN CUT DOWN BY THE REANIMATED DEAD.
PHYSICAL STRENGTH ALONE IS NOT POWER.
I LEARNED THAT PROWESS ALONE DOESN'T GUARANTEE SURVIVAL.
THAT SOME ARE DEFENDED BY FATE.
HE FLED...THAT WAY.
ON FOOT...
DUNCAN...
NO. GO. I'LL BE FINE. TOOK THE ANTIDOTE ALREADY.
TAKE WHAT'S LEFT... IT'S NOT MUCH... BUT TAKE IT AND **END** THIS.

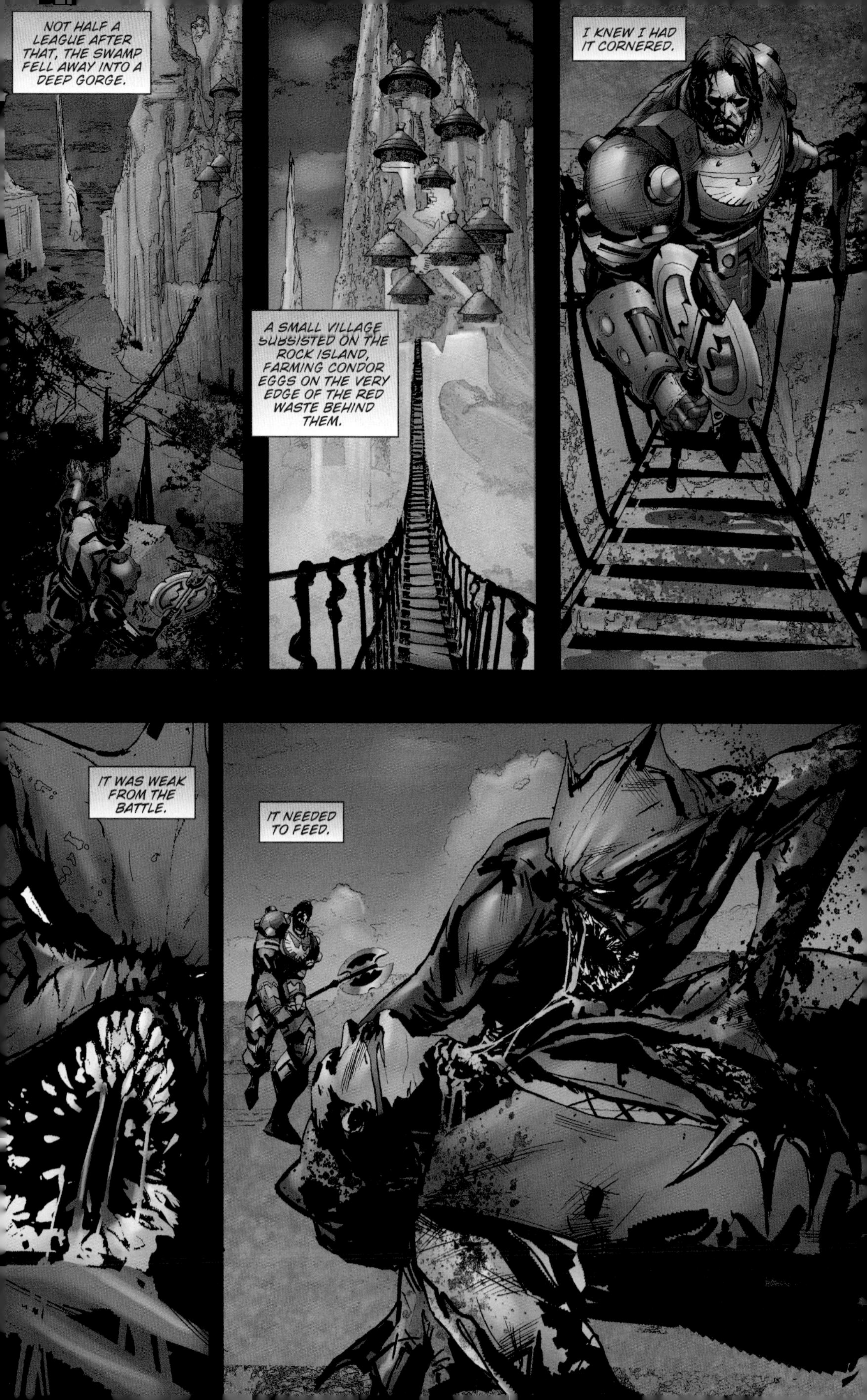
NOT HALF A LEAGUE AFTER THAT, THE SWAMP FELL AWAY INTO A DEEP GORGE.
A SMALL VILLAGE SUBSISTED ON THE ROCK ISLAND, FARMING CONDOR EGGS ON THE VERY EDGE OF THE RED WASTE BEHIND THEM.
I KNEW I HAD IT CORNERED.
IT WAS WEAK FROM THE BATTLE.
IT NEEDED TO FEED.

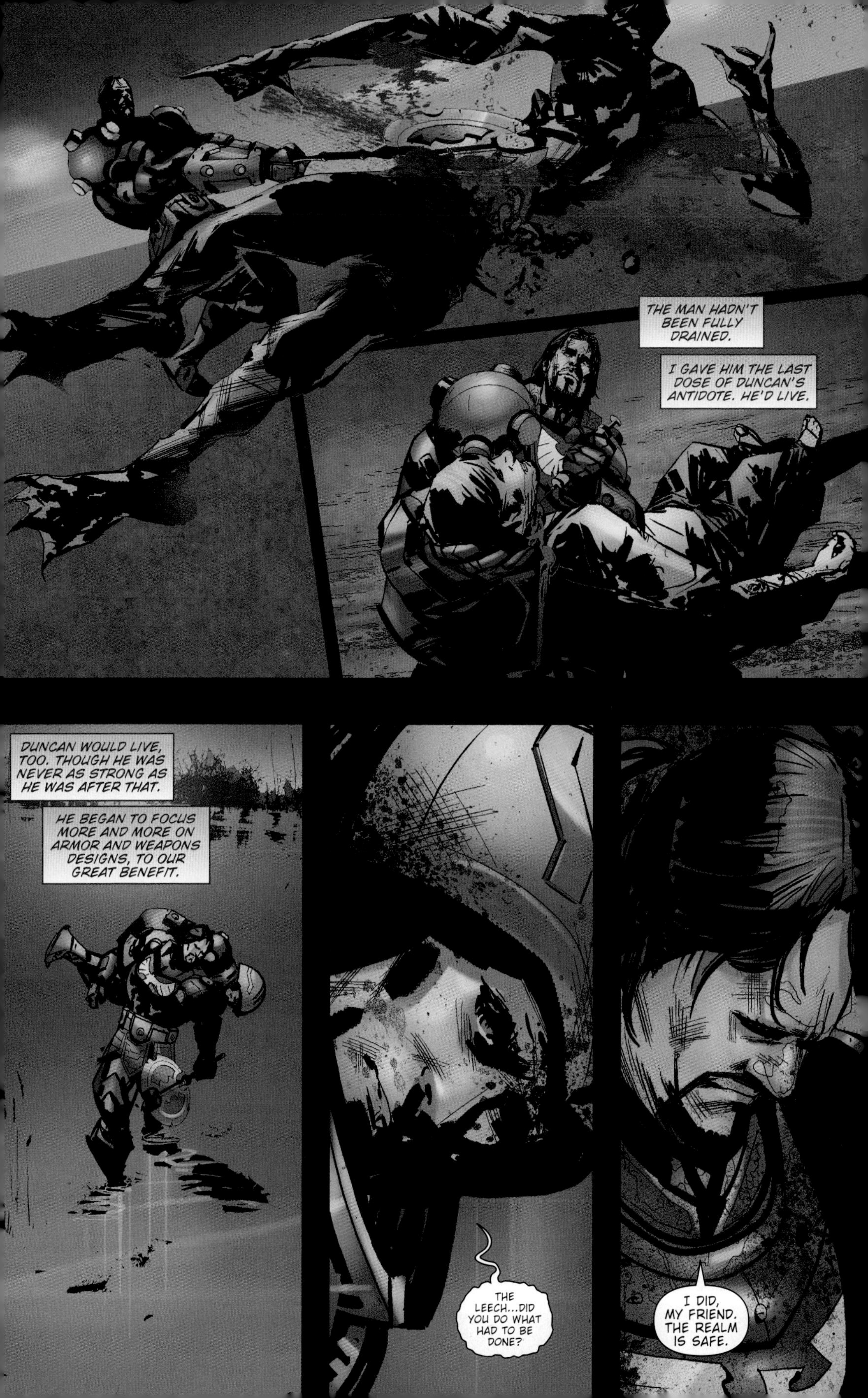
THE MAN HADN'T BEEN FULLY DRAINED.
I GAVE HIM THE LAST DOSE OF DUNCAN'S ANTIDOTE. HE'D LIVE.
DUNCAN WOULD LIVE, TOO. THOUGH HE WAS NEVER AS STRONG AS HE WAS AFTER THAT.
HE BEGAN TO FOCUS MORE AND MORE ON ARMOR AND WEAPONS DESIGNS, TO OUR GREAT BENEFIT.
THE LEECH...DID YOU DO WHAT HAD TO BE DONE?
I DID, MY FRIEND. THE REALM IS SAFE.

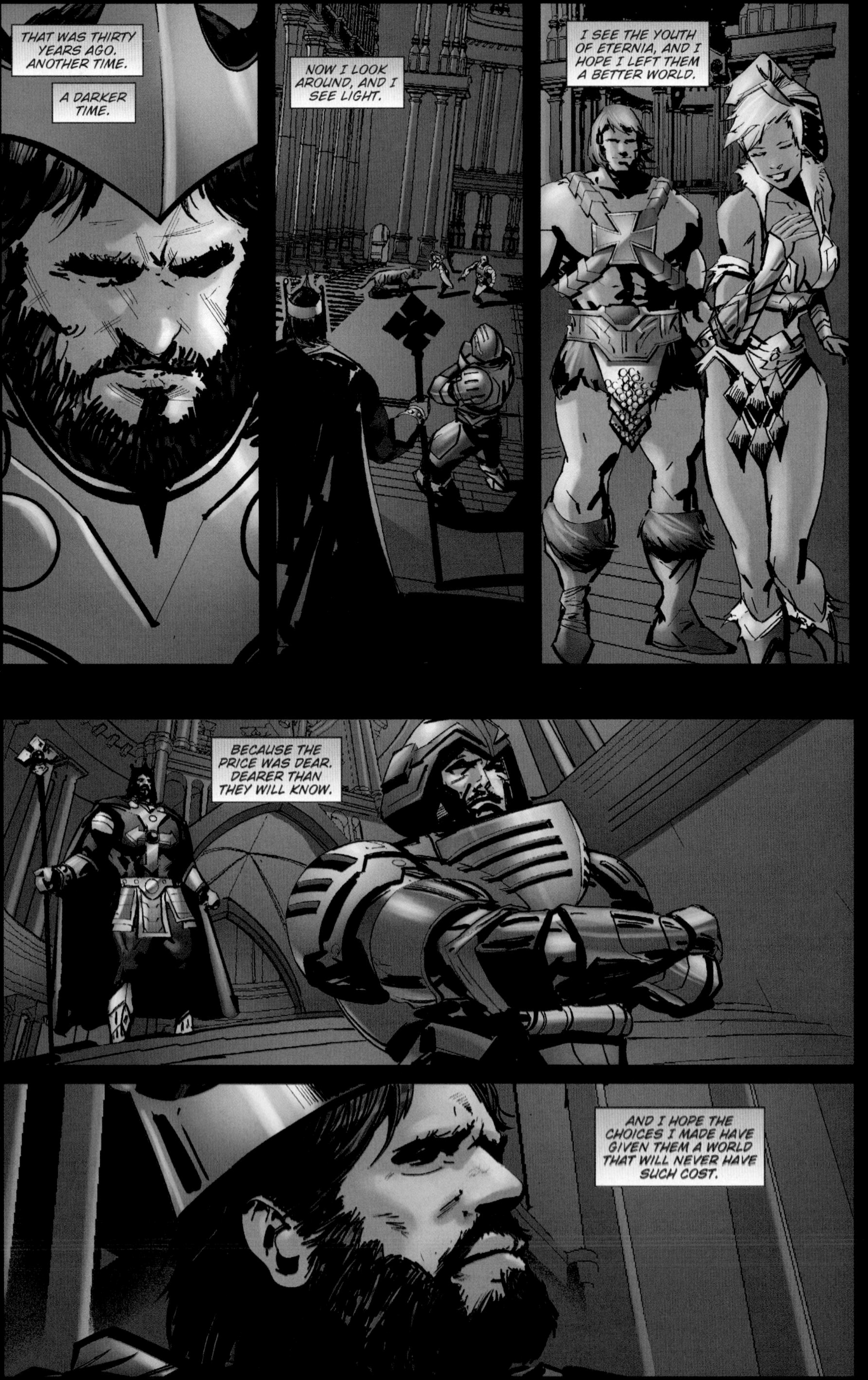
THAT WAS THIRTY YEARS AGO. ANOTHER TIME.
A DARKER TIME.
NOW I LOOK AROUND, AND I SEE LIGHT.
I SEE THE YOUTH OF ETERNIA, AND I HOPE I LEFT THEM A BETTER WORLD.
BECAUSE THE PRICE WAS DEAR. DEARER THAN THEY WILL KNOW.
AND I HOPE THE CHOICES I MADE HAVE GIVEN THEM A WORLD THAT WILL NEVER HAVE SUCH COST.

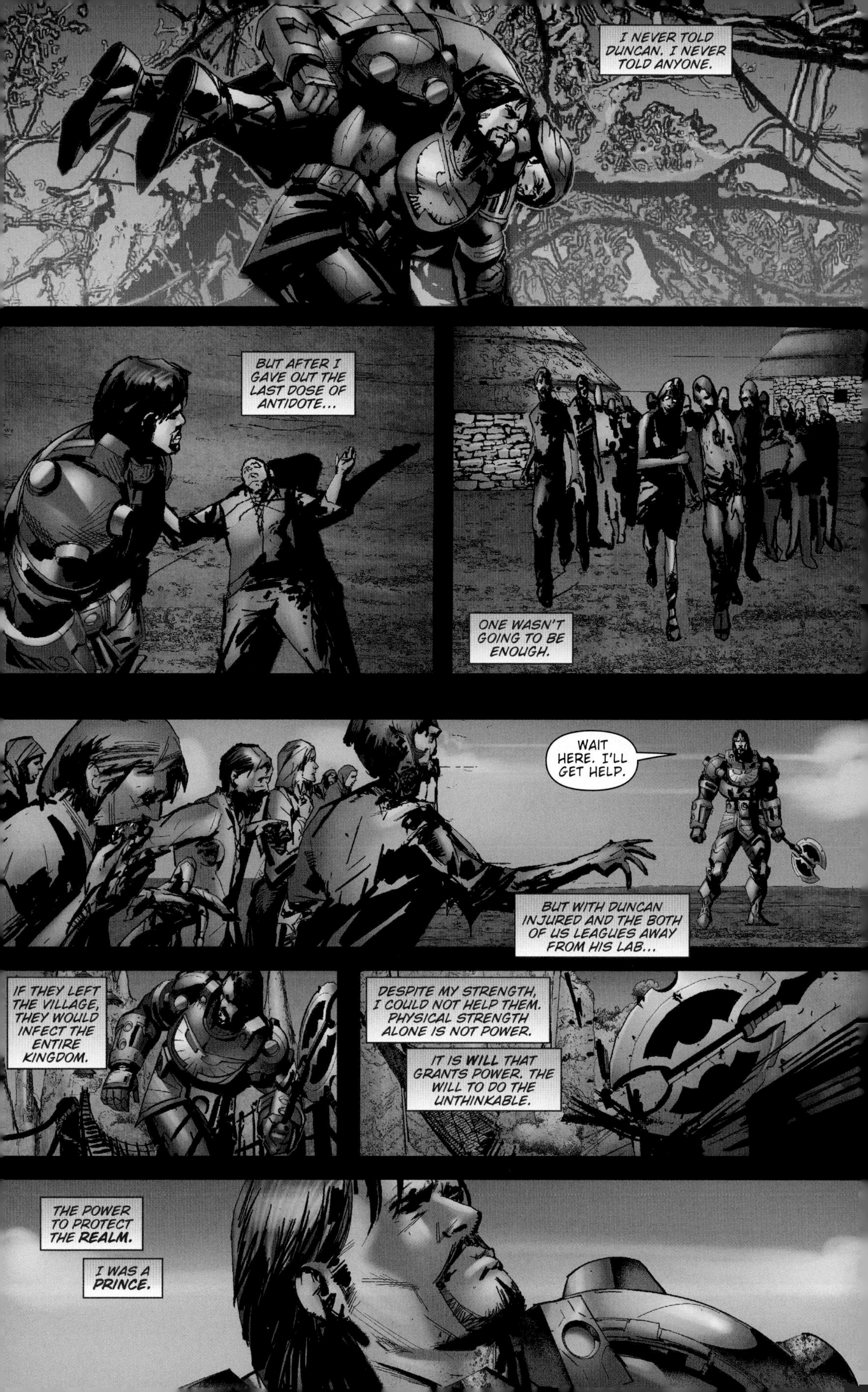
I NEVER TOLD DUNCAN. I NEVER TOLD ANYONE.
BUT AFTER I GAVE OUT THE LAST DOSE OF ANTIDOTE...
ONE WASN'T GOING TO BE ENOUGH.
WAIT HERE. I'LL GET HELP.
BUT WITH DUNCAN INJURED AND THE BOTH OF US LEAGUES AWAY FROM HIS LAB...
IF THEY LEFT THE VILLAGE, THEY WOULD INFECT THE ENTIRE KINGDOM.
DESPITE MY STRENGTH, I COULD NOT HELP THEM. PHYSICAL STRENGTH ALONE IS NOT POWER.
IT IS WILL THAT GRANTS POWER. THE WILL TO DO THE UNTHINKABLE.
THE POWER TO PROTECT THE REALM.
I WAS A PRINCE.

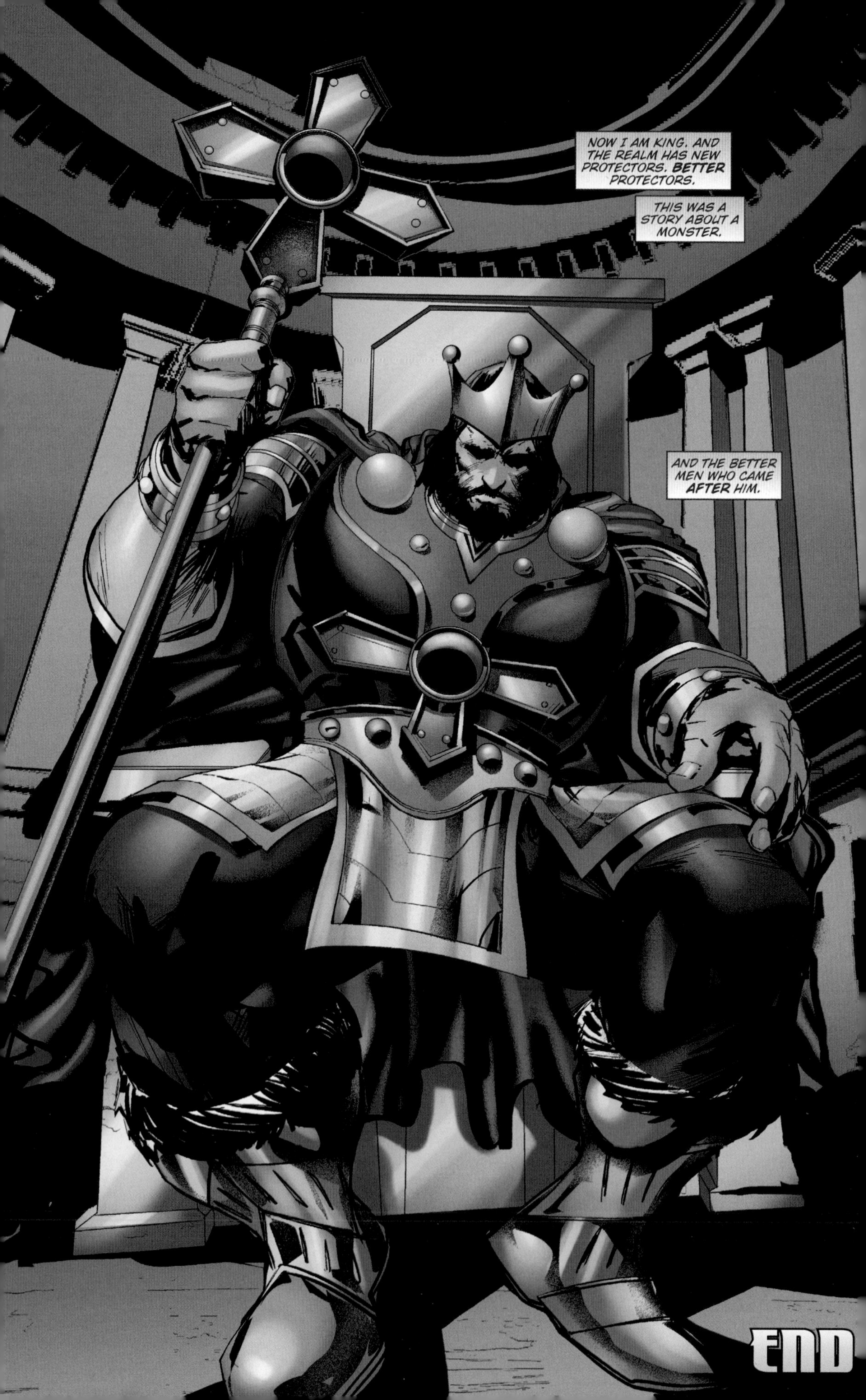
NOW I AM KING. AND THE REALM HAS NEW PROTECTORS. **BETTER** PROTECTORS.
THIS WAS A STORY ABOUT A MONSTER.
AND THE BETTER MEN WHO CAME **AFTER** HIM.
END

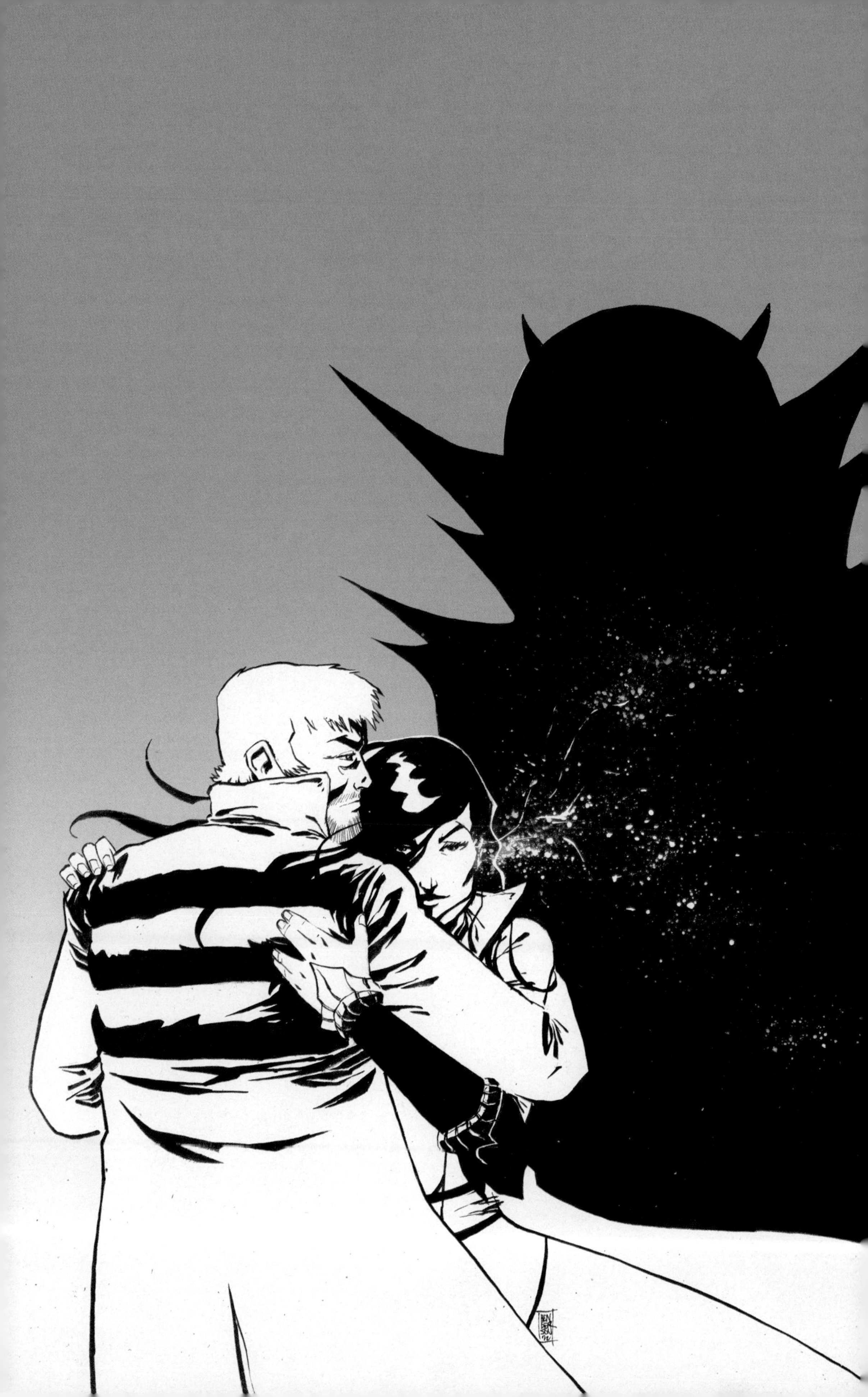

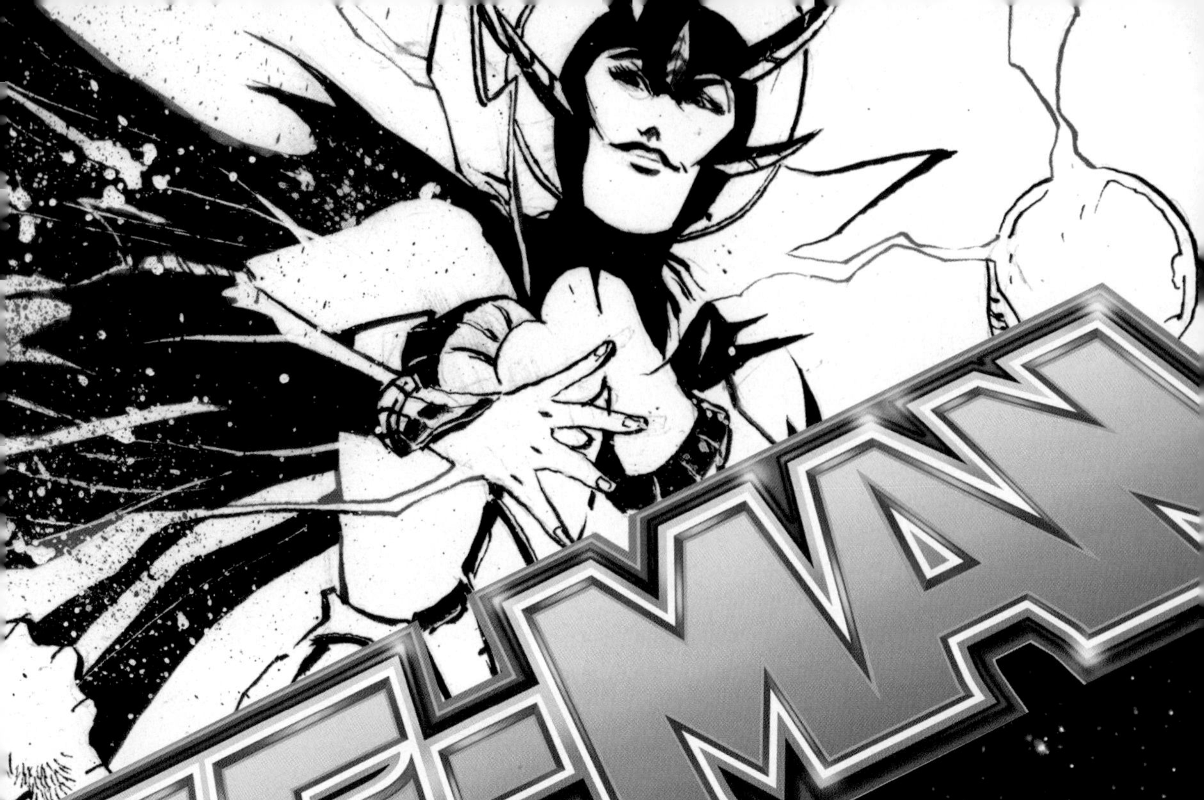

HE-MAN

EVIL-LYN

Kyle Higgins Writer
Mike Henderson Artist
Dezi Sienty Letterer

Cover Art by **Mike Henderson**

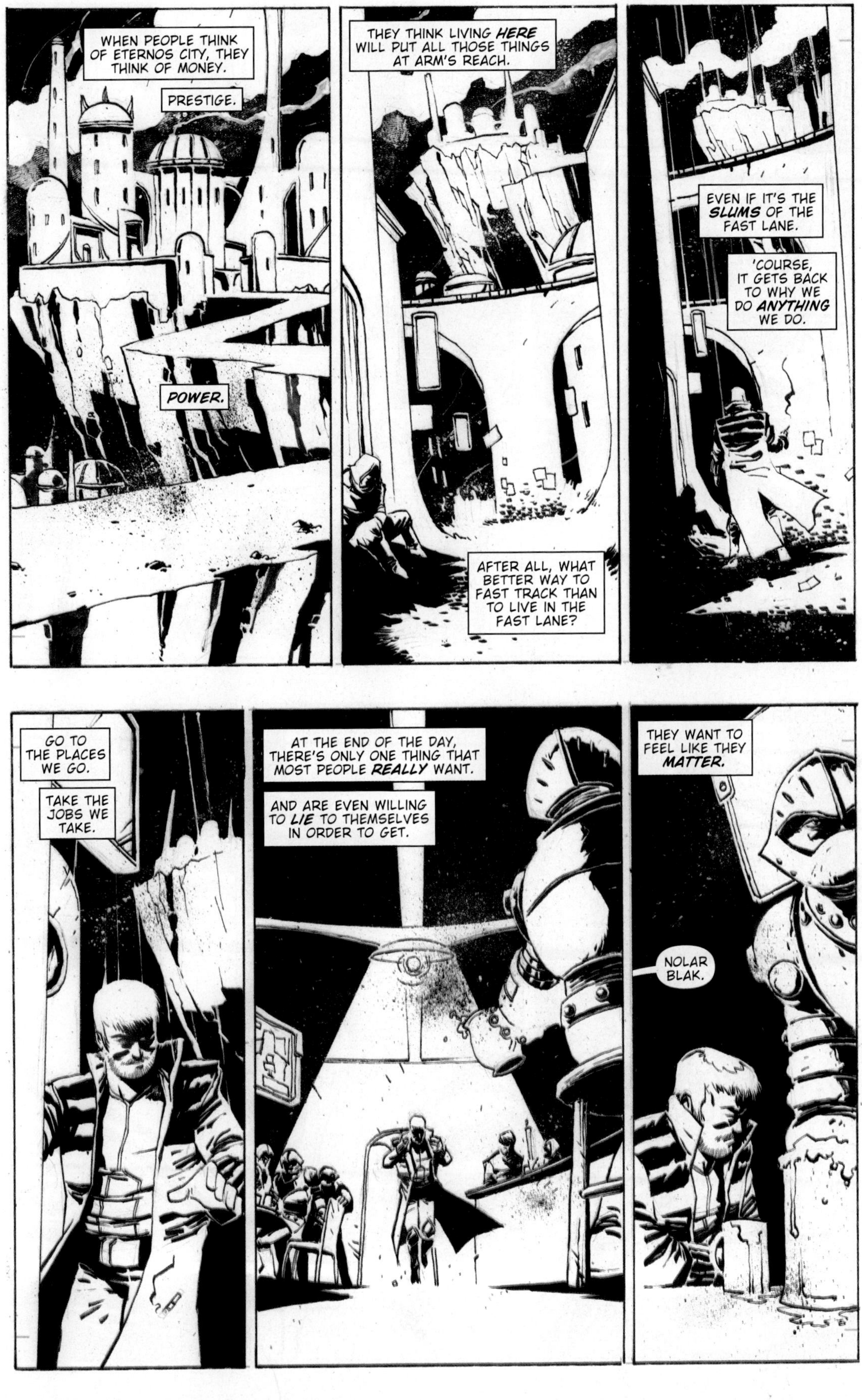
WHEN PEOPLE THINK OF ETERNOS CITY, THEY THINK OF MONEY.
PRESTIGE.
POWER.
THEY THINK LIVING HERE WILL PUT ALL THOSE THINGS AT ARM'S REACH.
AFTER ALL, WHAT BETTER WAY TO FAST TRACK THAN TO LIVE IN THE FAST LANE?
EVEN IF IT'S THE SLUMS OF THE FAST LANE.
'COURSE, IT GETS BACK TO WHY WE DO ANYTHING WE DO.
GO TO THE PLACES WE GO.
TAKE THE JOBS WE TAKE.
AT THE END OF THE DAY, THERE'S ONLY ONE THING THAT MOST PEOPLE REALLY WANT.
AND ARE EVEN WILLING TO LIE TO THEMSELVES IN ORDER TO GET.
THEY WANT TO FEEL LIKE THEY MATTER.
NOLAR BLAK.

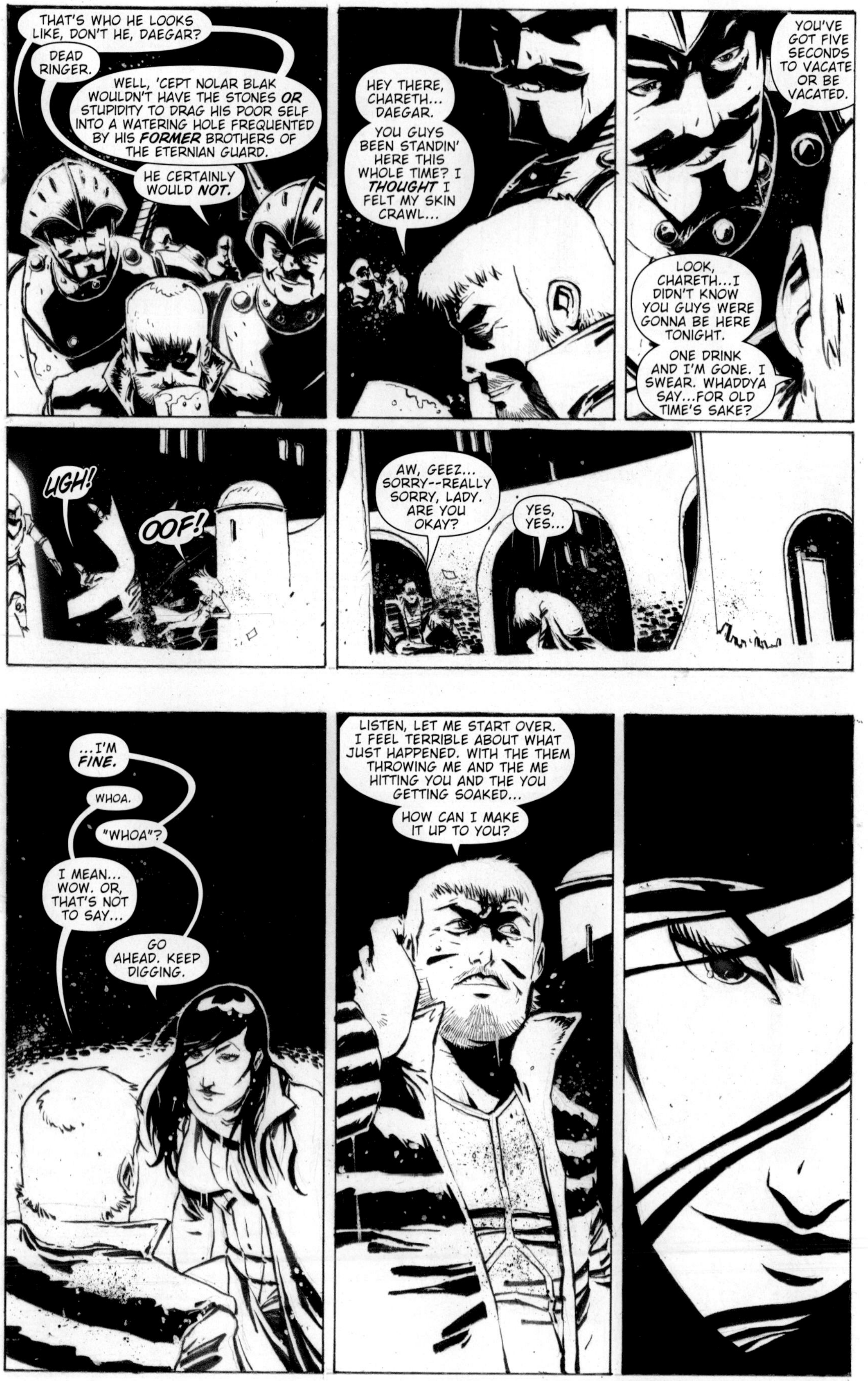
THAT'S WHO HE LOOKS LIKE, DON'T HE, DAEGAR?
DEAD RINGER.
WELL, 'CEPT NOLAR BLAK WOULDN'T HAVE THE STONES OR STUPIDITY TO DRAG HIS POOR SELF INTO A WATERING HOLE FREQUENTED BY HIS FORMER BROTHERS OF THE ETERNIAN GUARD.
HE CERTAINLY WOULD NOT.
HEY THERE, CHARETH... DAEGAR.
YOU GUYS BEEN STANDIN' HERE THIS WHOLE TIME? I THOUGHT I FELT MY SKIN CRAWL...
YOU'VE GOT FIVE SECONDS TO VACATE OR BE VACATED.
LOOK, CHARETH...I DIDN'T KNOW YOU GUYS WERE GONNA BE HERE TONIGHT.
ONE DRINK AND I'M GONE. I SWEAR. WHADDYA SAY...FOR OLD TIME'S SAKE?
UGH!
OOF!
AW, GEEZ... SORRY--REALLY SORRY, LADY. ARE YOU OKAY?
YES, YES...
...I'M FINE.
WHOA.
"WHOA"?
I MEAN... WOW. OR, THAT'S NOT TO SAY...
GO AHEAD. KEEP DIGGING.
LISTEN, LET ME START OVER. I FEEL TERRIBLE ABOUT WHAT JUST HAPPENED. WITH THE THEM THROWING ME AND THE ME HITTING YOU AND THE YOU GETTING SOAKED...
HOW CAN I MAKE IT UP TO YOU?

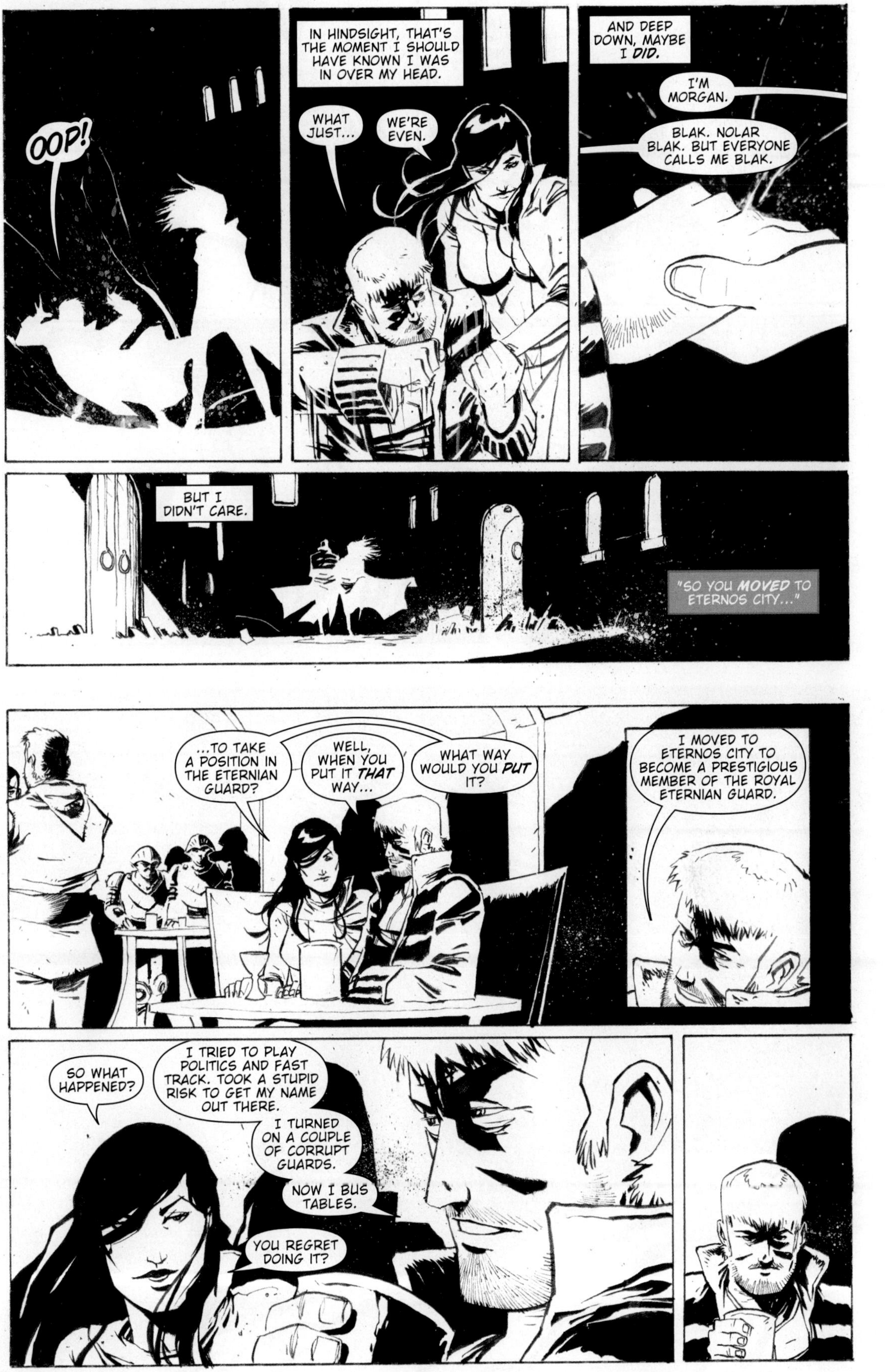
OOP!
IN HINDSIGHT, THAT'S THE MOMENT I SHOULD HAVE KNOWN I WAS IN OVER MY HEAD.
WHAT JUST...
WE'RE EVEN.
AND DEEP DOWN, MAYBE I DID.
I'M MORGAN.
BLAK. NOLAR BLAK. BUT EVERYONE CALLS ME BLAK.
BUT I DIDN'T CARE.
"SO YOU MOVED TO ETERNOS CITY..."
...TO TAKE A POSITION IN THE ETERNIAN GUARD?
WELL, WHEN YOU PUT IT THAT WAY...
WHAT WAY WOULD YOU PUT IT?
I MOVED TO ETERNOS CITY TO BECOME A PRESTIGIOUS MEMBER OF THE ROYAL ETERNIAN GUARD.
SO WHAT HAPPENED?
I TRIED TO PLAY POLITICS AND FAST TRACK. TOOK A STUPID RISK TO GET MY NAME OUT THERE.
I TURNED ON A COUPLE OF CORRUPT GUARDS.
NOW I BUS TABLES.
YOU REGRET DOING IT?

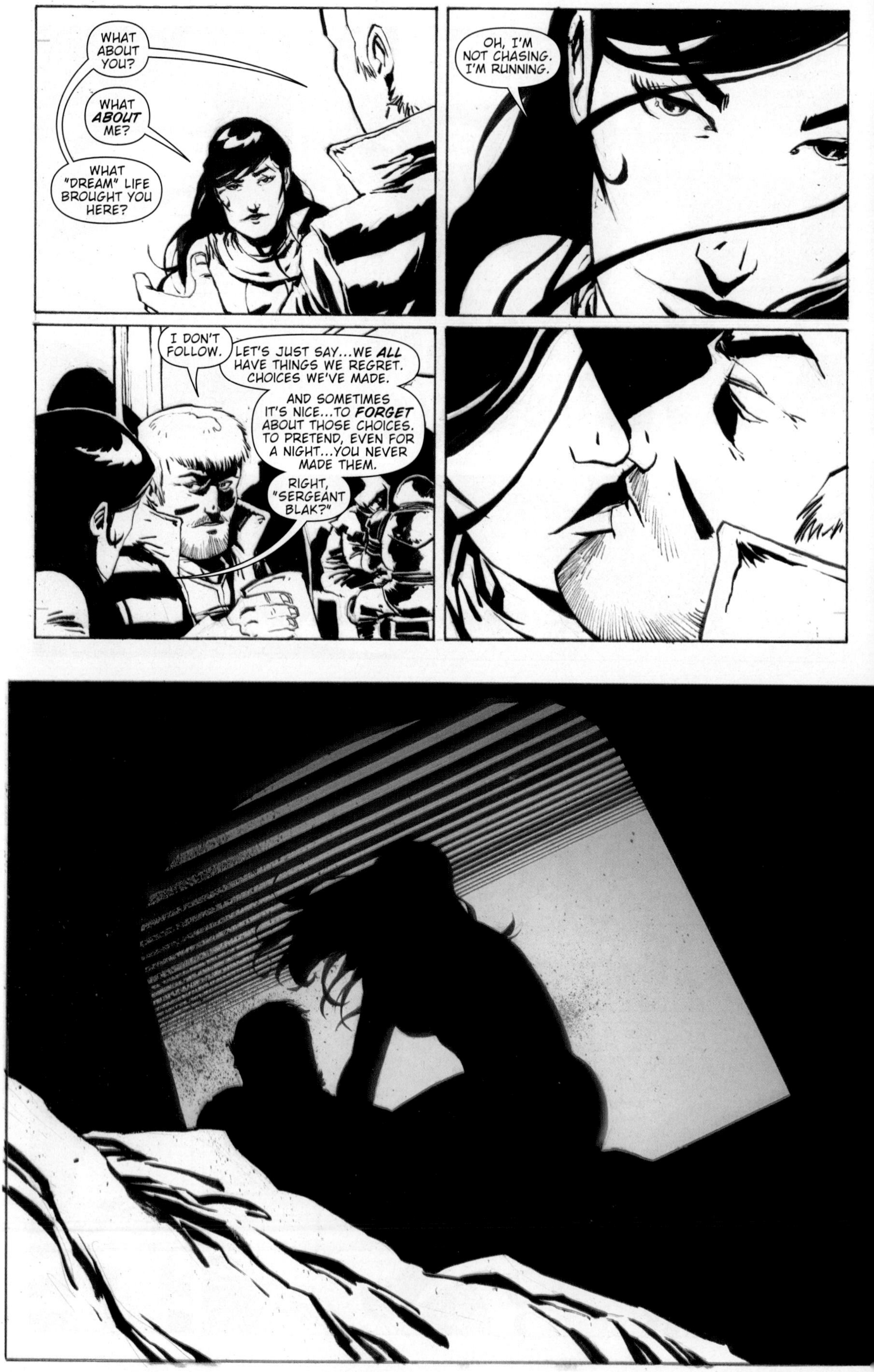
WHAT ABOUT YOU?
WHAT ABOUT ME?
WHAT "DREAM" LIFE BROUGHT YOU HERE?
OH, I'M NOT CHASING. I'M RUNNING.
I DON'T FOLLOW.
LET'S JUST SAY...WE ALL HAVE THINGS WE REGRET. CHOICES WE'VE MADE.
AND SOMETIMES IT'S NICE...TO FORGET ABOUT THOSE CHOICES. TO PRETEND, EVEN FOR A NIGHT...YOU NEVER MADE THEM.
RIGHT, "SERGEANT BLAK?"

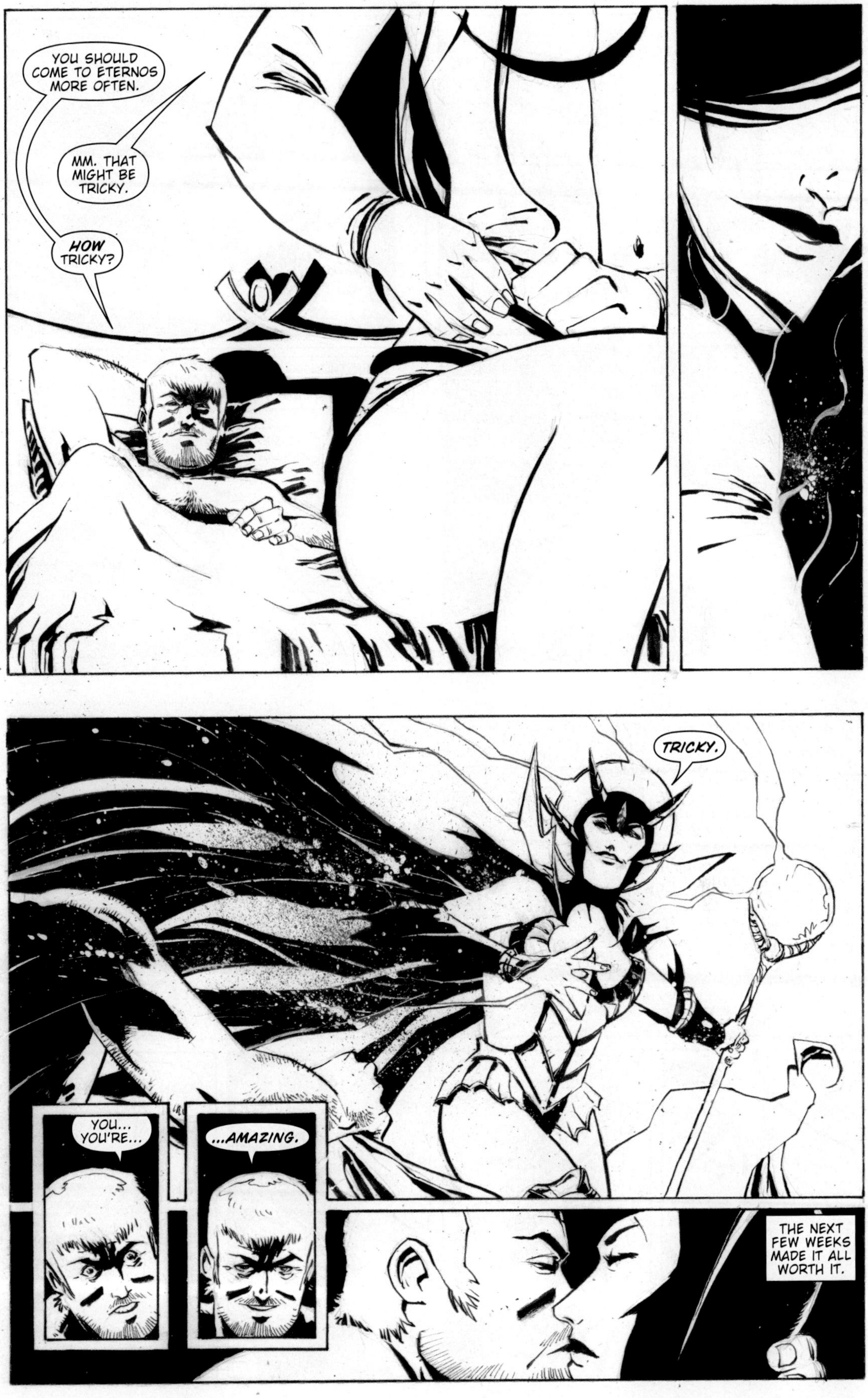

YOU SHOULD COME TO ETERNOS MORE OFTEN.
MM. THAT MIGHT BE TRICKY.
HOW TRICKY?
TRICKY.
YOU... YOU'RE...
...AMAZING.
THE NEXT FEW WEEKS MADE IT ALL WORTH IT.

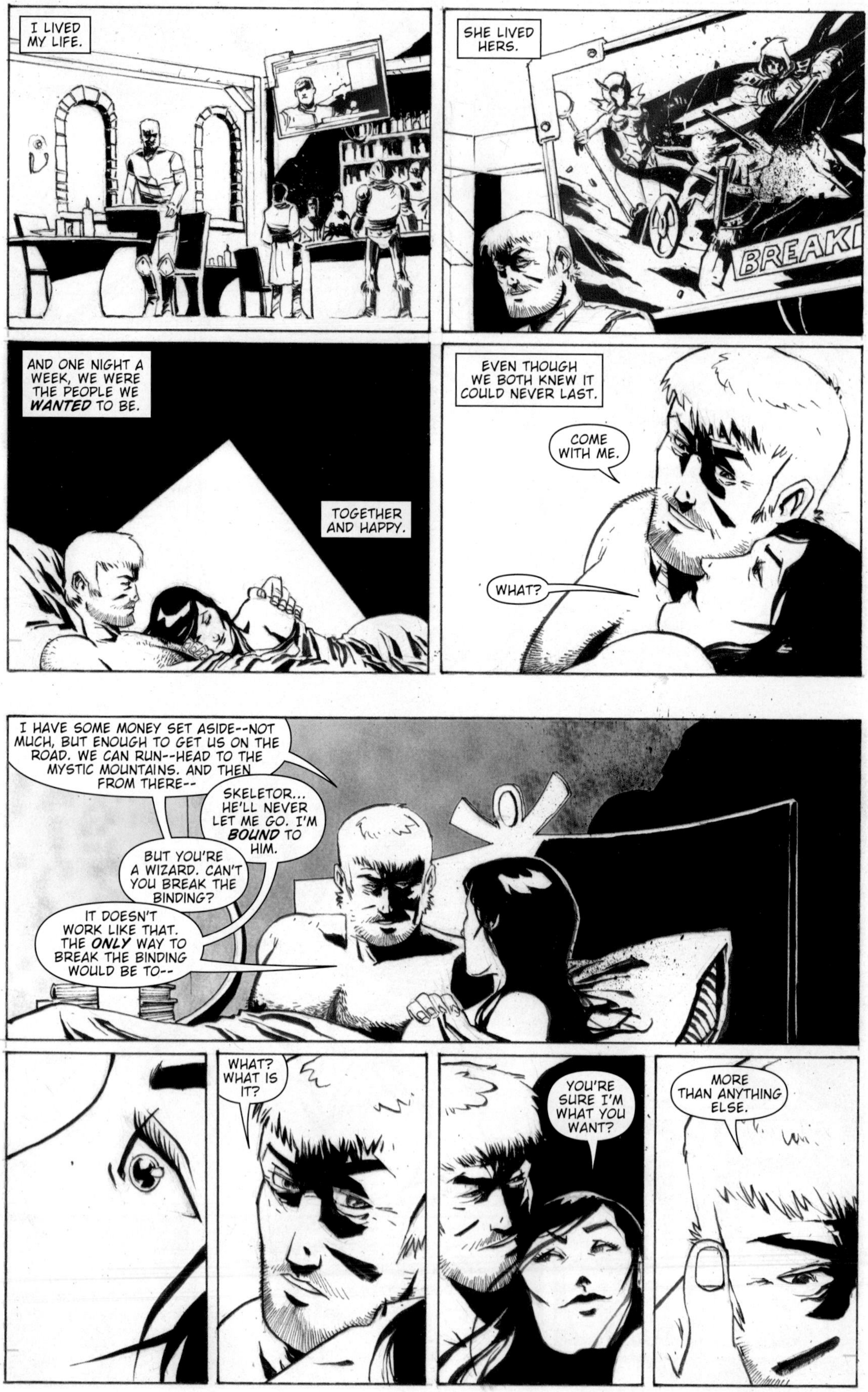
I LIVED MY LIFE.
SHE LIVED HERS.
BREAK
AND ONE NIGHT A WEEK, WE WERE THE PEOPLE WE WANTED TO BE.
TOGETHER AND HAPPY.
EVEN THOUGH WE BOTH KNEW IT COULD NEVER LAST.
COME WITH ME.
WHAT?
I HAVE SOME MONEY SET ASIDE--NOT MUCH, BUT ENOUGH TO GET US ON THE ROAD. WE CAN RUN--HEAD TO THE MYSTIC MOUNTAINS. AND THEN FROM THERE--
SKELETOR... HE'LL NEVER LET ME GO. I'M BOUND TO HIM.
BUT YOU'RE A WIZARD. CAN'T YOU BREAK THE BINDING?
IT DOESN'T WORK LIKE THAT. THE ONLY WAY TO BREAK THE BINDING WOULD BE TO--
WHAT? WHAT IS IT?
YOU'RE SURE I'M WHAT YOU WANT?
MORE THAN ANYTHING ELSE.

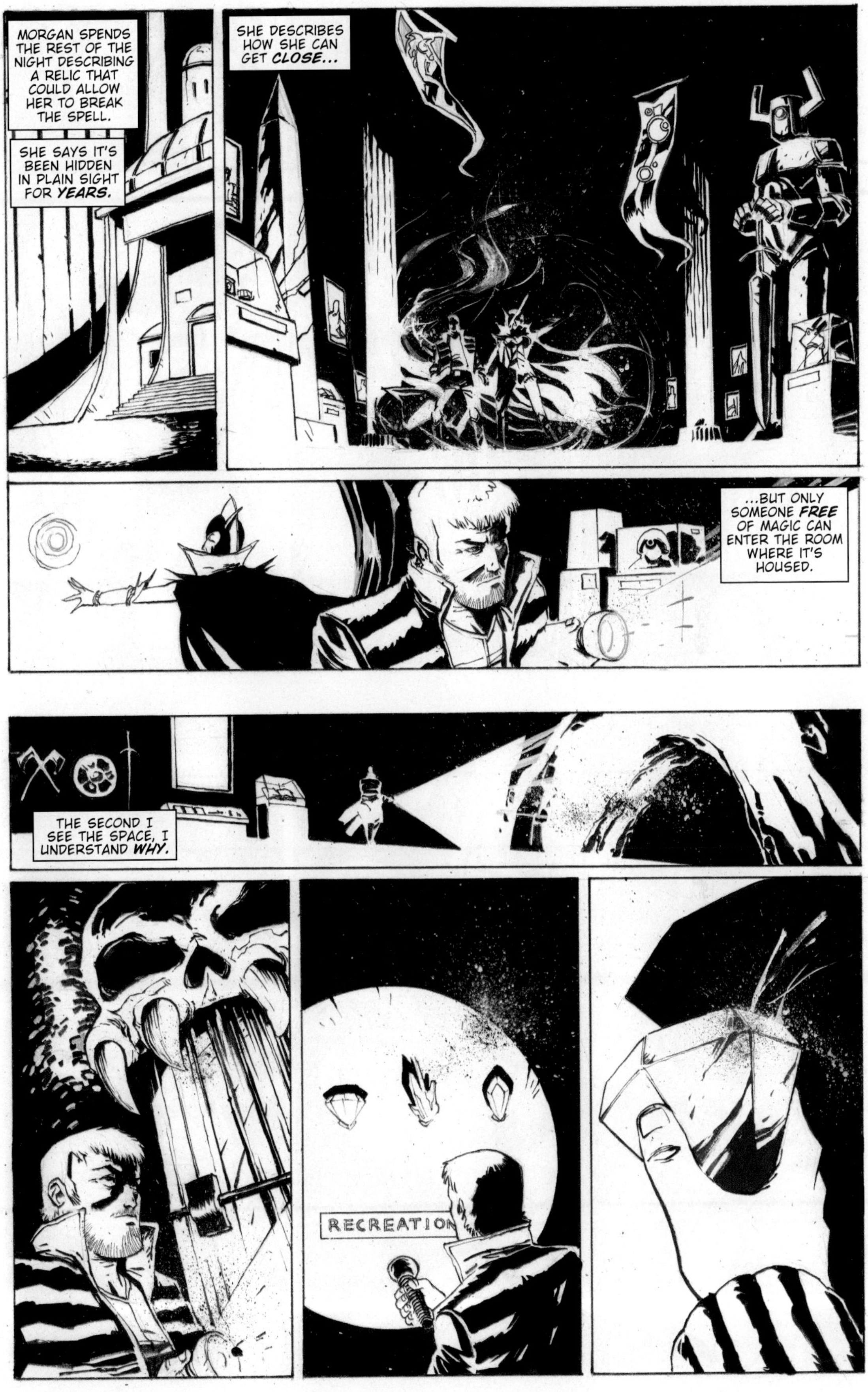
MORGAN SPENDS THE REST OF THE NIGHT DESCRIBING A RELIC THAT COULD ALLOW HER TO BREAK THE SPELL.
SHE SAYS IT'S BEEN HIDDEN IN PLAIN SIGHT FOR *YEARS.*
SHE DESCRIBES HOW SHE CAN GET *CLOSE...*
...BUT ONLY SOMEONE *FREE* OF MAGIC CAN ENTER THE ROOM WHERE IT'S HOUSED.
THE SECOND I SEE THE SPACE, I UNDERSTAND *WHY.*
RECREATION

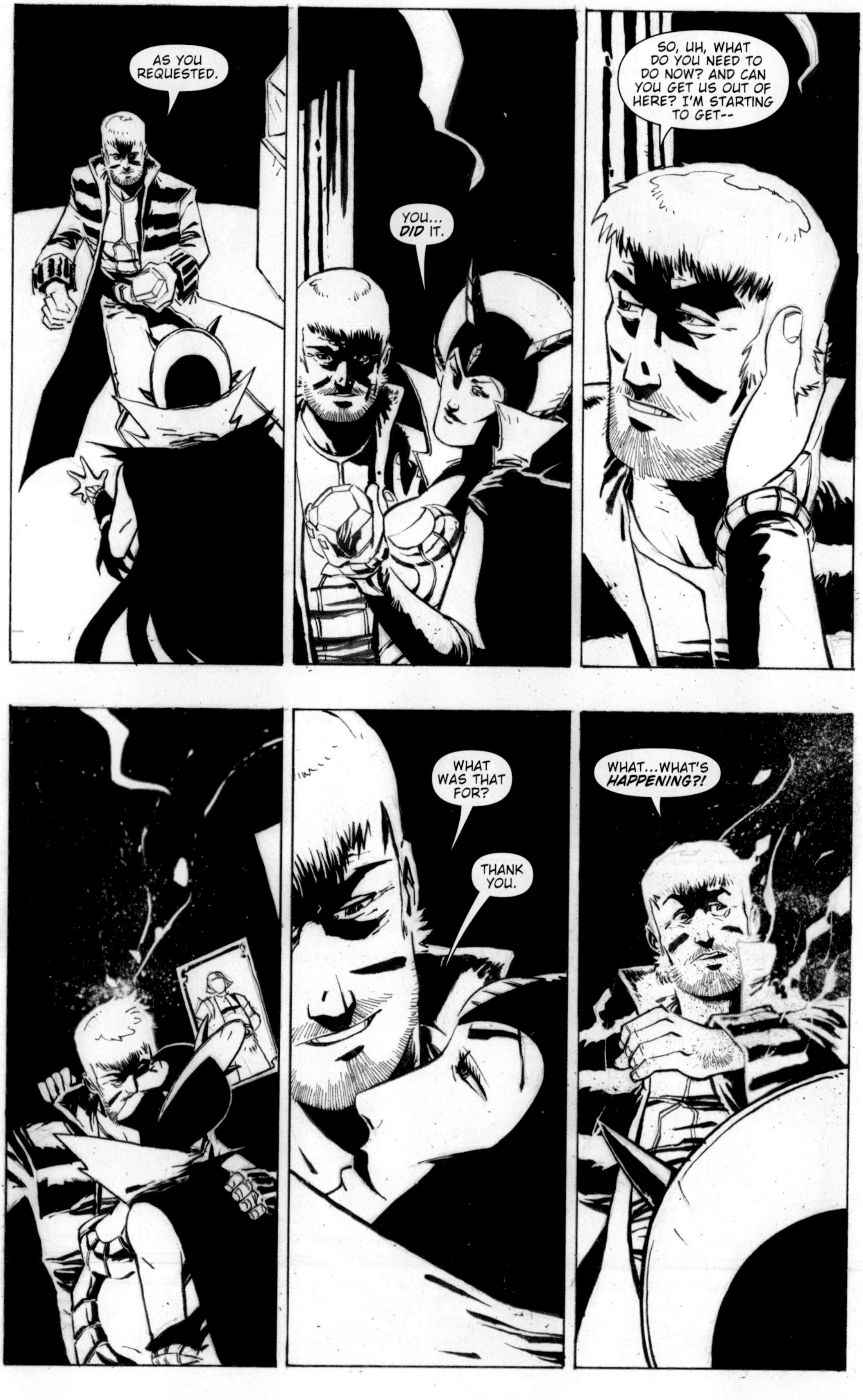
AS YOU REQUESTED.
YOU... *DID* IT.
SO, UH, WHAT DO YOU NEED TO DO NOW? AND CAN YOU GET US OUT OF HERE? I'M STARTING TO GET--
WHAT WAS THAT FOR?
THANK YOU.
WHAT...WHAT'S *HAPPENING?!*

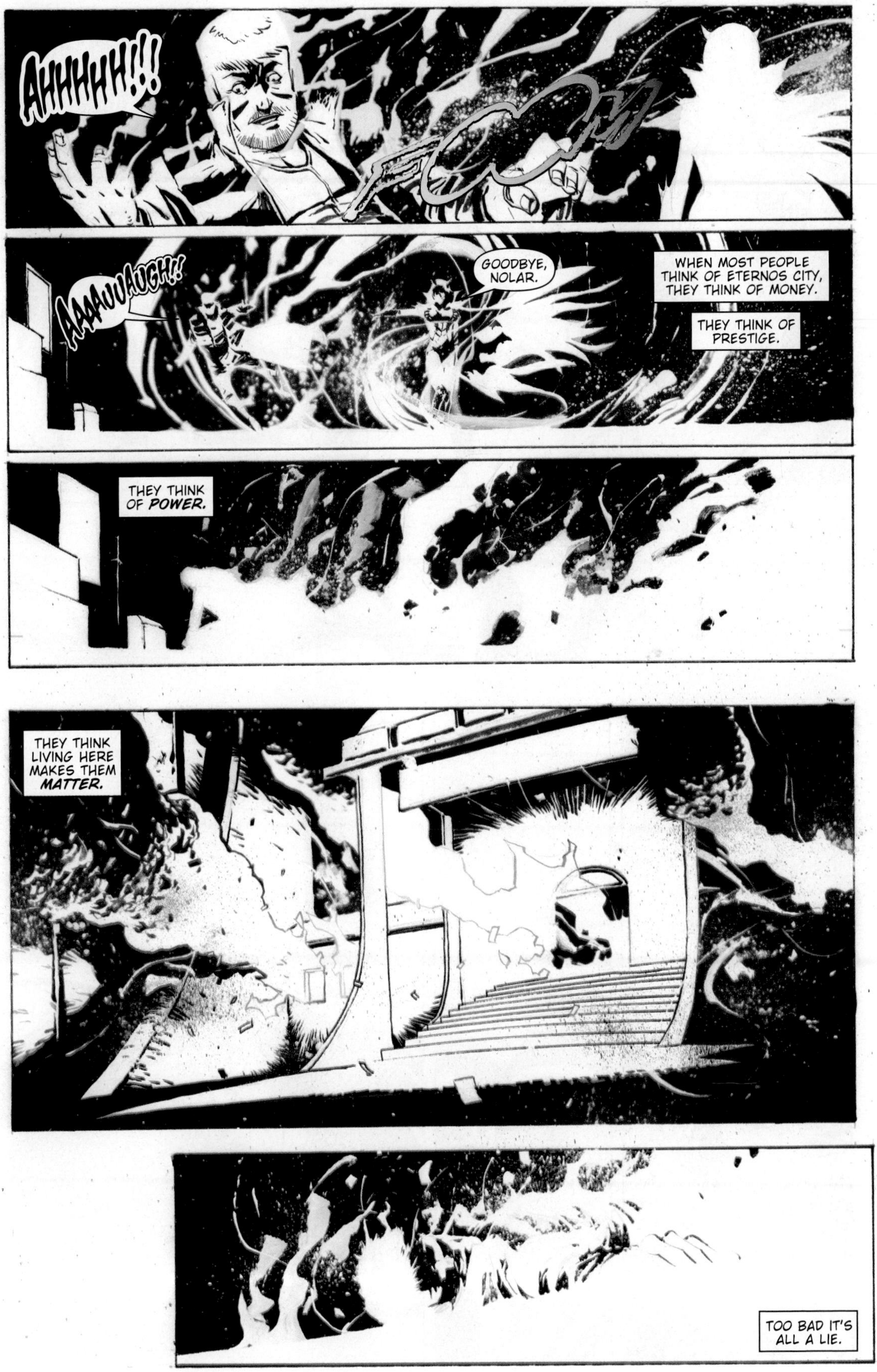
AHHHHH!!!
FOOM
AAAAUUAUGH!!
GOODBYE, NOLAR.
WHEN MOST PEOPLE THINK OF ETERNOS CITY, THEY THINK OF MONEY.
THEY THINK OF PRESTIGE.
THEY THINK OF POWER.
THEY THINK LIVING HERE MAKES THEM MATTER.
TOO BAD IT'S ALL A LIE.

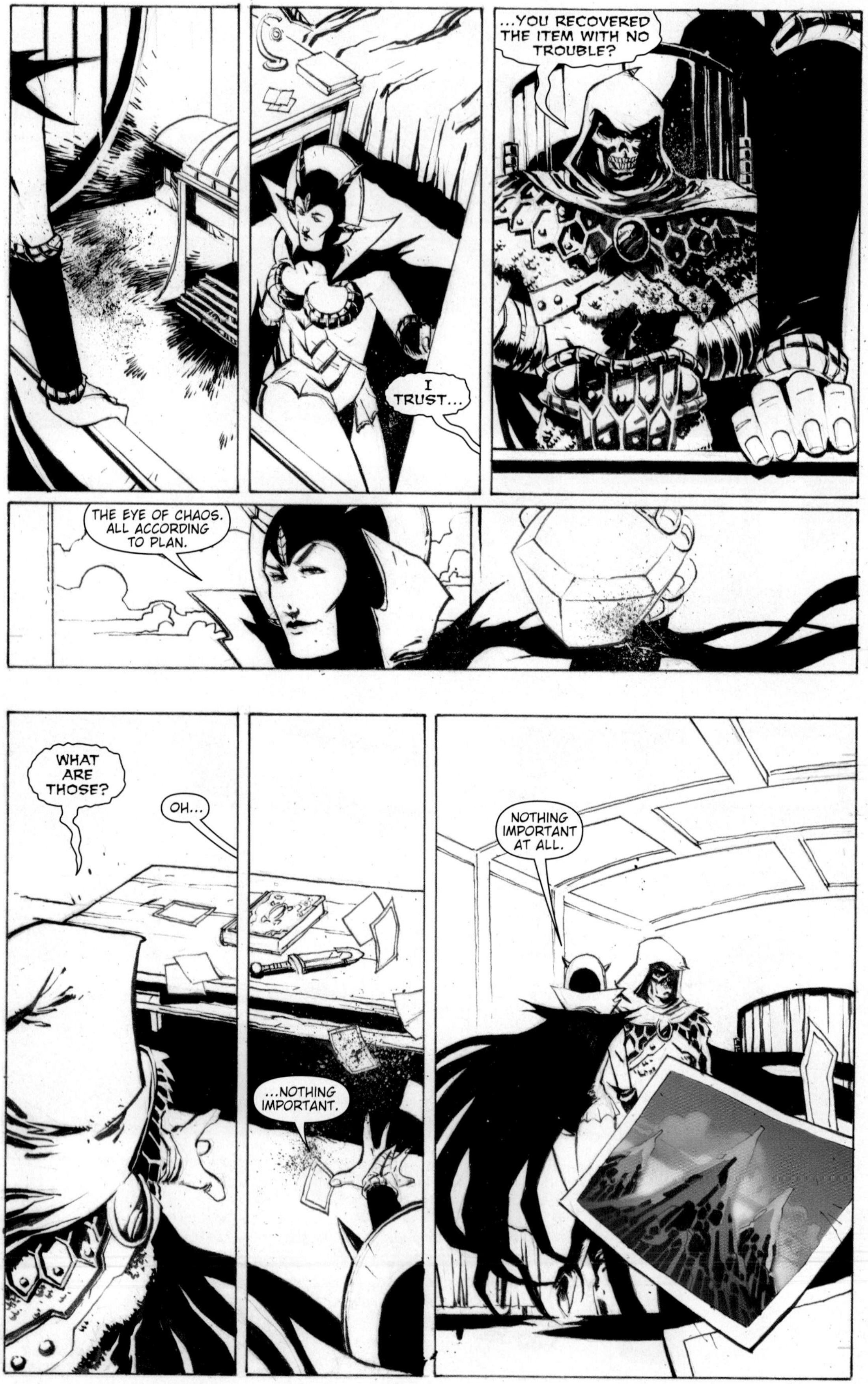
I TRUST...
...YOU RECOVERED THE ITEM WITH NO TROUBLE?
THE EYE OF CHAOS. ALL ACCORDING TO PLAN.
WHAT ARE THOSE?
OH...
...NOTHING IMPORTANT.
NOTHING IMPORTANT AT ALL.

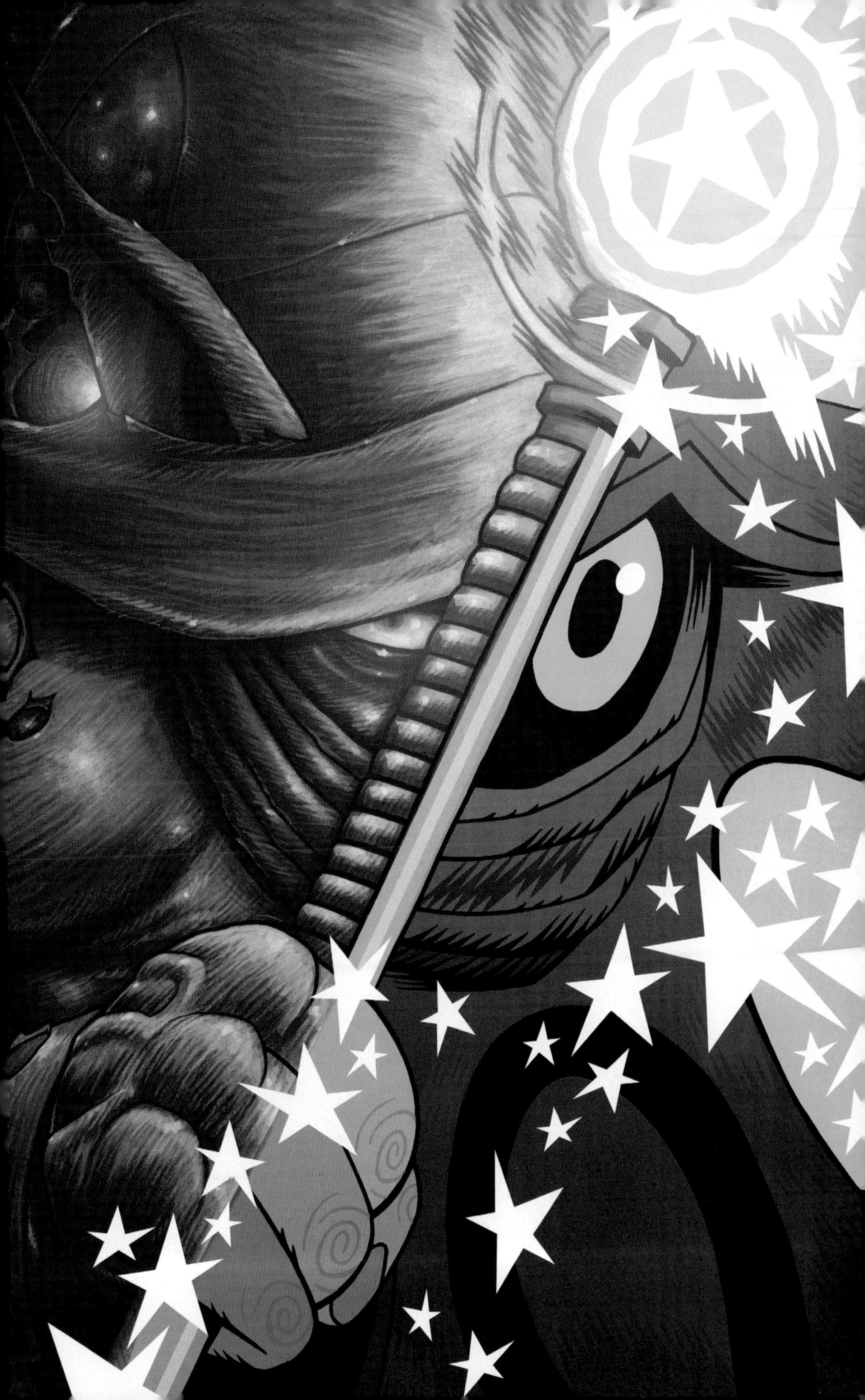

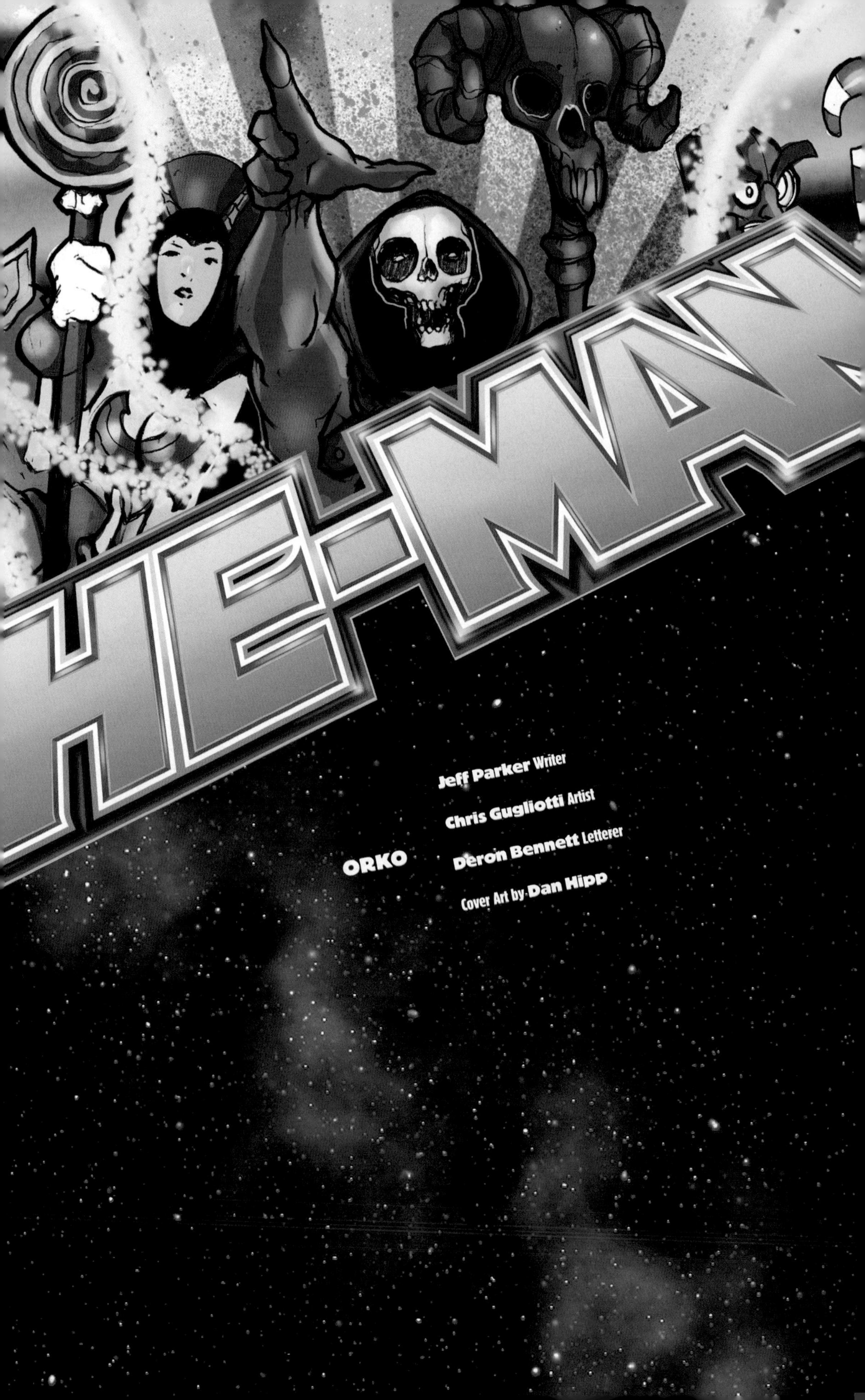
HE-MAN
ORKO
Jeff Parker Writer
Chris Gugliotti Artist
Deron Bennett Letterer
Cover Art by Dan Hipp

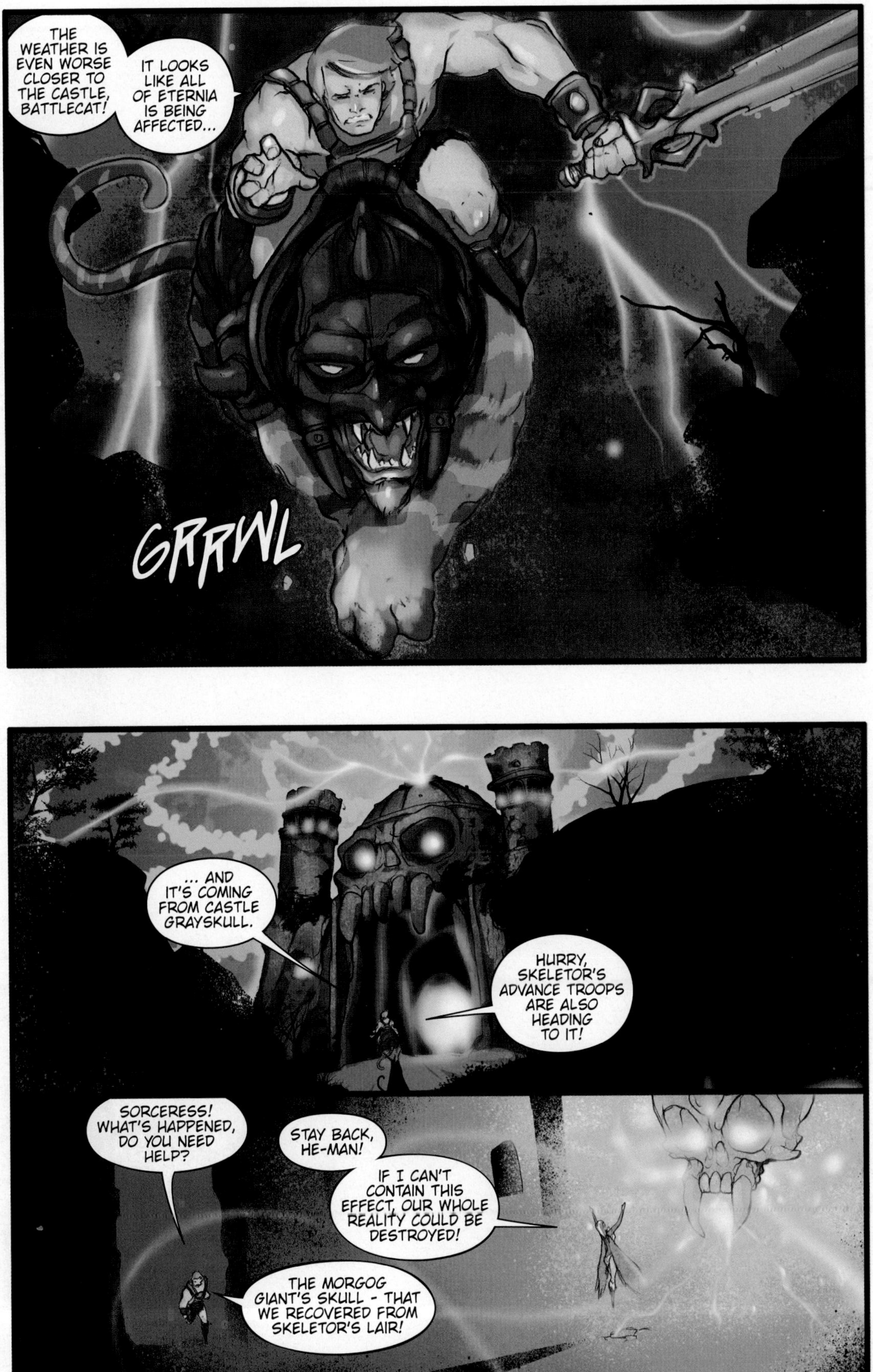
THE WEATHER IS EVEN WORSE CLOSER TO THE CASTLE, BATTLECAT!
IT LOOKS LIKE ALL OF ETERNIA IS BEING AFFECTED...
GRRWL
... AND IT'S COMING FROM CASTLE GRAYSKULL.
HURRY, SKELETOR'S ADVANCE TROOPS ARE ALSO HEADING TO IT!
SORCERESS! WHAT'S HAPPENED, DO YOU NEED HELP?
STAY BACK, HE-MAN!
IF I CAN'T CONTAIN THIS EFFECT, OUR WHOLE REALITY COULD BE DESTROYED!
THE MORGOG GIANT'S SKULL - THAT WE RECOVERED FROM SKELETOR'S LAIR!

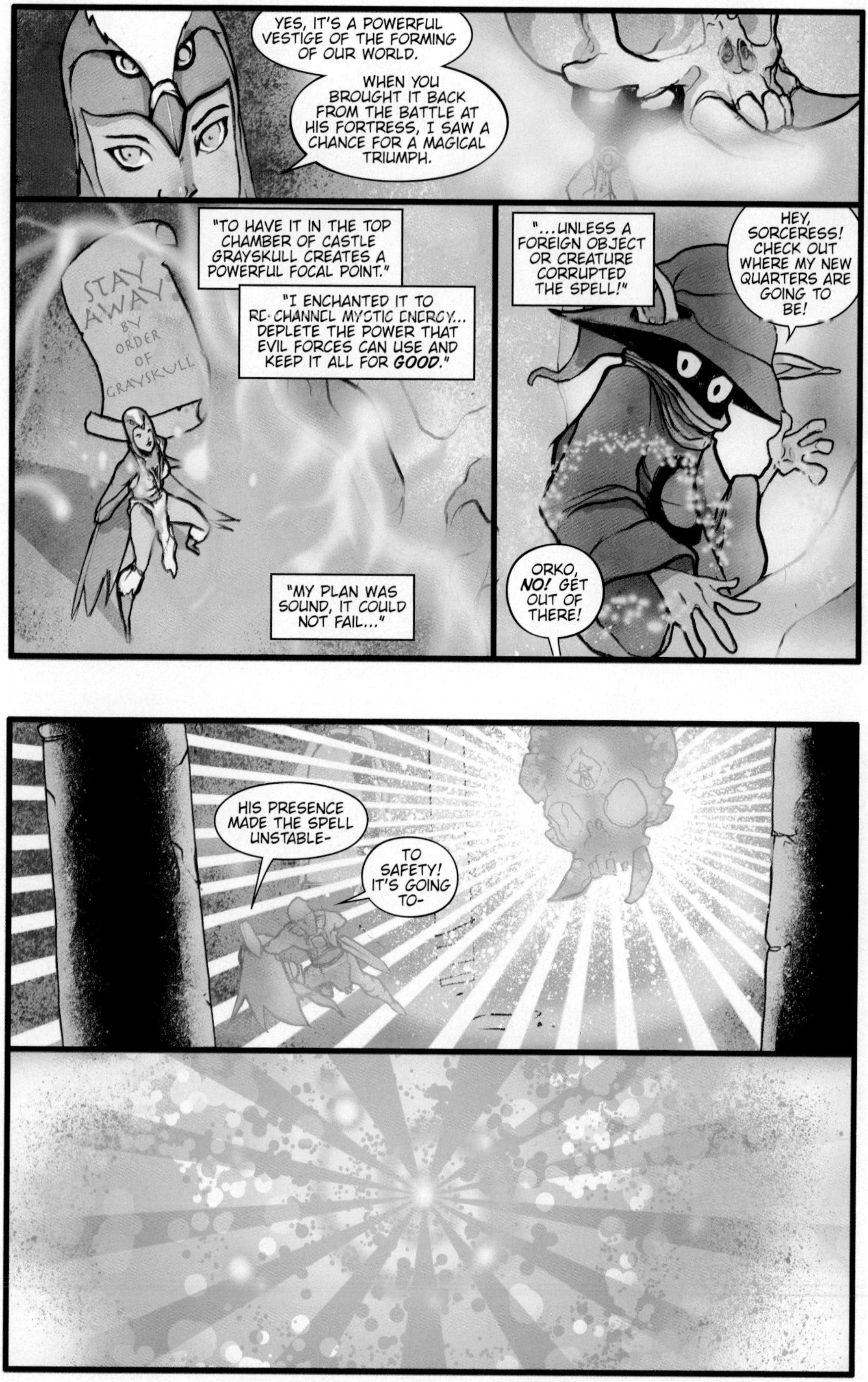
YES, IT'S A POWERFUL VESTIGE OF THE FORMING OF OUR WORLD.
WHEN YOU BROUGHT IT BACK FROM THE BATTLE AT HIS FORTRESS, I SAW A CHANCE FOR A MAGICAL TRIUMPH.
"TO HAVE IT IN THE TOP CHAMBER OF CASTLE GRAYSKULL CREATES A POWERFUL FOCAL POINT."
STAY AWAY! BY ORDER OF GRAYSKULL
"I ENCHANTED IT TO RE-CHANNEL MYSTIC ENERGY... DEPLETE THE POWER THAT EVIL FORCES CAN USE AND KEEP IT ALL FOR GOOD."
"MY PLAN WAS SOUND, IT COULD NOT FAIL..."
"...UNLESS A FOREIGN OBJECT OR CREATURE CORRUPTED THE SPELL!"
HEY, SORCERESS! CHECK OUT WHERE MY NEW QUARTERS ARE GOING TO BE!
ORKO, NO! GET OUT OF THERE!
HIS PRESENCE MADE THE SPELL UNSTABLE-
TO SAFETY! IT'S GOING TO-

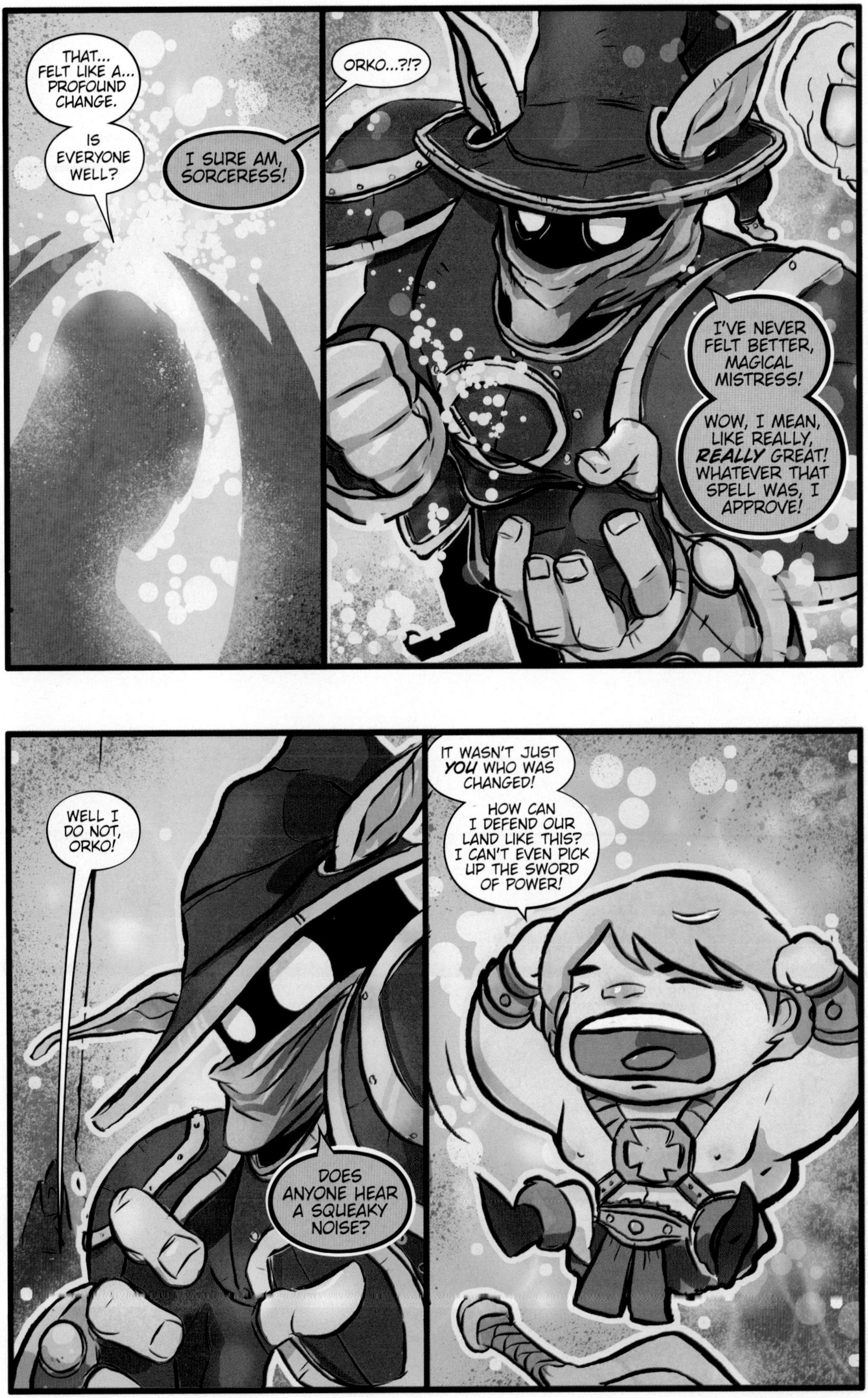
THAT... FELT LIKE A... PROFOUND CHANGE.
IS EVERYONE WELL?
ORKO...?!?
I SURE AM, SORCERESS!
I'VE NEVER FELT BETTER, MAGICAL MISTRESS!
WOW, I MEAN, LIKE REALLY, REALLY GREAT! WHATEVER THAT SPELL WAS, I APPROVE!
WELL I DO NOT, ORKO!
DOES ANYONE HEAR A SQUEAKY NOISE?
IT WASN'T JUST YOU WHO WAS CHANGED!
HOW CAN I DEFEND OUR LAND LIKE THIS? I CAN'T EVEN PICK UP THE SWORD OF POWER!

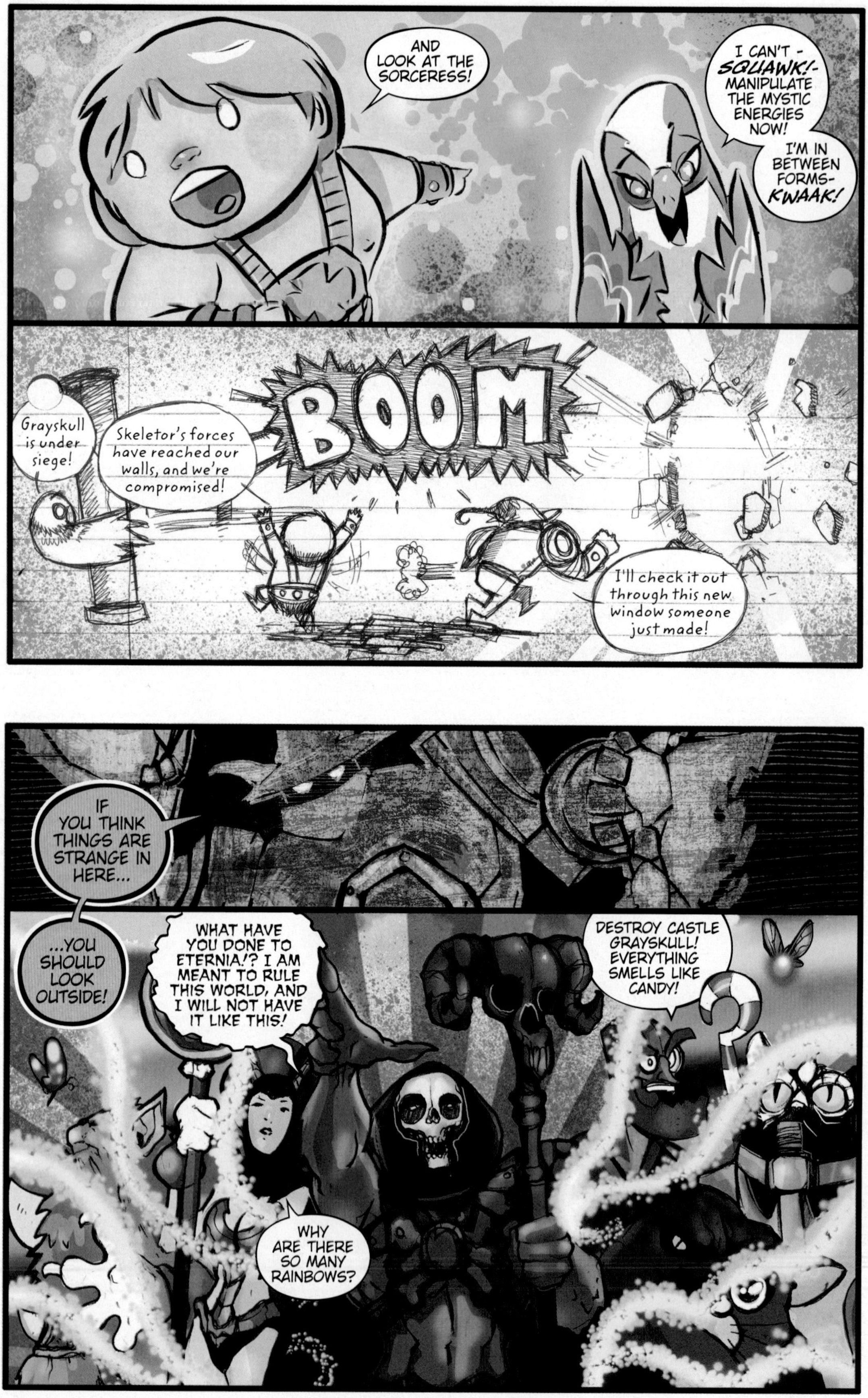
AND LOOK AT THE SORCERESS!
I CAN'T - SQUAWK! - MANIPULATE THE MYSTIC ENERGIES NOW!
I'M IN BETWEEN FORMS- KWAAK!
BOOM
Grayskull is under siege!
Skeletor's forces have reached our walls, and we're compromised!
I'll check it out through this new window someone just made!
IF YOU THINK THINGS ARE STRANGE IN HERE...
...YOU SHOULD LOOK OUTSIDE!
WHAT HAVE YOU DONE TO ETERNIA!? I AM MEANT TO RULE THIS WORLD, AND I WILL NOT HAVE IT LIKE THIS!
DESTROY CASTLE GRAYSKULL! EVERYTHING SMELLS LIKE CANDY!
WHY ARE THERE SO MANY RAINBOWS?

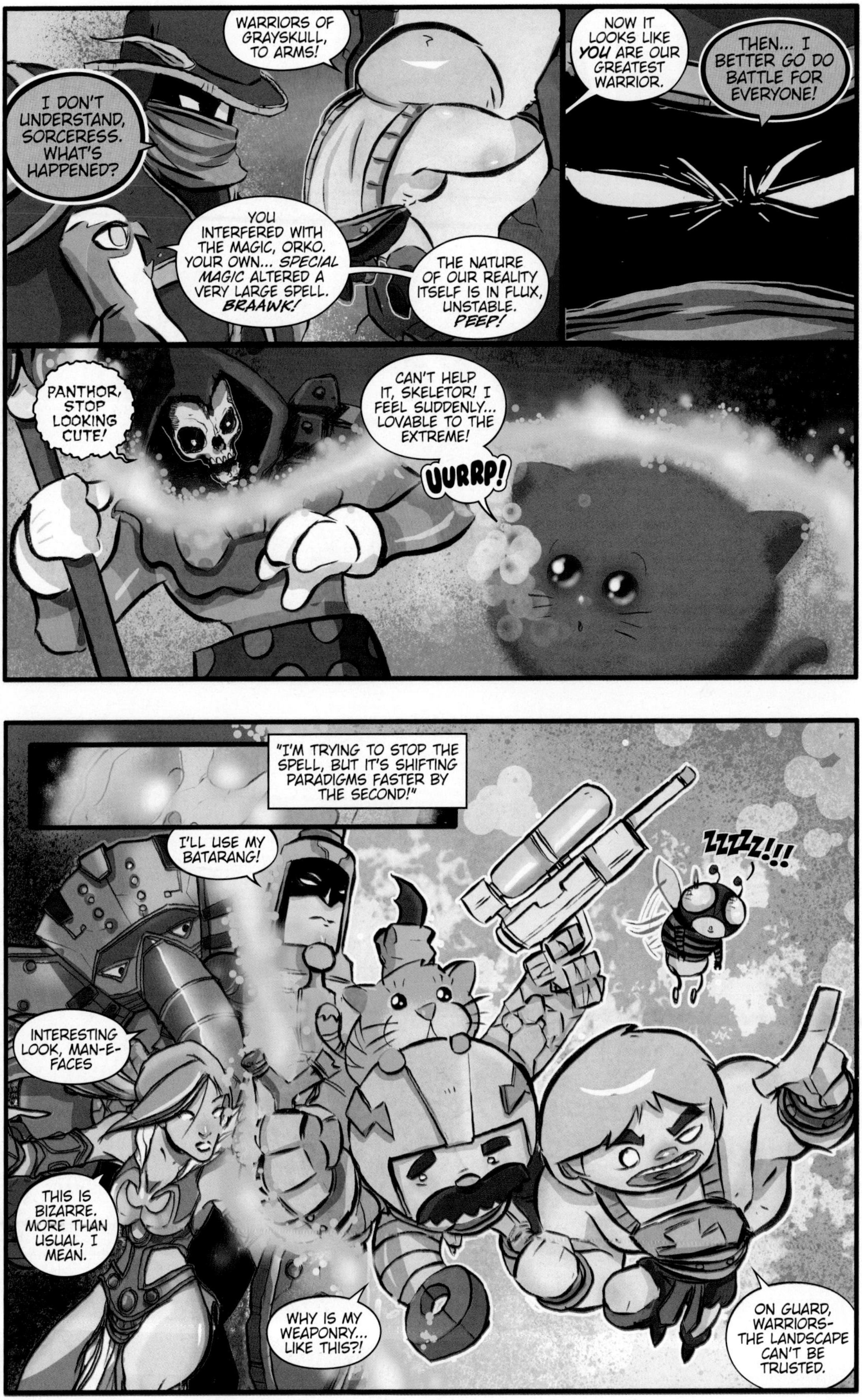
WARRIORS OF GRAYSKULL, TO ARMS!
I DON'T UNDERSTAND, SORCERESS. WHAT'S HAPPENED?
YOU INTERFERED WITH THE MAGIC, ORKO. YOUR OWN... SPECIAL MAGIC ALTERED A VERY LARGE SPELL. BRAAWK!
THE NATURE OF OUR REALITY ITSELF IS IN FLUX, UNSTABLE. PEEP!
NOW IT LOOKS LIKE YOU ARE OUR GREATEST WARRIOR.
THEN... I BETTER GO DO BATTLE FOR EVERYONE!
PANTHOR, STOP LOOKING CUTE!
CAN'T HELP IT, SKELETOR! I FEEL SUDDENLY... LOVABLE TO THE EXTREME!
UURRP!
"I'M TRYING TO STOP THE SPELL, BUT IT'S SHIFTING PARADIGMS FASTER BY THE SECOND!"
I'LL USE MY BATARANG!
ZZZZZ!!!
INTERESTING LOOK, MAN-E-FACES
THIS IS BIZARRE. MORE THAN USUAL, I MEAN.
WHY IS MY WEAPONRY... LIKE THIS?!
ON GUARD, WARRIORS- THE LANDSCAPE CAN'T BE TRUSTED.

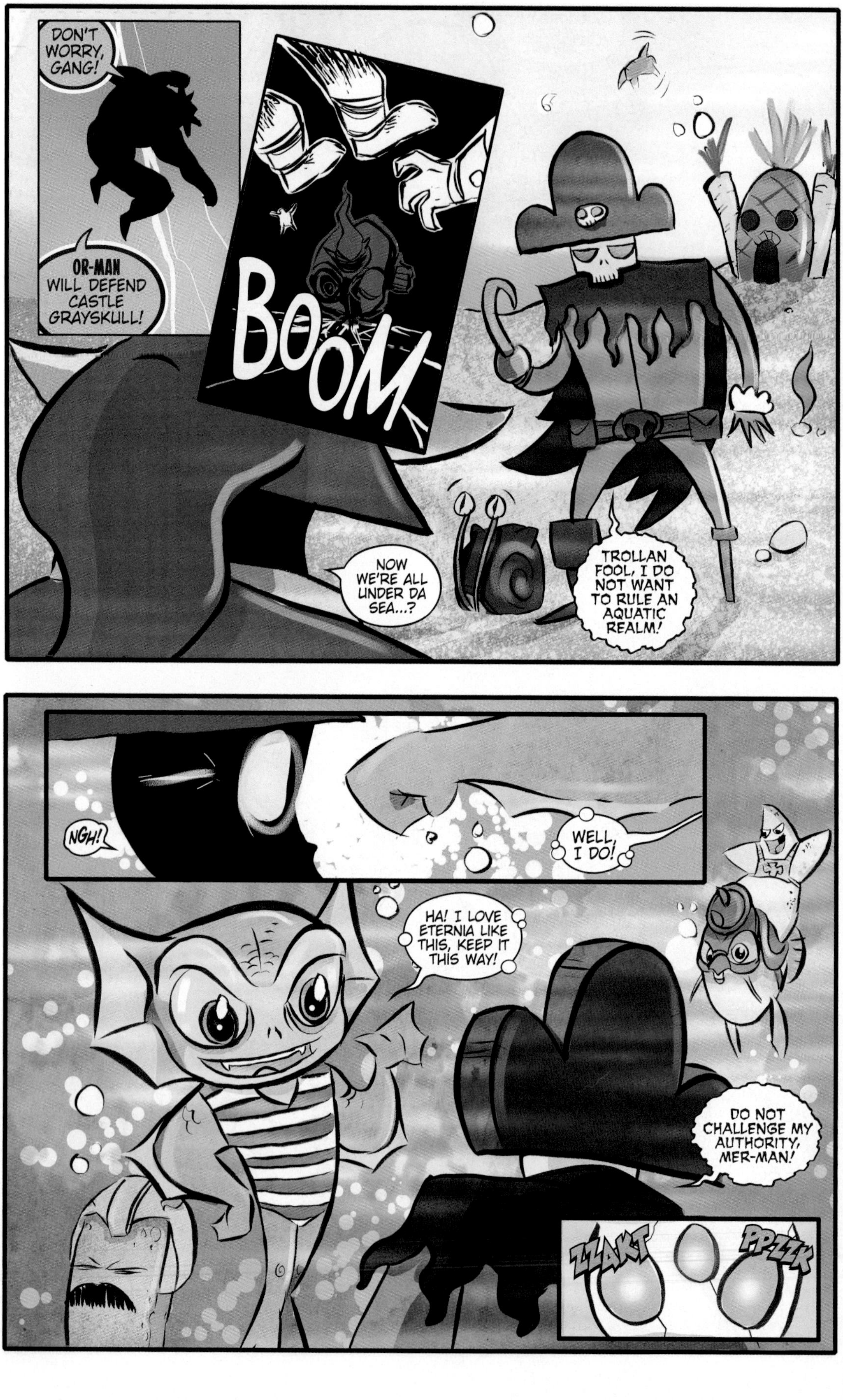
DON'T WORRY, GANG!
OR-MAN WILL DEFEND CASTLE GRAYSKULL!
BOOM
NOW WE'RE ALL UNDER DA SEA...?
TROLLAN FOOL, I DO NOT WANT TO RULE AN AQUATIC REALM!
NGH!
WELL, I DO!
HA! I LOVE ETERNIA LIKE THIS, KEEP IT THIS WAY!
DO NOT CHALLENGE MY AUTHORITY, MER-MAN!
ZZAKT
PPZZK

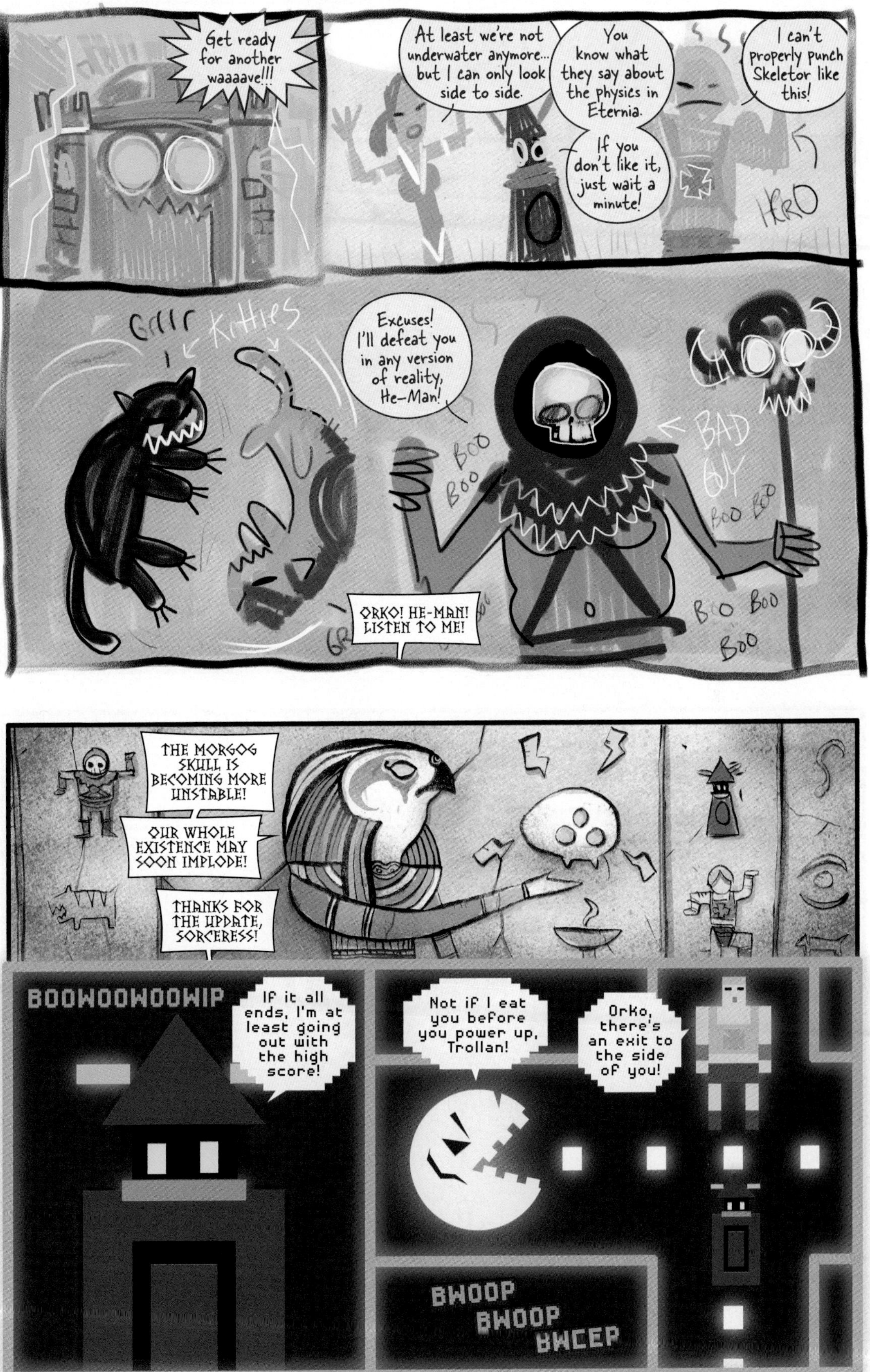

Get ready for another waaaave!!!
At least we're not underwater anymore... but I can only look side to side.
You know what they say about the physics in Eternia.
If you don't like it, just wait a minute!
I can't properly punch Skeletor like this!
HERO
Grrr
Kitties
Excuses! I'll defeat you in any version of reality, He-Man!
BOO BOO
BAD GUY
BOO BOO
ORKO! HE-MAN! LISTEN TO ME!
BOO BOO BOO
THE MORGOG SKULL IS BECOMING MORE UNSTABLE!
OUR WHOLE EXISTENCE MAY SOON IMPLODE!
THANKS FOR THE UPDATE, SORCERESS!
BOOWOOWOOWIP
If it all ends, I'm at least going out with the high score!
Not if I eat you before you power up, Trollan!
Orko, there's an exit to the side of you!
BWOOP
BWOOP
BWEEP

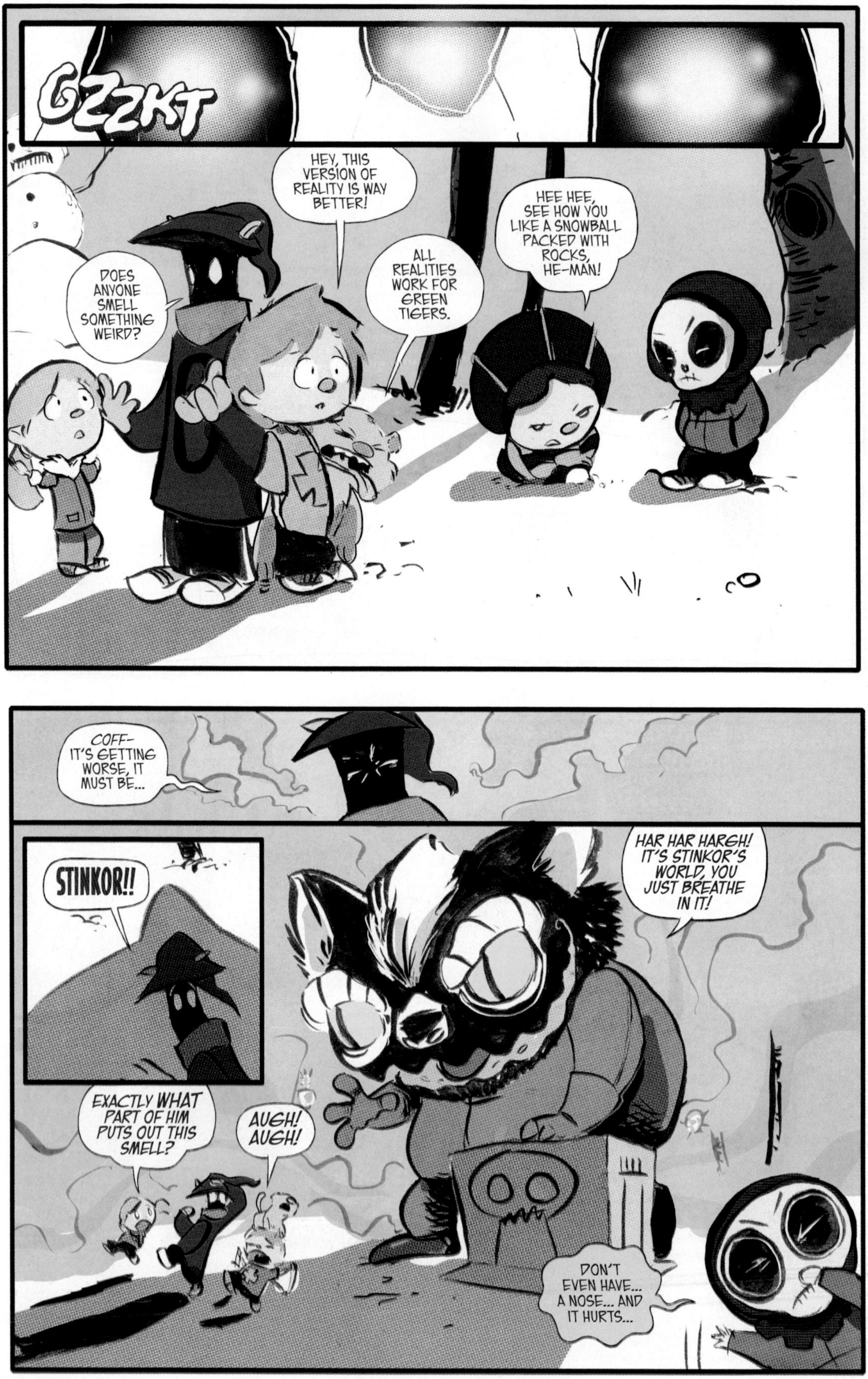
GZZKT
DOES ANYONE SMELL SOMETHING WEIRD?
HEY, THIS VERSION OF REALITY IS WAY BETTER!
ALL REALITIES WORK FOR GREEN TIGERS.
HEE HEE, SEE HOW YOU LIKE A SNOWBALL PACKED WITH ROCKS, HE-MAN!
COFF- IT'S GETTING WORSE, IT MUST BE...
STINKOR!!
HAR HAR HARGH! IT'S STINKOR'S WORLD, YOU JUST BREATHE IN IT!
EXACTLY WHAT PART OF HIM PUTS OUT THIS SMELL?
AUGH! AUGH!
DON'T EVEN HAVE... A NOSE... AND IT HURTS...

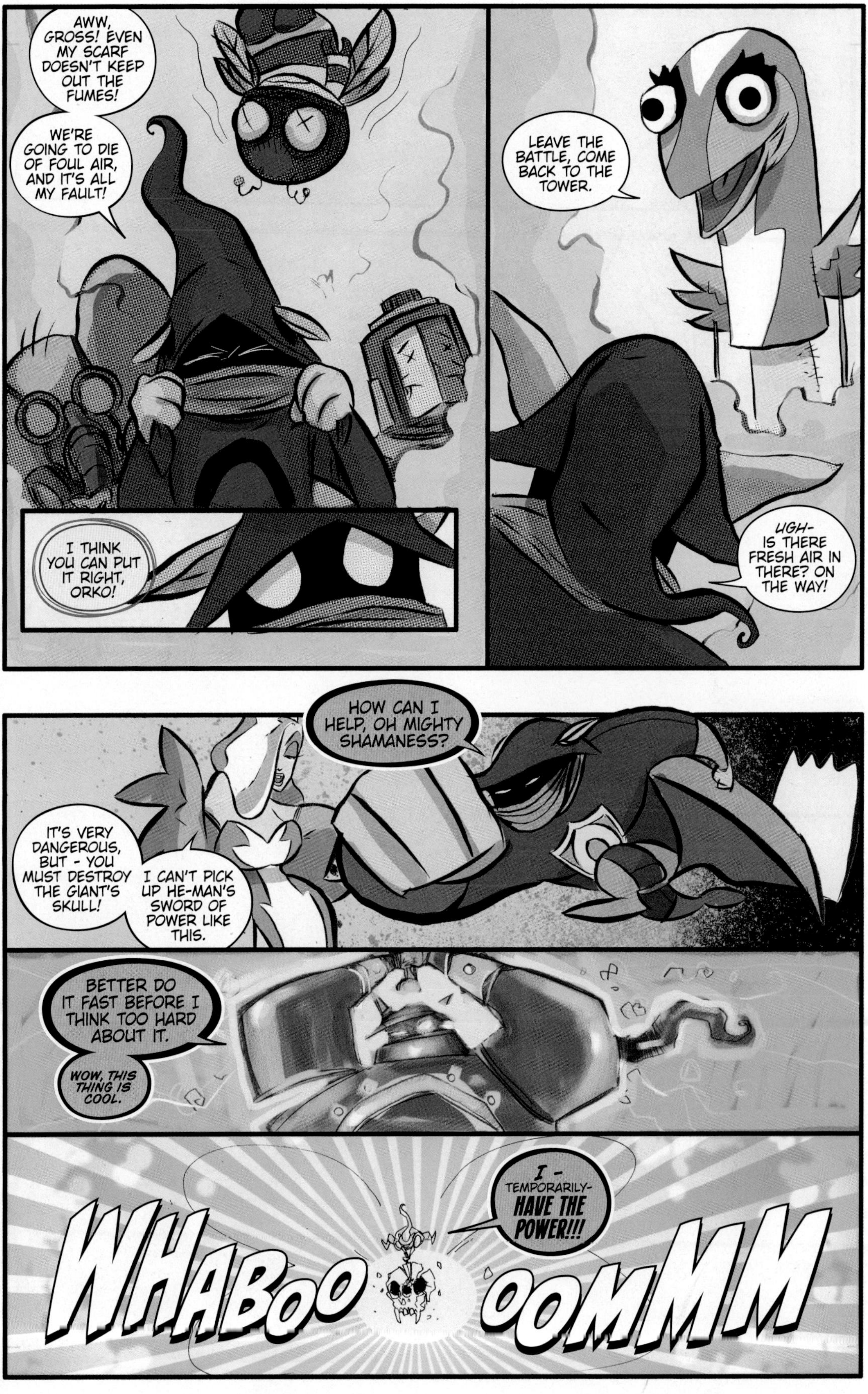
AWW, GROSS! EVEN MY SCARF DOESN'T KEEP OUT THE FUMES!
WE'RE GOING TO DIE OF FOUL AIR, AND IT'S ALL MY FAULT!
I THINK YOU CAN PUT IT RIGHT, ORKO!
LEAVE THE BATTLE, COME BACK TO THE TOWER.
UGH- IS THERE FRESH AIR IN THERE? ON THE WAY!
HOW CAN I HELP, OH MIGHTY SHAMANESS?
IT'S VERY DANGEROUS, BUT - YOU MUST DESTROY THE GIANT'S SKULL!
I CAN'T PICK UP HE-MAN'S SWORD OF POWER LIKE THIS.
BETTER DO IT FAST BEFORE I THINK TOO HARD ABOUT IT.
WOW, THIS THING IS COOL.
I - TEMPORARILY- HAVE THE POWER!!!
WHABOO OOMMM

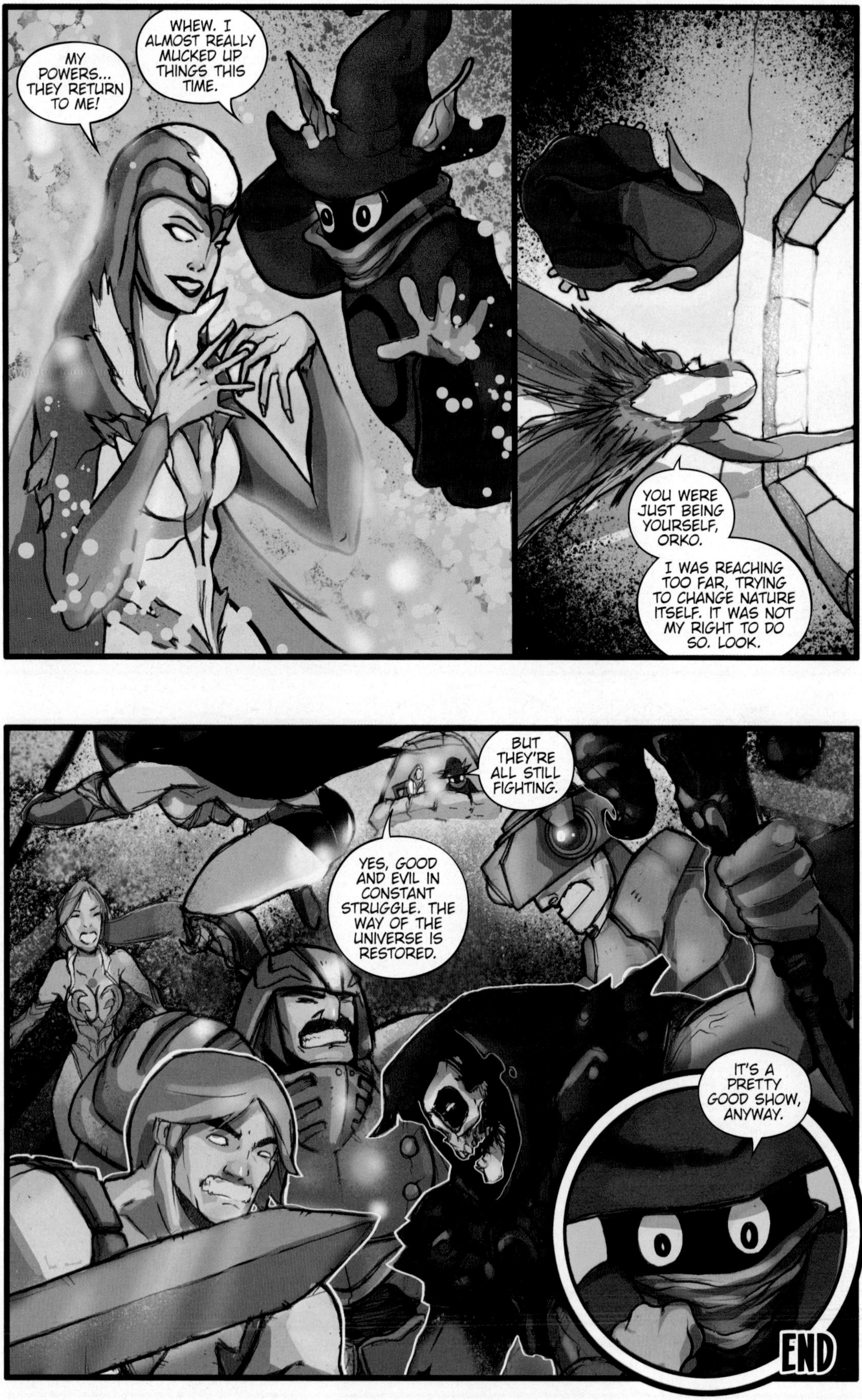
MY POWERS... THEY RETURN TO ME!
WHEW. I ALMOST REALLY MUCKED UP THINGS THIS TIME.
YOU WERE JUST BEING YOURSELF, ORKO.
I WAS REACHING TOO FAR, TRYING TO CHANGE NATURE ITSELF. IT WAS NOT MY RIGHT TO DO SO. LOOK.
BUT THEY'RE ALL STILL FIGHTING.
YES, GOOD AND EVIL IN CONSTANT STRUGGLE. THE WAY OF THE UNIVERSE IS RESTORED.
IT'S A PRETTY GOOD SHOW, ANYWAY.
END

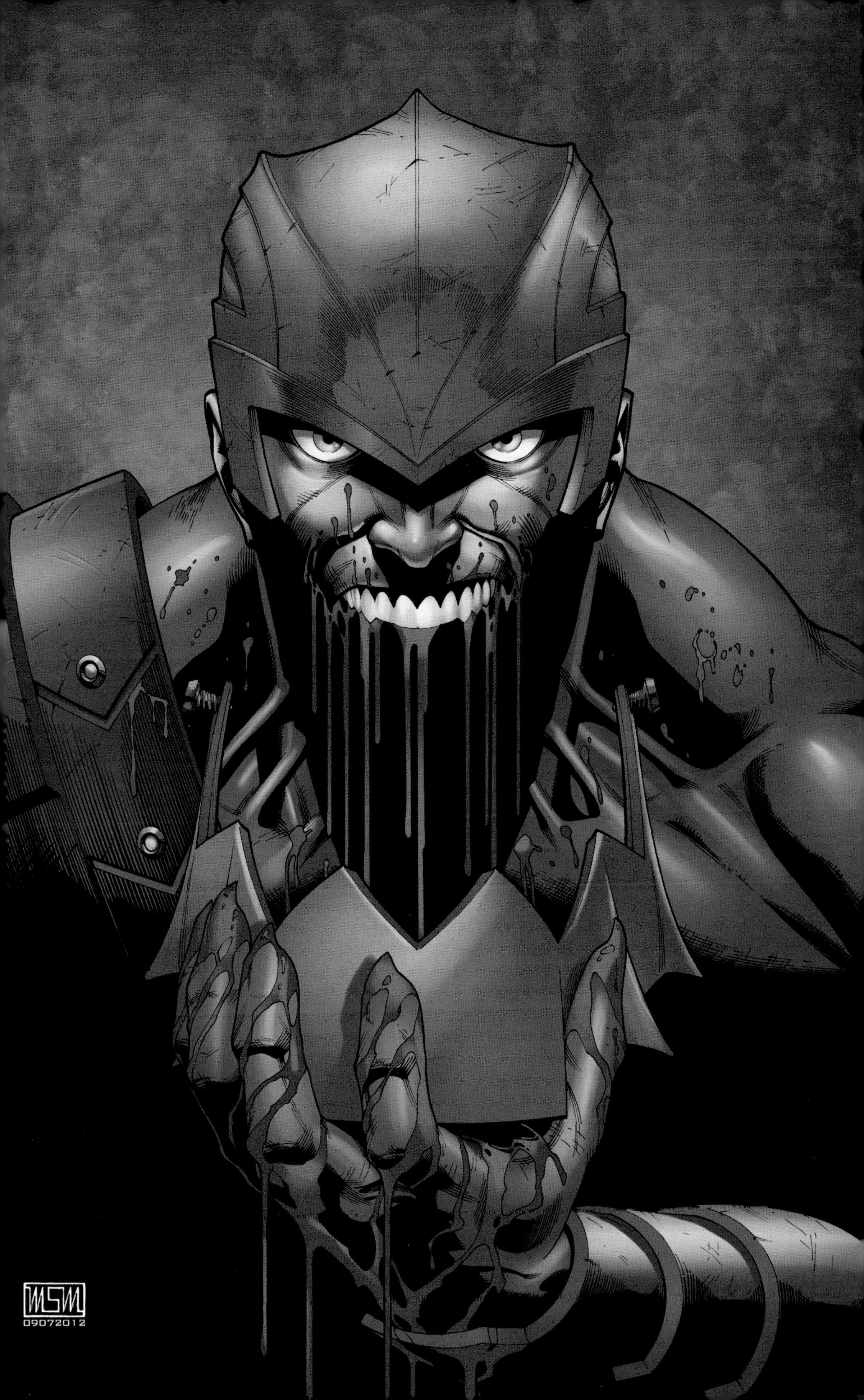
MSM
09072012

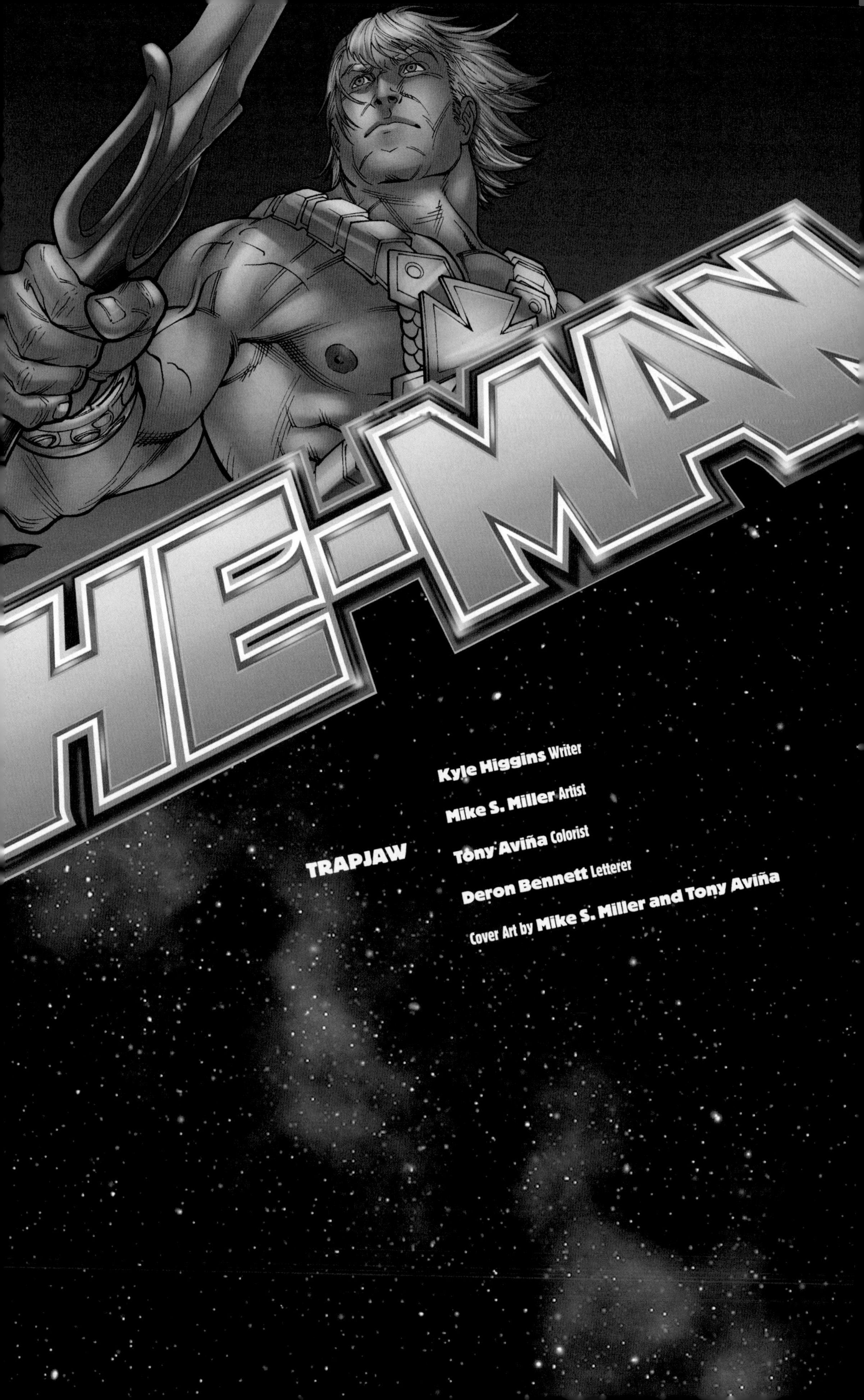
HE-MAN
TRAPJAW
Kyle Higgins Writer
Mike S. Miller Artist
Tony Aviña Colorist
Deron Bennett Letterer
Cover Art by Mike S. Miller and Tony Aviña

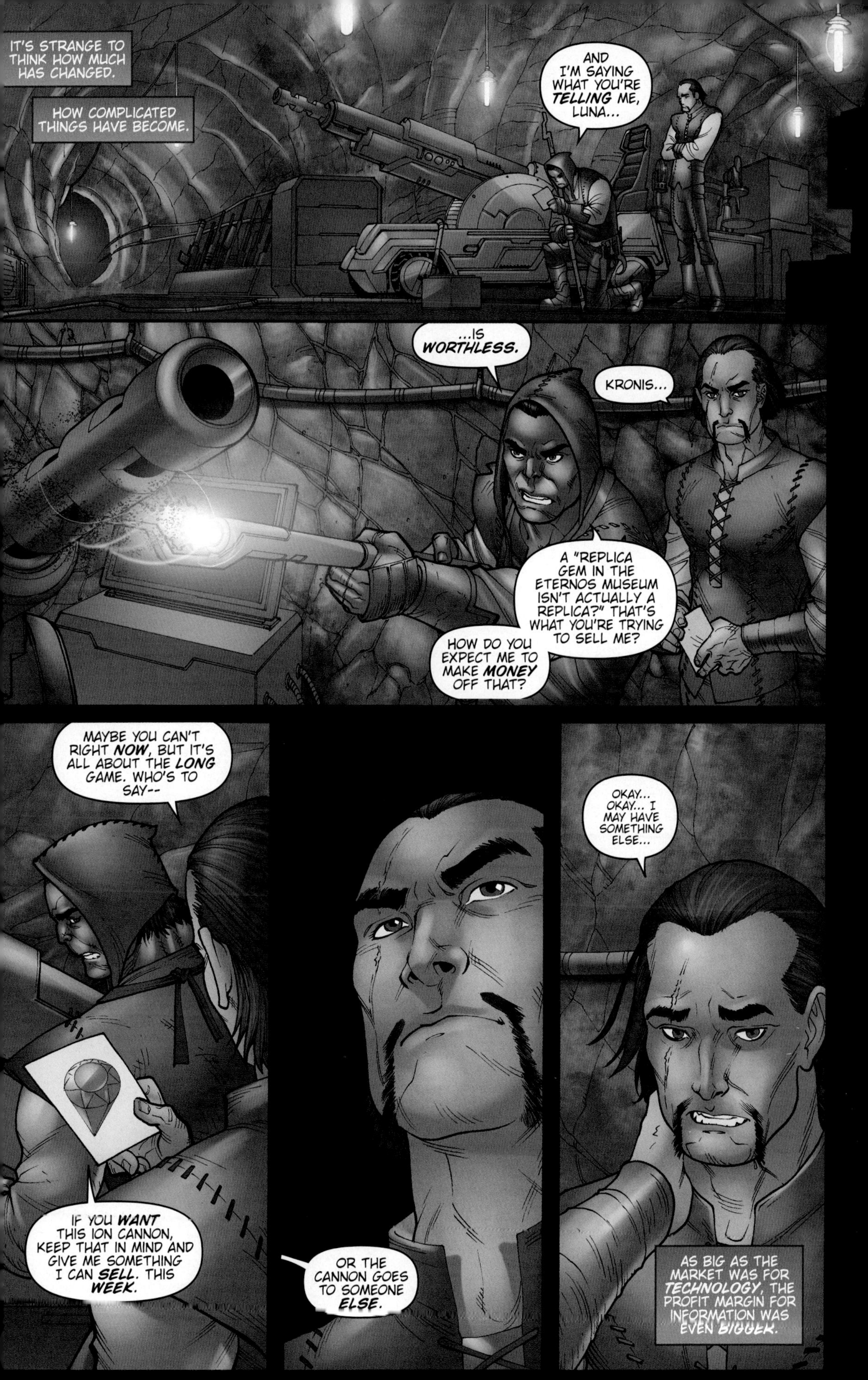
IT'S STRANGE TO THINK HOW MUCH HAS CHANGED.
HOW COMPLICATED THINGS HAVE BECOME.
AND I'M SAYING WHAT YOU'RE TELLING ME, LUNA...
...IS WORTHLESS.
KRONIS...
A "REPLICA GEM IN THE ETERNOS MUSEUM ISN'T ACTUALLY A REPLICA?" THAT'S WHAT YOU'RE TRYING TO SELL ME?
HOW DO YOU EXPECT ME TO MAKE MONEY OFF THAT?
MAYBE YOU CAN'T RIGHT NOW, BUT IT'S ALL ABOUT THE LONG GAME. WHO'S TO SAY--
IF YOU WANT THIS ION CANNON, KEEP THAT IN MIND AND GIVE ME SOMETHING I CAN SELL. THIS WEEK.
OR THE CANNON GOES TO SOMEONE ELSE.
OKAY... OKAY... I MAY HAVE SOMETHING ELSE...
AS BIG AS THE MARKET WAS FOR TECHNOLOGY, THE PROFIT MARGIN FOR INFORMATION WAS EVEN BIGGER.

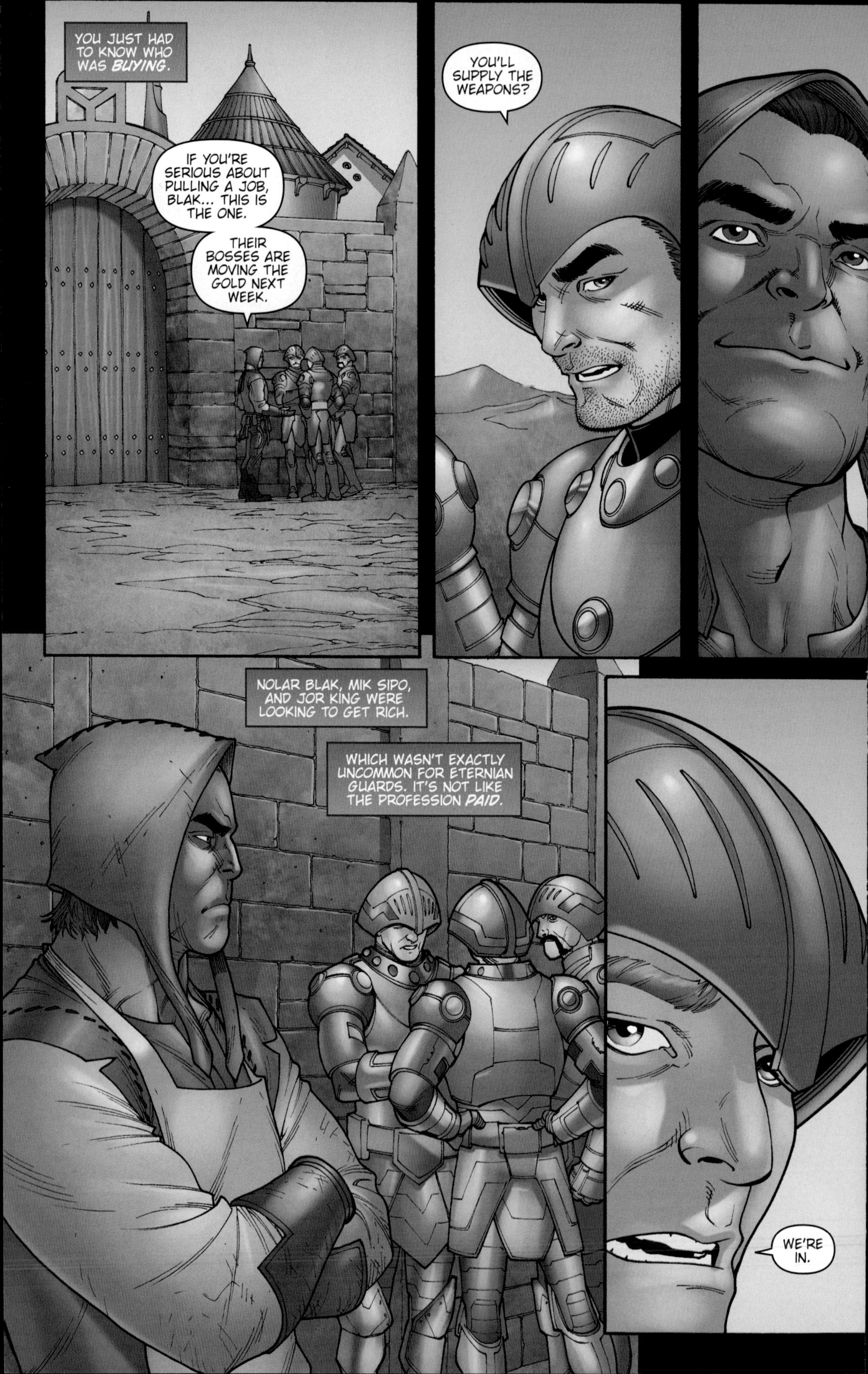
YOU JUST HAD TO KNOW WHO WAS *BUYING*.
IF YOU'RE SERIOUS ABOUT PULLING A JOB, BLAK... THIS IS THE ONE.
THEIR BOSSES ARE MOVING THE GOLD NEXT WEEK.
YOU'LL SUPPLY THE WEAPONS?
NOLAR BLAK, MIK SIPO, AND JOR KING WERE LOOKING TO GET RICH.
WHICH WASN'T EXACTLY UNCOMMON FOR ETERNIAN GUARDS. IT'S NOT LIKE THE PROFESSION *PAID*.
WE'RE IN.

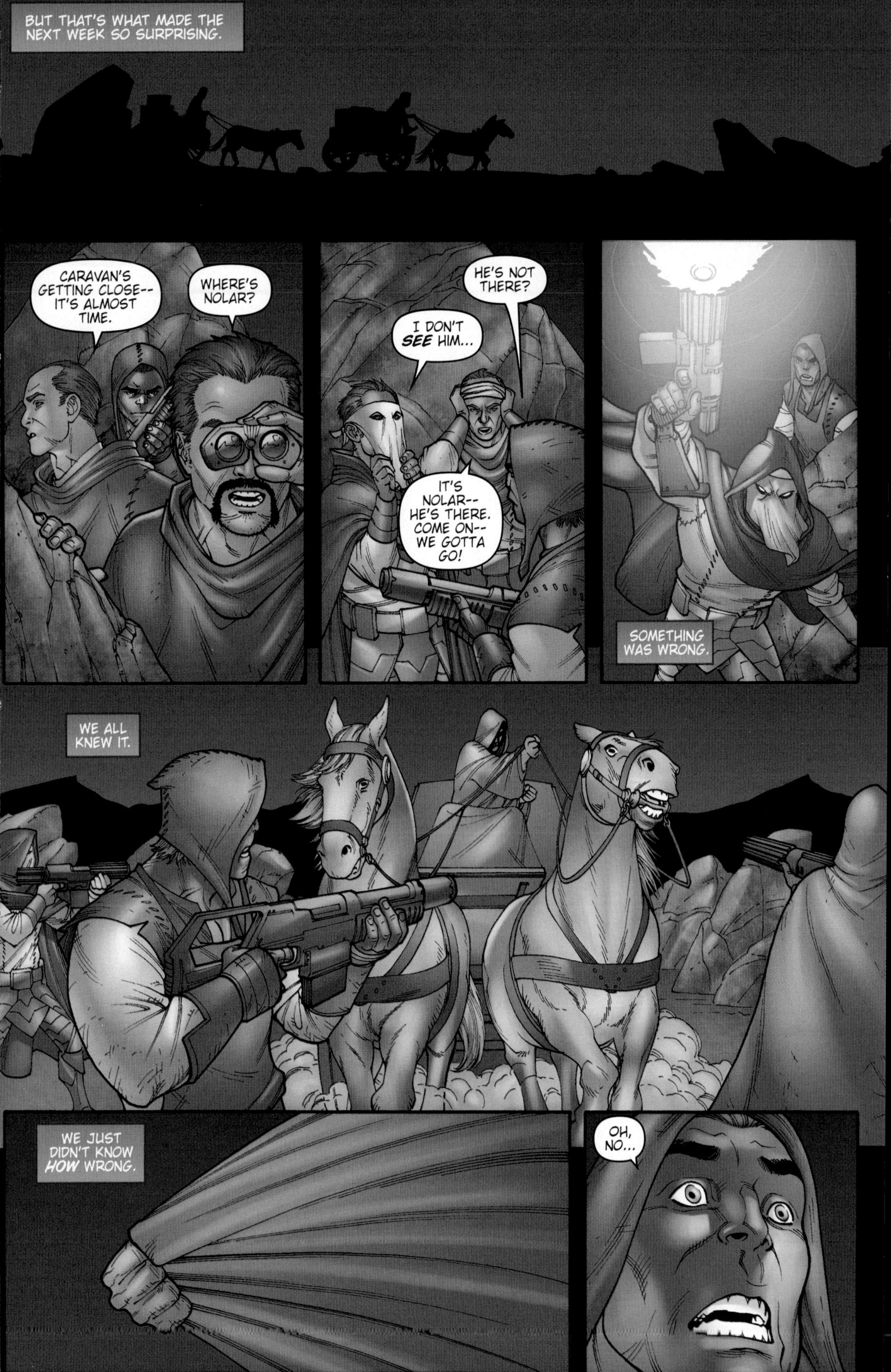
BUT THAT'S WHAT MADE THE NEXT WEEK SO SURPRISING.
CARAVAN'S GETTING CLOSE-- IT'S ALMOST TIME.
WHERE'S NOLAR?
HE'S NOT THERE?
I DON'T **SEE** HIM...
IT'S NOLAR-- HE'S THERE. COME ON-- WE GOTTA GO!
SOMETHING WAS WRONG.
WE ALL KNEW IT.
WE JUST DIDN'T KNOW ***HOW*** WRONG.
OH, NO...

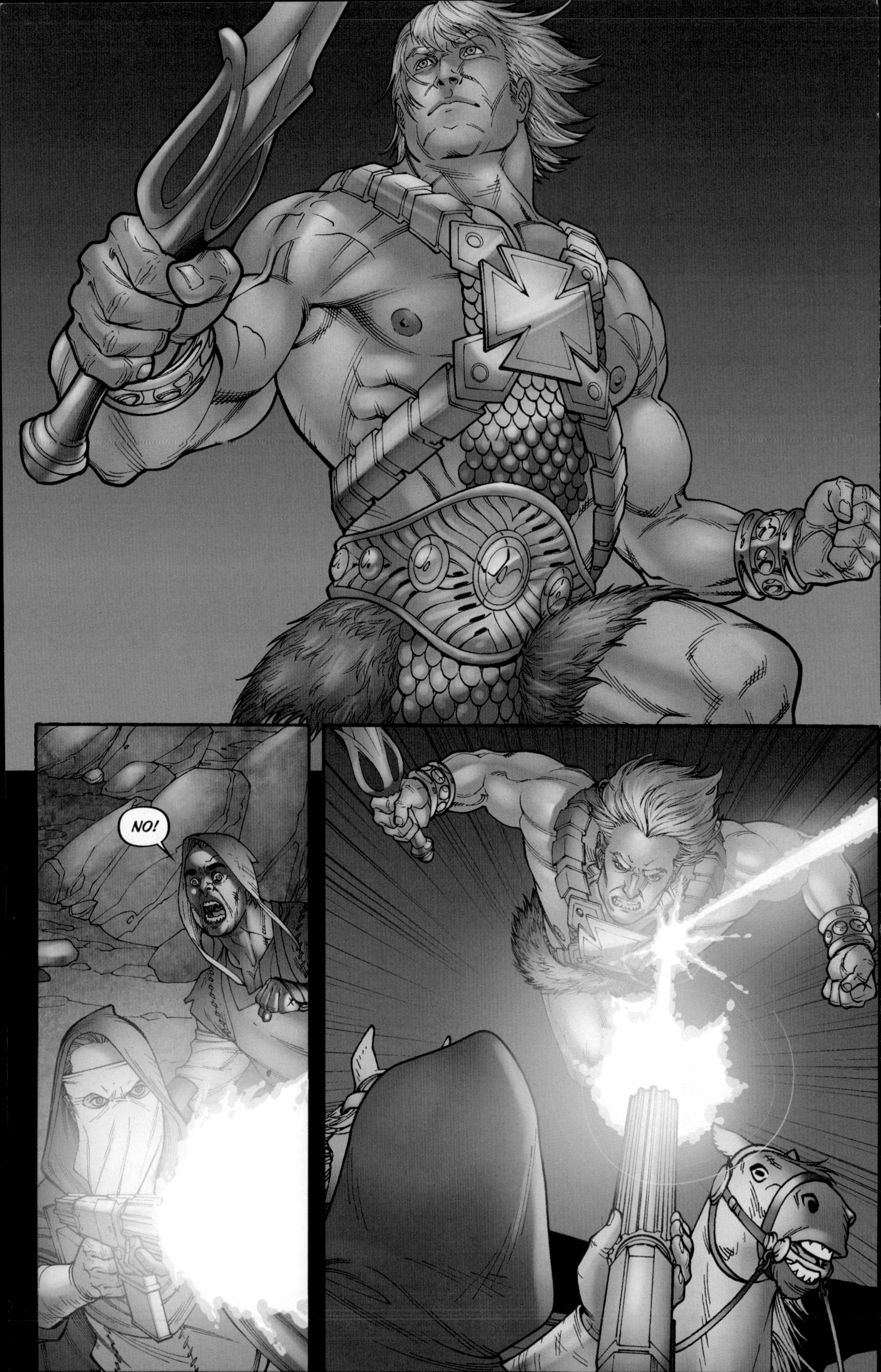
NO!

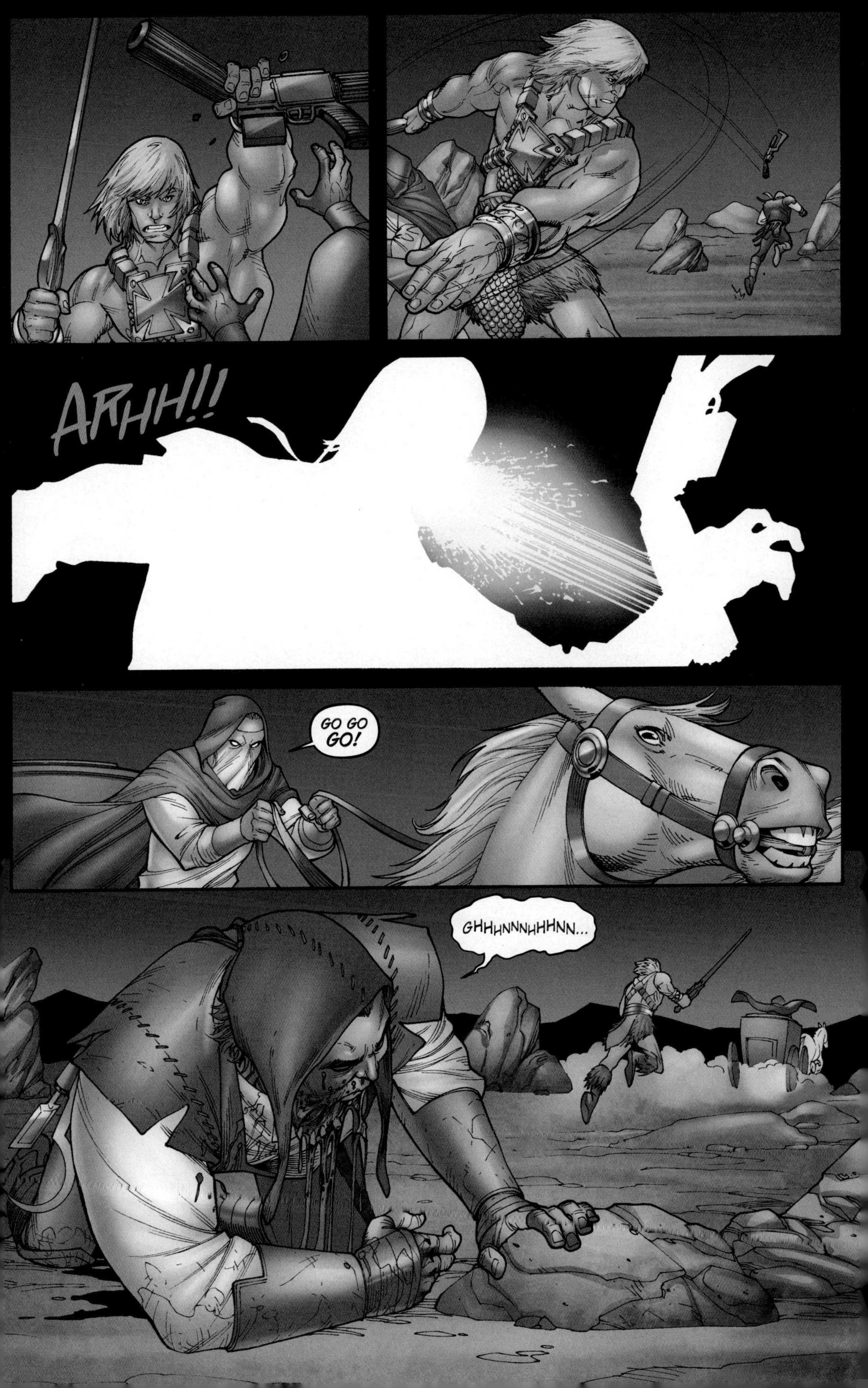
ARHH!!
GO GO GO!
GHHHNNNHHHNN...

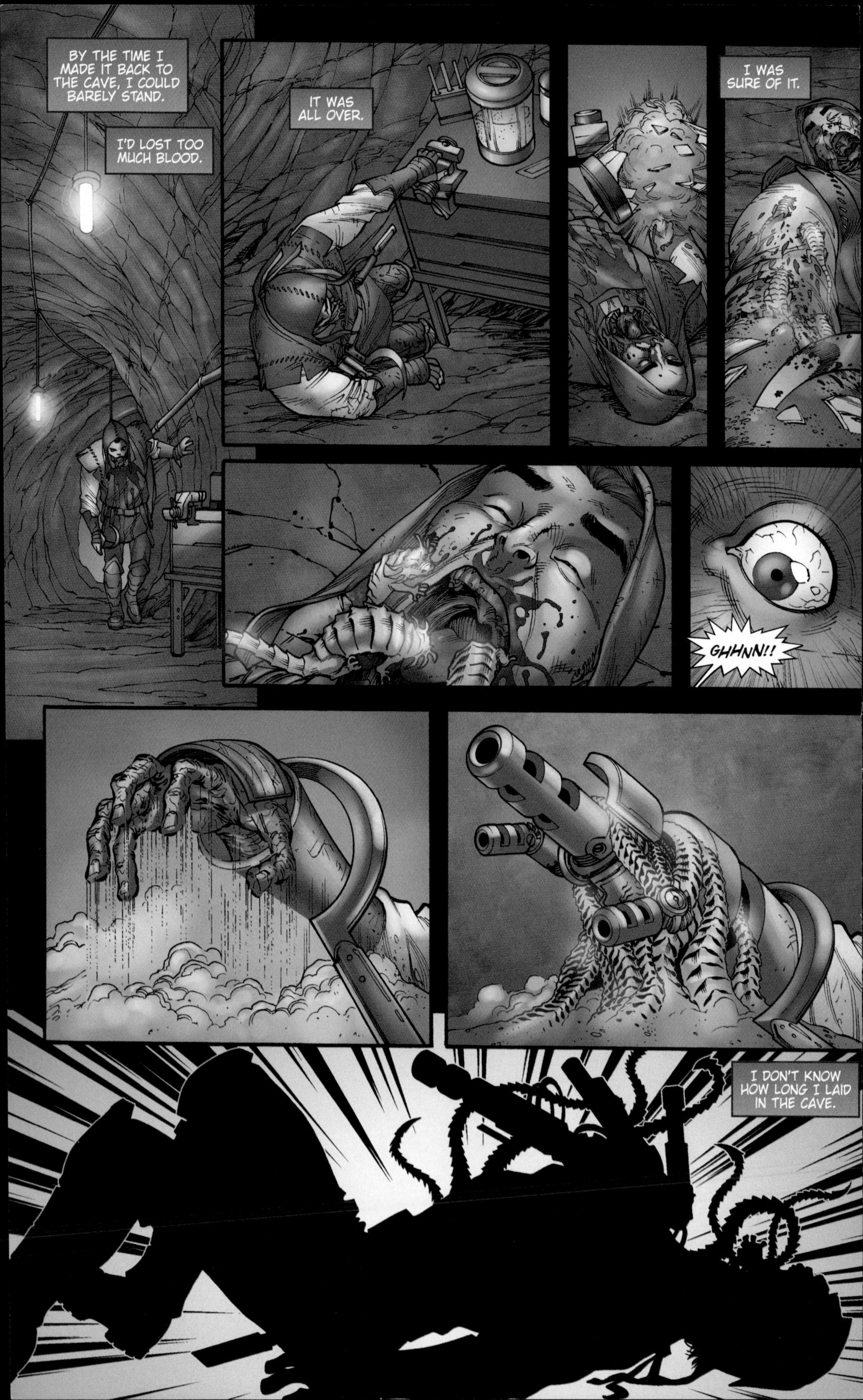

BY THE TIME I MADE IT BACK TO THE CAVE, I COULD BARELY STAND.
I'D LOST TOO MUCH BLOOD.
IT WAS ALL OVER.
I WAS SURE OF IT.
GHHNN!!
I DON'T KNOW HOW LONG I LAID IN THE CAVE.

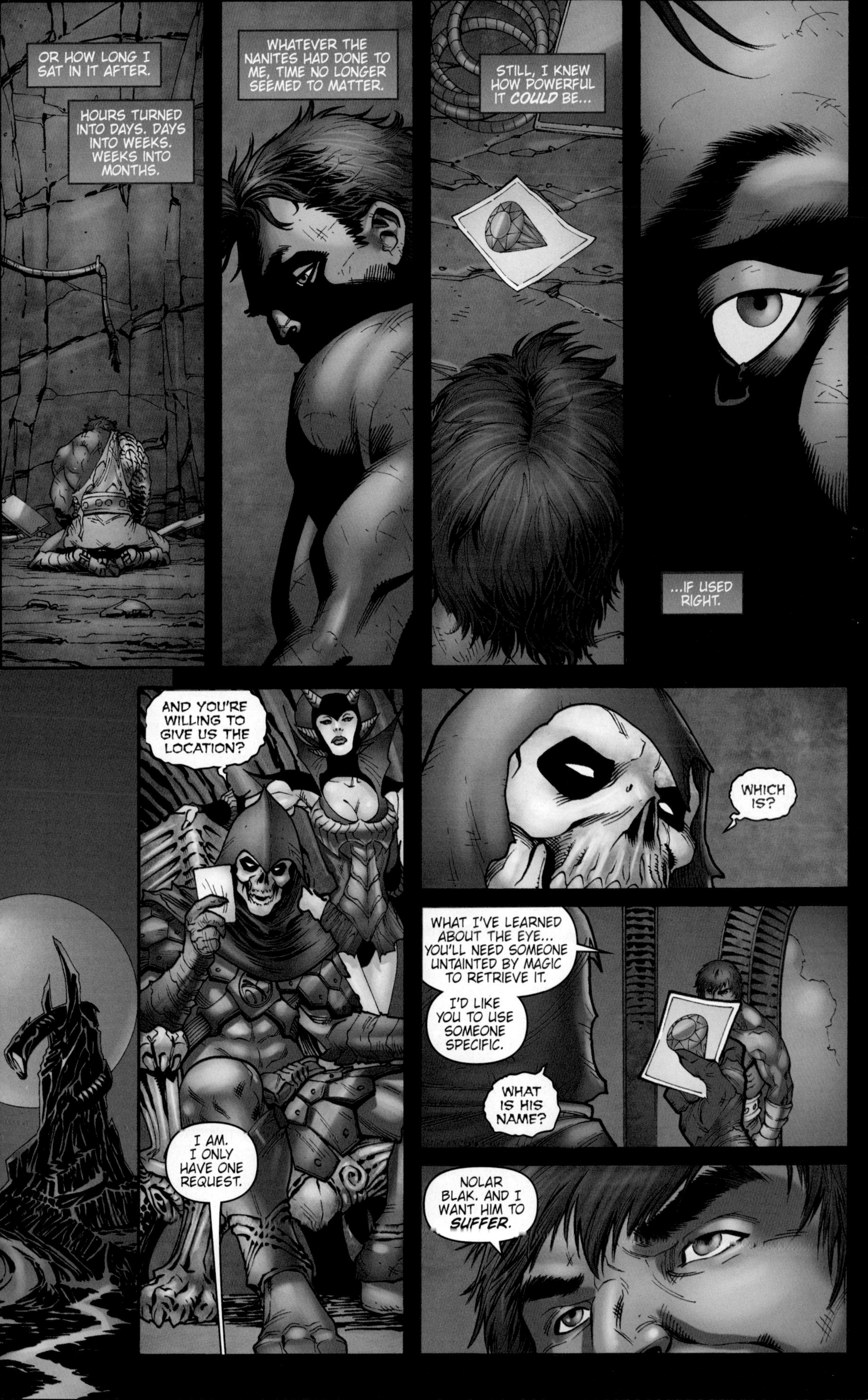
OR HOW LONG I SAT IN IT AFTER.
HOURS TURNED INTO DAYS. DAYS INTO WEEKS. WEEKS INTO MONTHS.
WHATEVER THE NANITES HAD DONE TO ME, TIME NO LONGER SEEMED TO MATTER.
STILL, I KNEW HOW POWERFUL IT COULD BE...
...IF USED RIGHT.
AND YOU'RE WILLING TO GIVE US THE LOCATION?
I AM. I ONLY HAVE ONE REQUEST.
WHICH IS?
WHAT I'VE LEARNED ABOUT THE EYE... YOU'LL NEED SOMEONE UNTAINTED BY MAGIC TO RETRIEVE IT.
I'D LIKE YOU TO USE SOMEONE SPECIFIC.
WHAT IS HIS NAME?
NOLAR BLAK. AND I WANT HIM TO SUFFER.

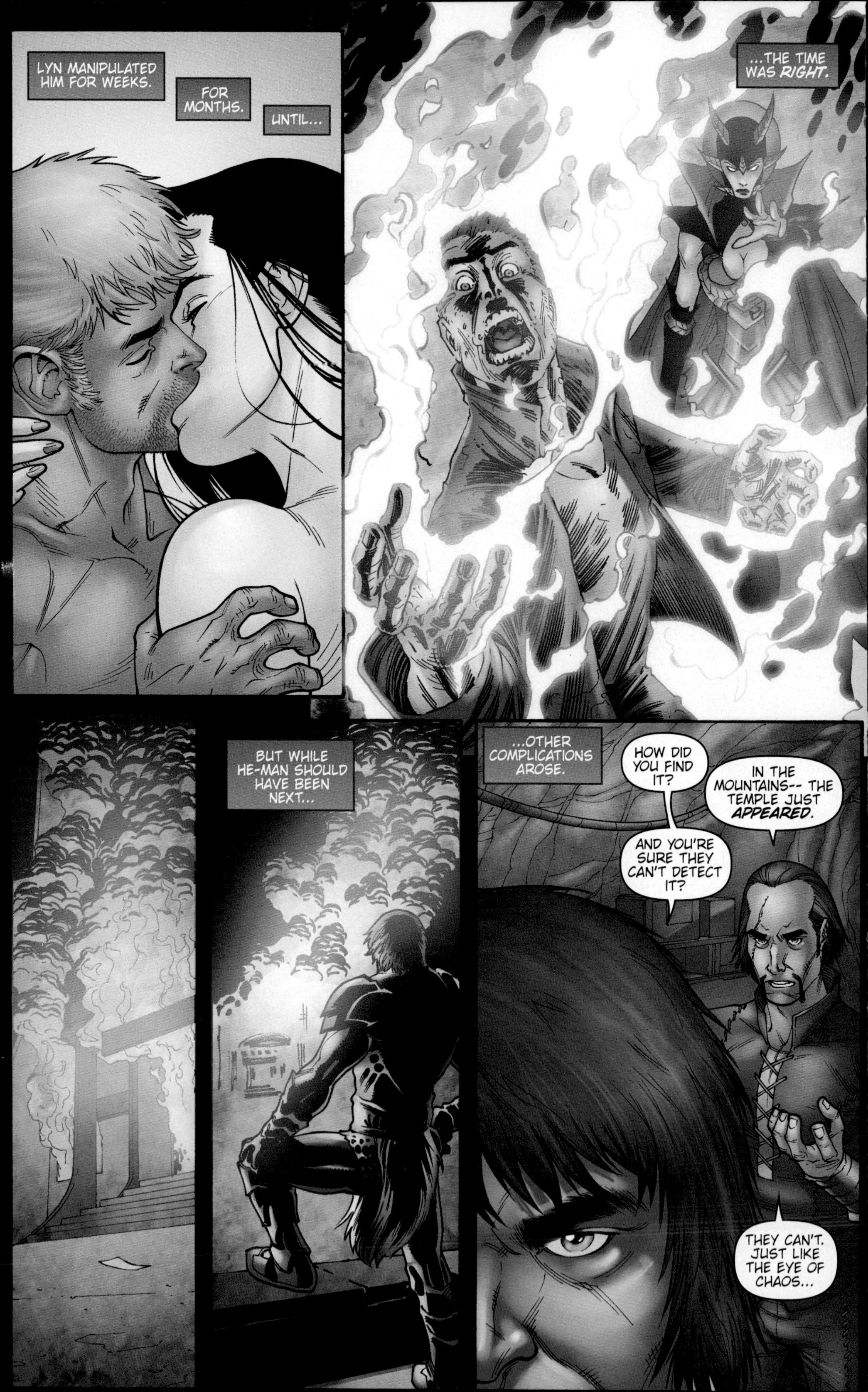
LYN MANIPULATED HIM FOR WEEKS.
FOR MONTHS.
UNTIL...
...THE TIME WAS RIGHT.
BUT WHILE HE-MAN SHOULD HAVE BEEN NEXT...
...OTHER COMPLICATIONS AROSE.
HOW DID YOU FIND IT?
IN THE MOUNTAINS-- THE TEMPLE JUST APPEARED.
AND YOU'RE SURE THEY CAN'T DETECT IT?
THEY CAN'T. JUST LIKE THE EYE OF CHAOS...

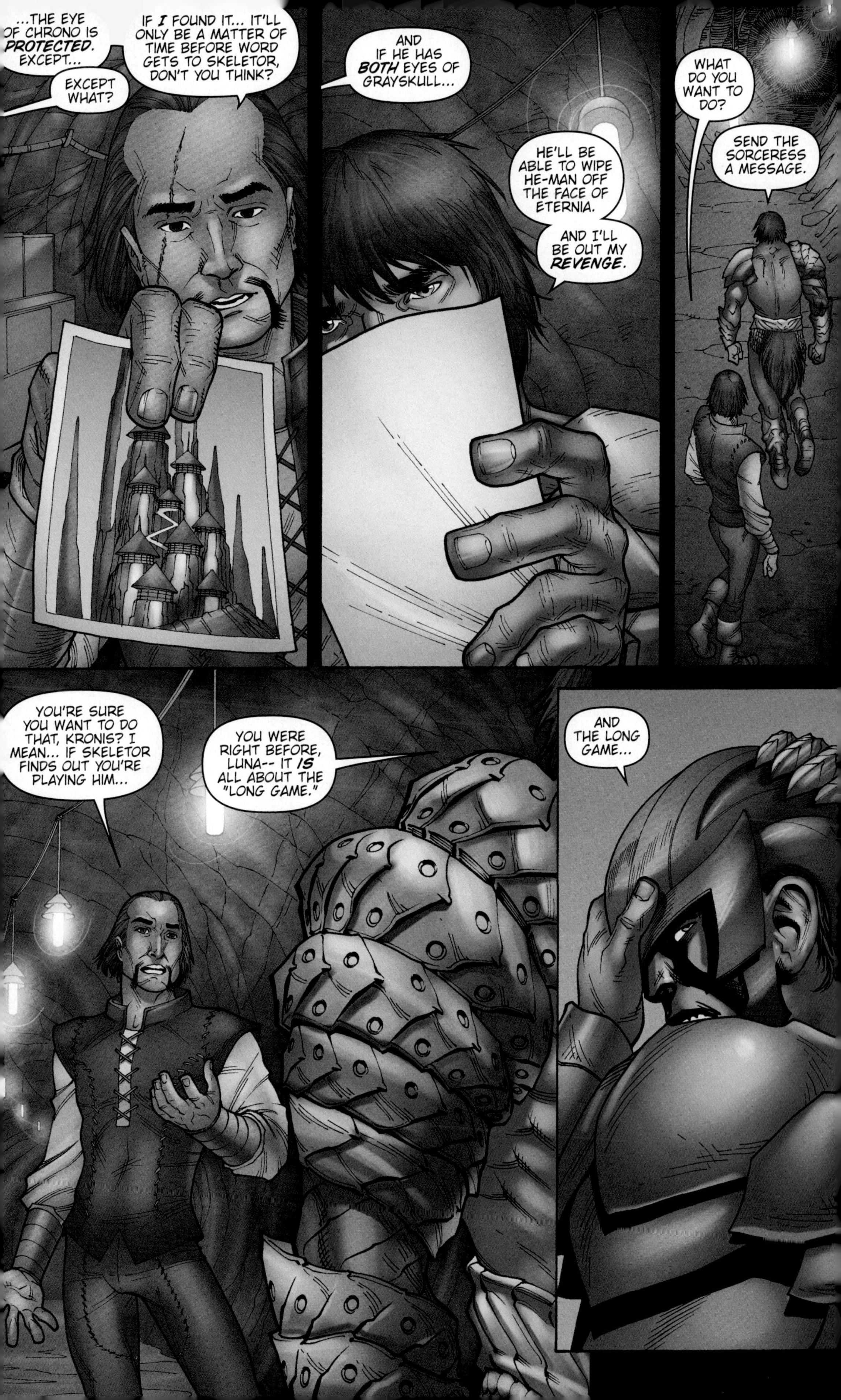
...THE EYE OF CHRONO IS *PROTECTED*. EXCEPT...
EXCEPT WHAT?
IF *I* FOUND IT... IT'LL ONLY BE A MATTER OF TIME BEFORE WORD GETS TO SKELETOR, DON'T YOU THINK?
AND IF HE HAS *BOTH* EYES OF GRAYSKULL...
HE'LL BE ABLE TO WIPE HE-MAN OFF THE FACE OF ETERNIA.
AND I'LL BE OUT MY *REVENGE*.
WHAT DO YOU WANT TO DO?
SEND THE SORCERESS A MESSAGE.
YOU'RE SURE YOU WANT TO DO THAT, KRONIS? I MEAN... IF SKELETOR FINDS OUT YOU'RE PLAYING HIM...
YOU WERE RIGHT BEFORE, LUNA-- IT *IS* ALL ABOUT THE "LONG GAME."
AND THE LONG GAME...

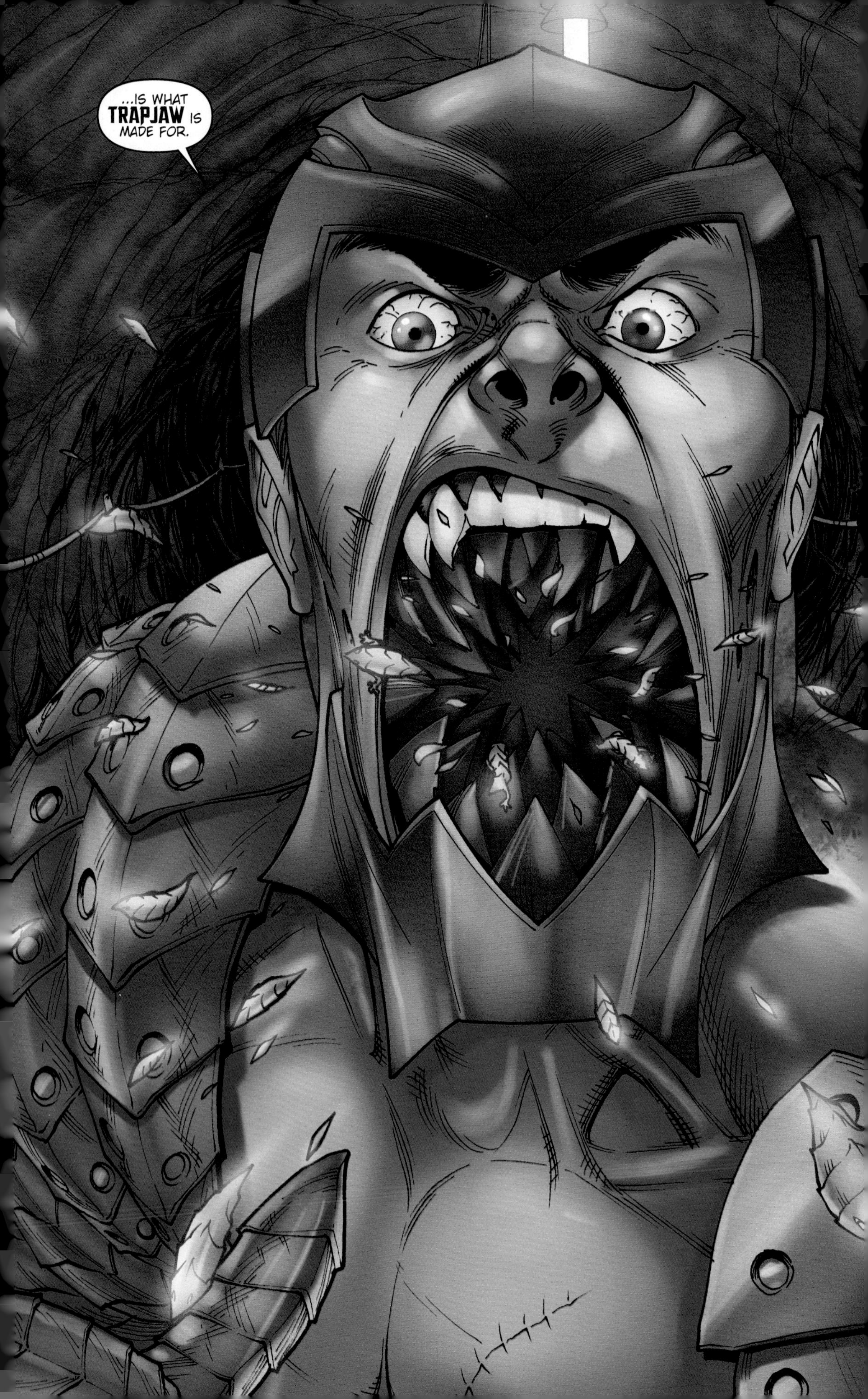
...IS WHAT TRAPJAW IS MADE FOR.

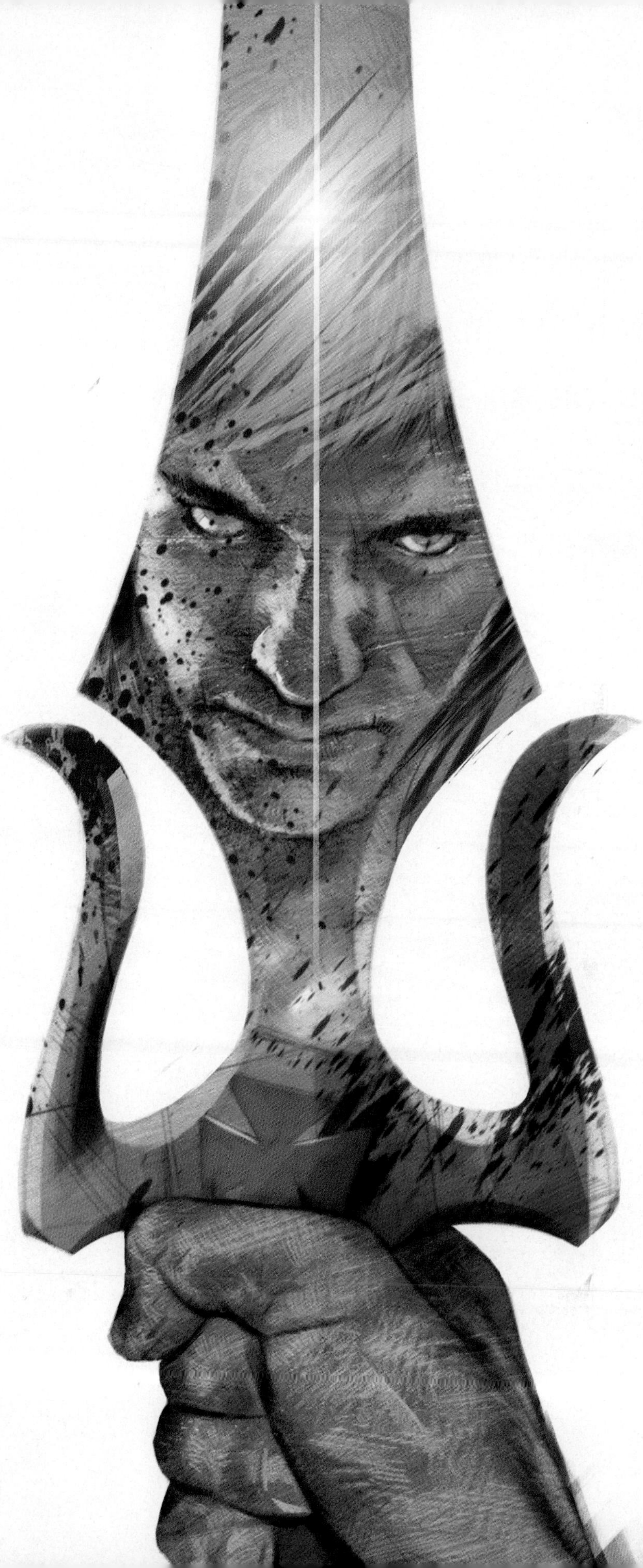

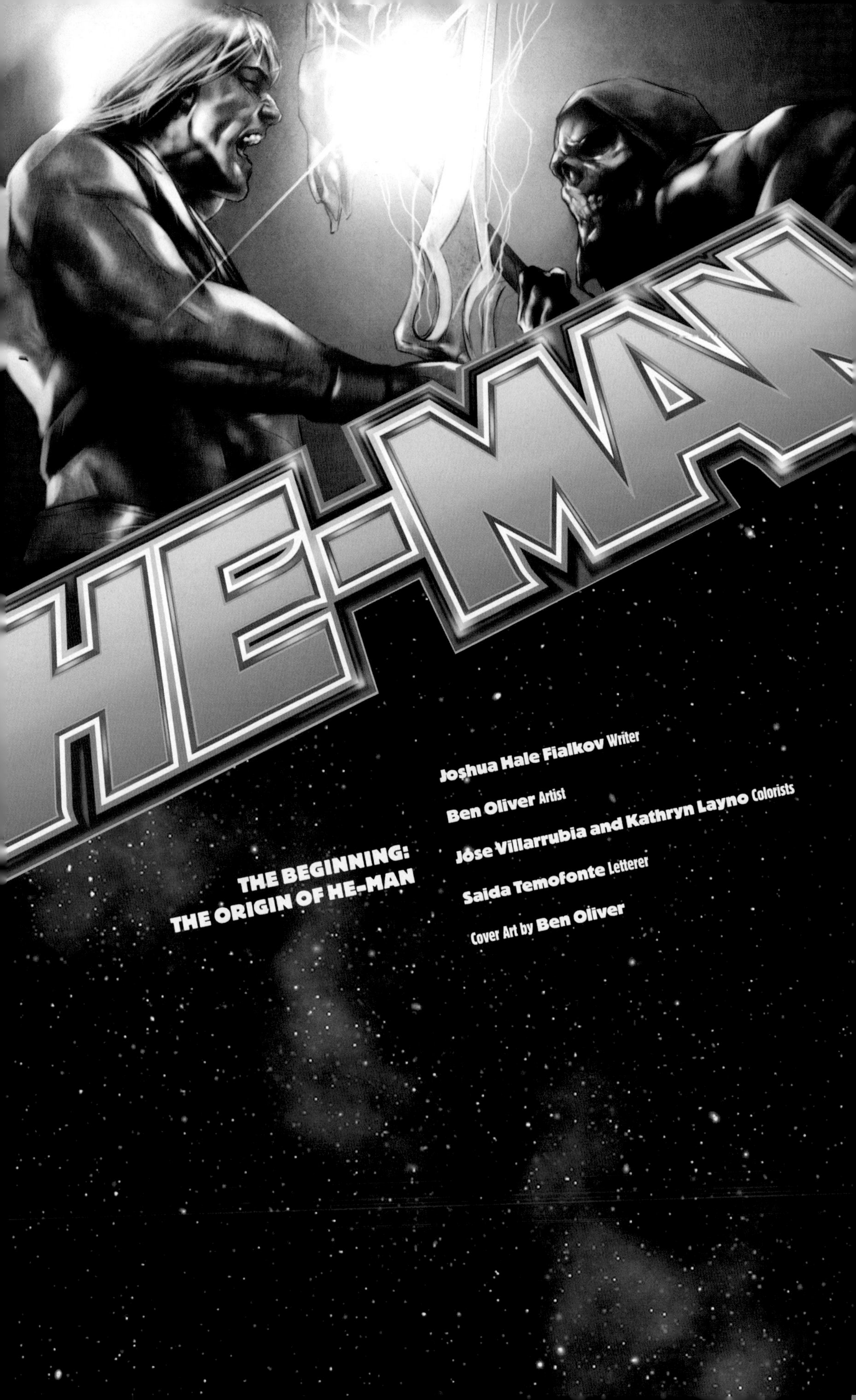
HE-MAN

THE BEGINNING: THE ORIGIN OF HE-MAN

Joshua Hale Fialkov Writer

Ben Oliver Artist

Jose Villarrubia and Kathryn Layno Colorists

Saida Temofonte Letterer

Cover Art by **Ben Oliver**

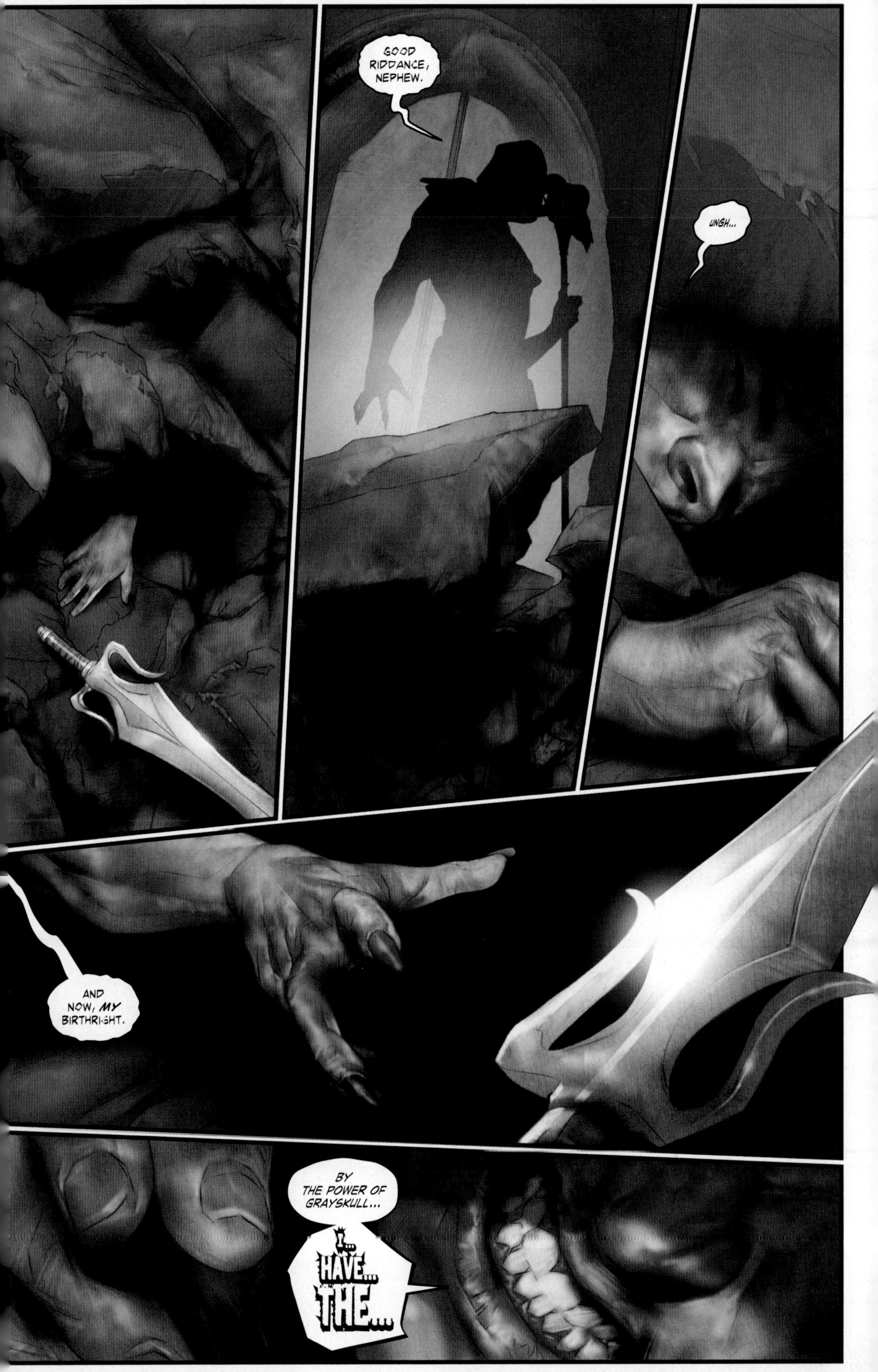
GOOD RIDDANCE, NEPHEW.
UNGH...
AND NOW, MY BIRTHRIGHT.
BY THE POWER OF GRAYSKULL...
I... HAVE... THE...

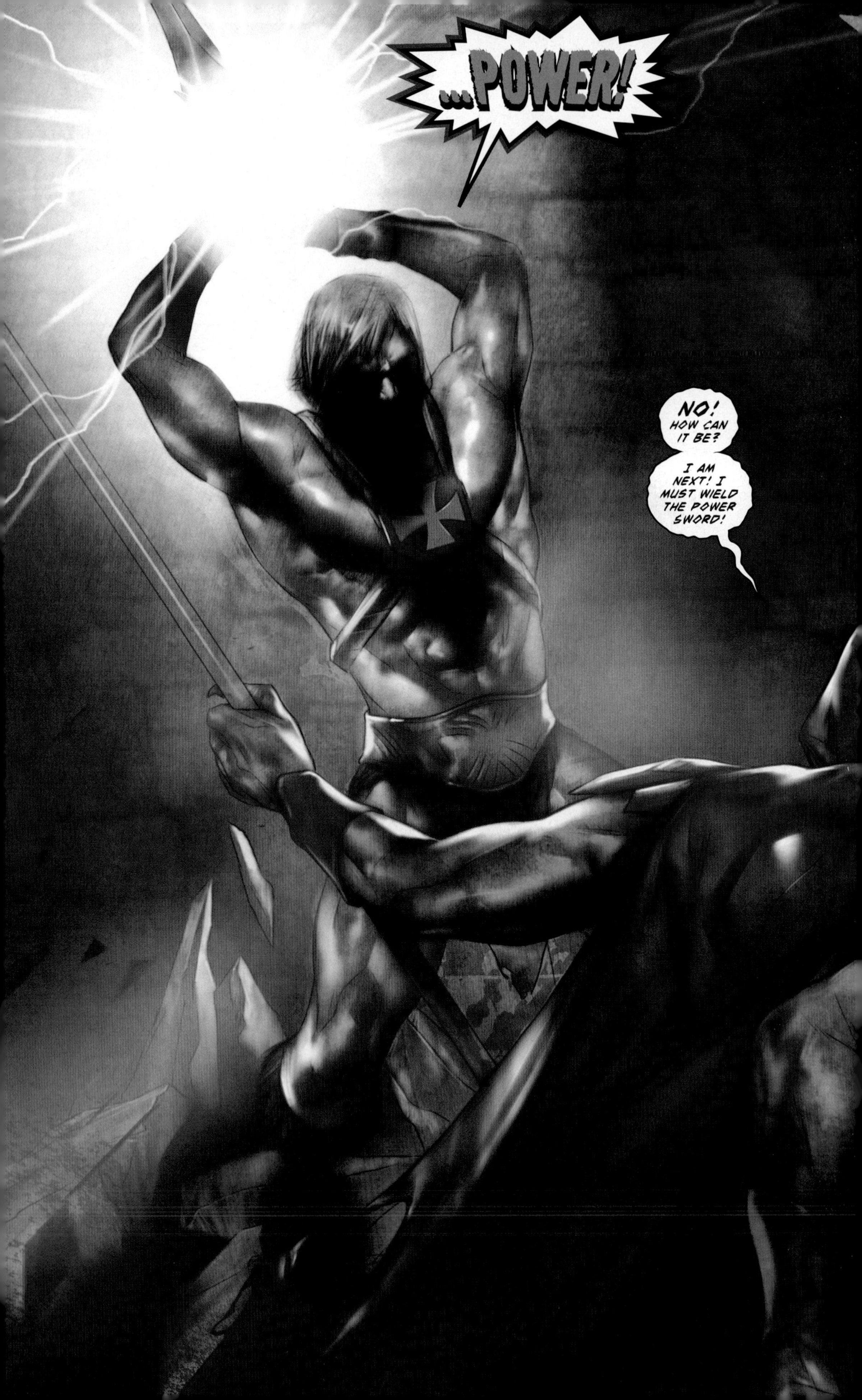
...POWER!
NO! HOW CAN IT BE?
I AM NEXT! I MUST WIELD THE POWER SWORD!

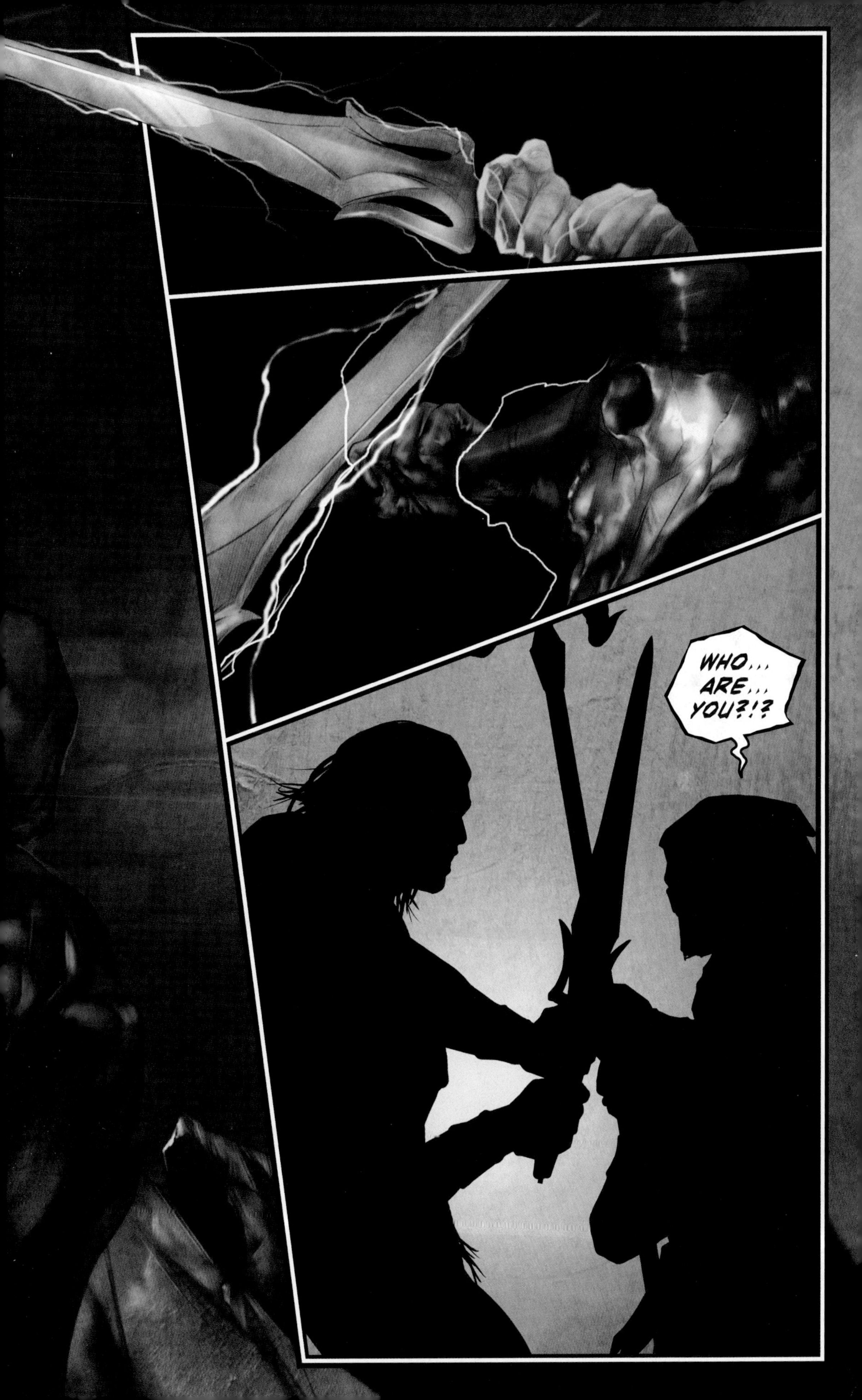
WHO... ARE... YOU?!?

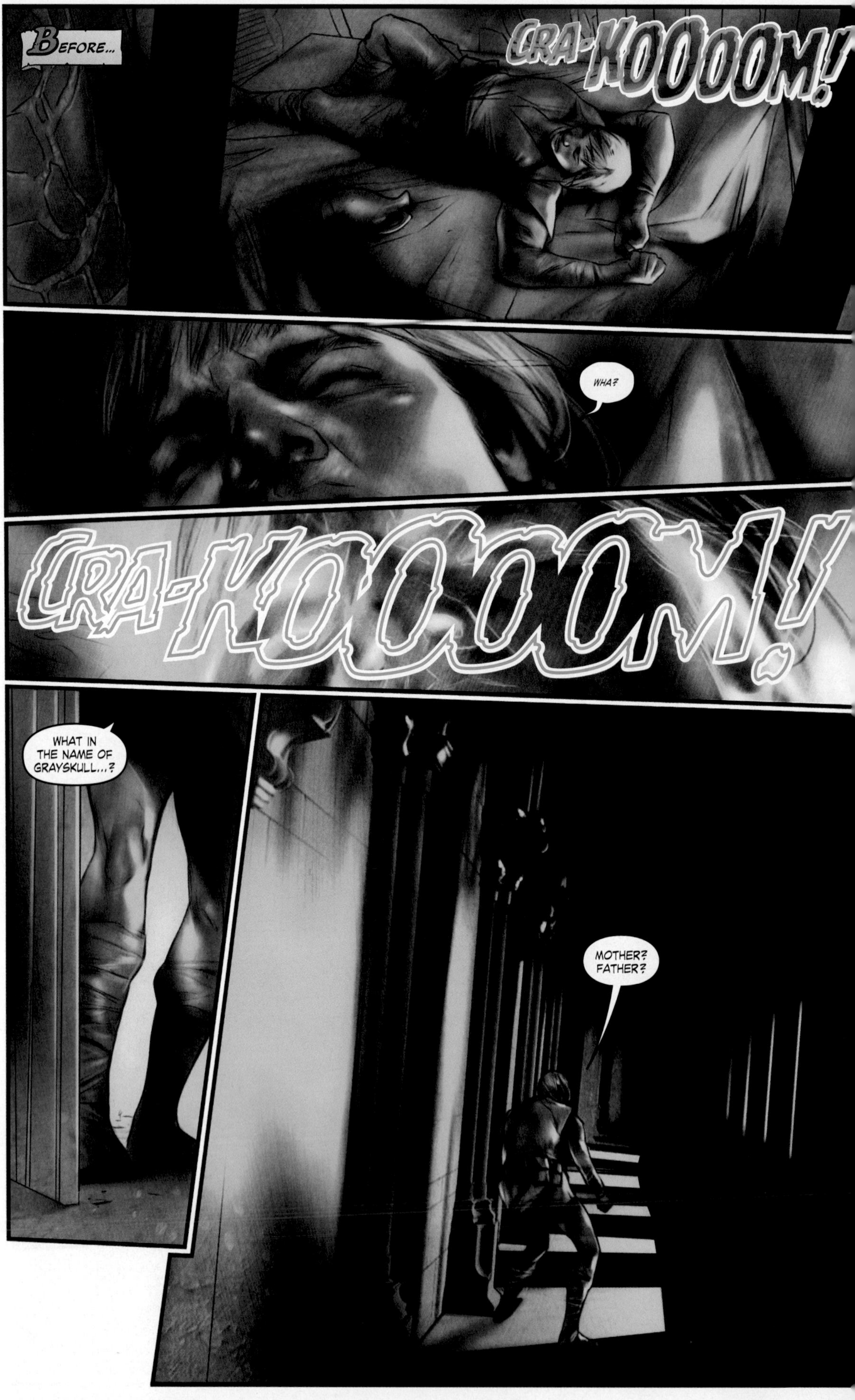
BEFORE...
CRA-KOOOOM!
WHA?
CRA-KOOOOM!!
WHAT IN THE NAME OF GRAYSKULL...?
MOTHER? FATHER?

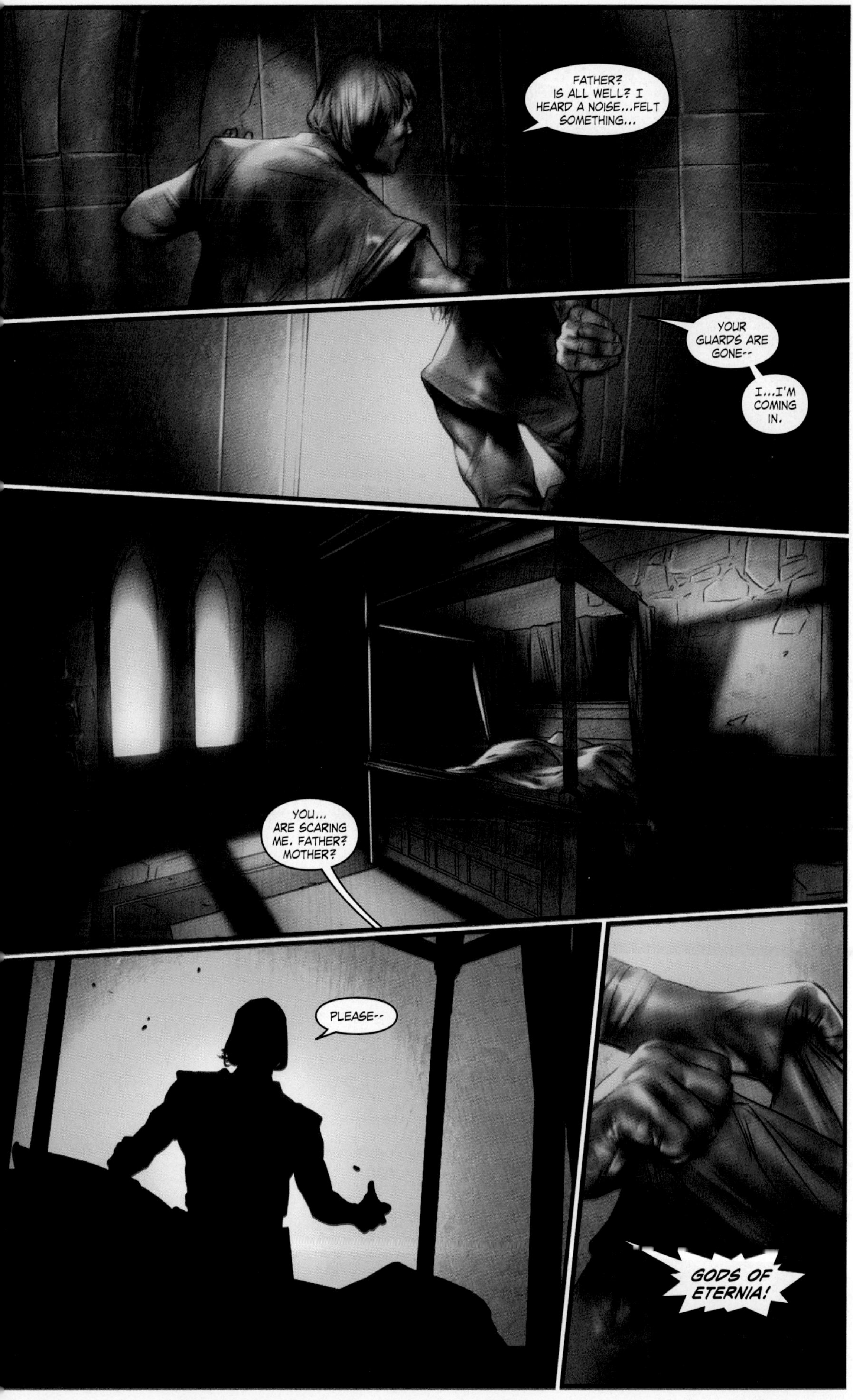
FATHER? IS ALL WELL? I HEARD A NOISE...FELT SOMETHING...
YOUR GUARDS ARE GONE--
I...I'M COMING IN.
YOU... ARE SCARING ME. FATHER? MOTHER?
PLEASE--
GODS OF ETERNIA!

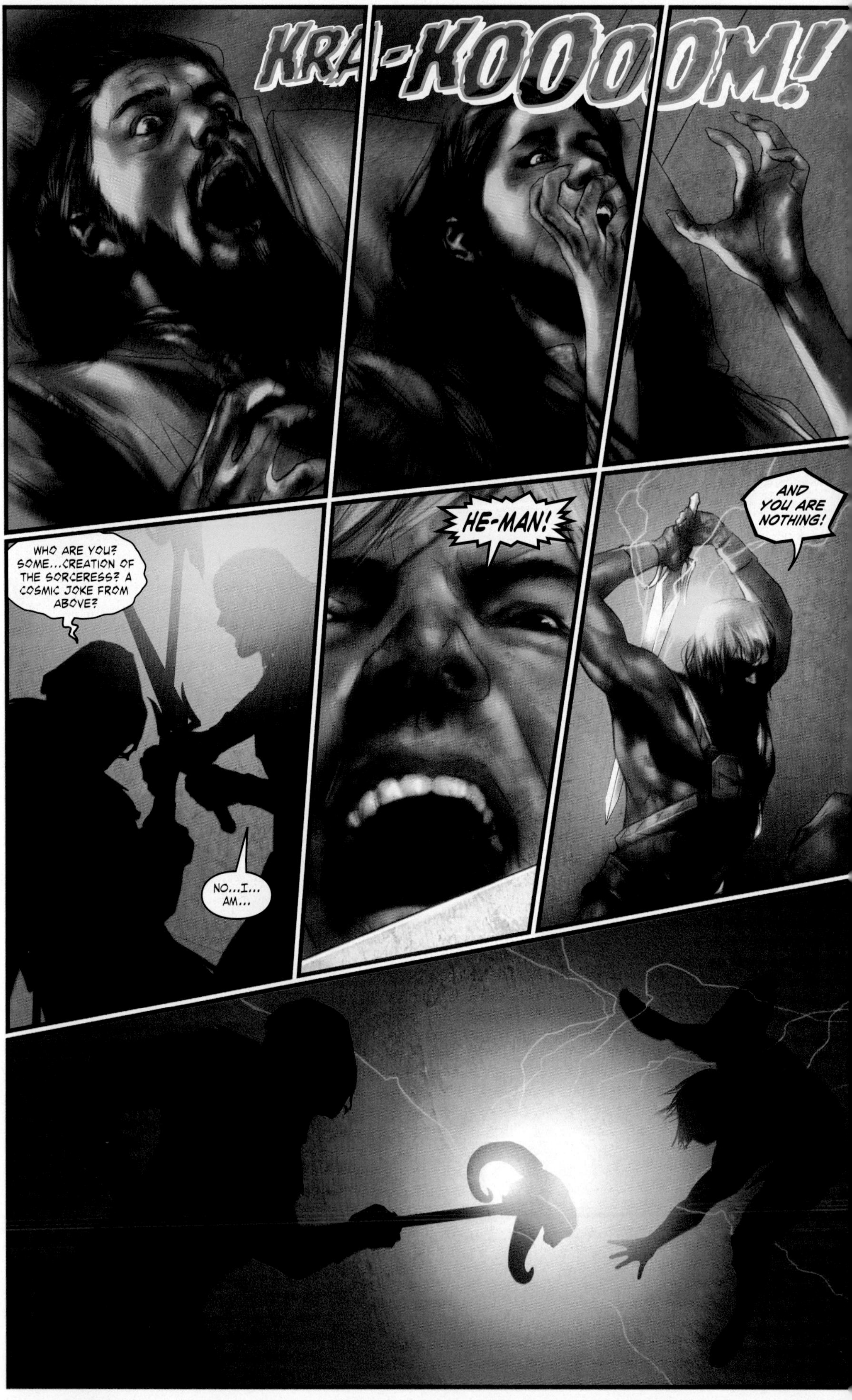
KRA-KOOOOOM!
WHO ARE YOU? SOME...CREATION OF THE SORCERESS? A COSMIC JOKE FROM ABOVE?
NO...I... AM...
HE-MAN!
AND YOU ARE NOTHING!

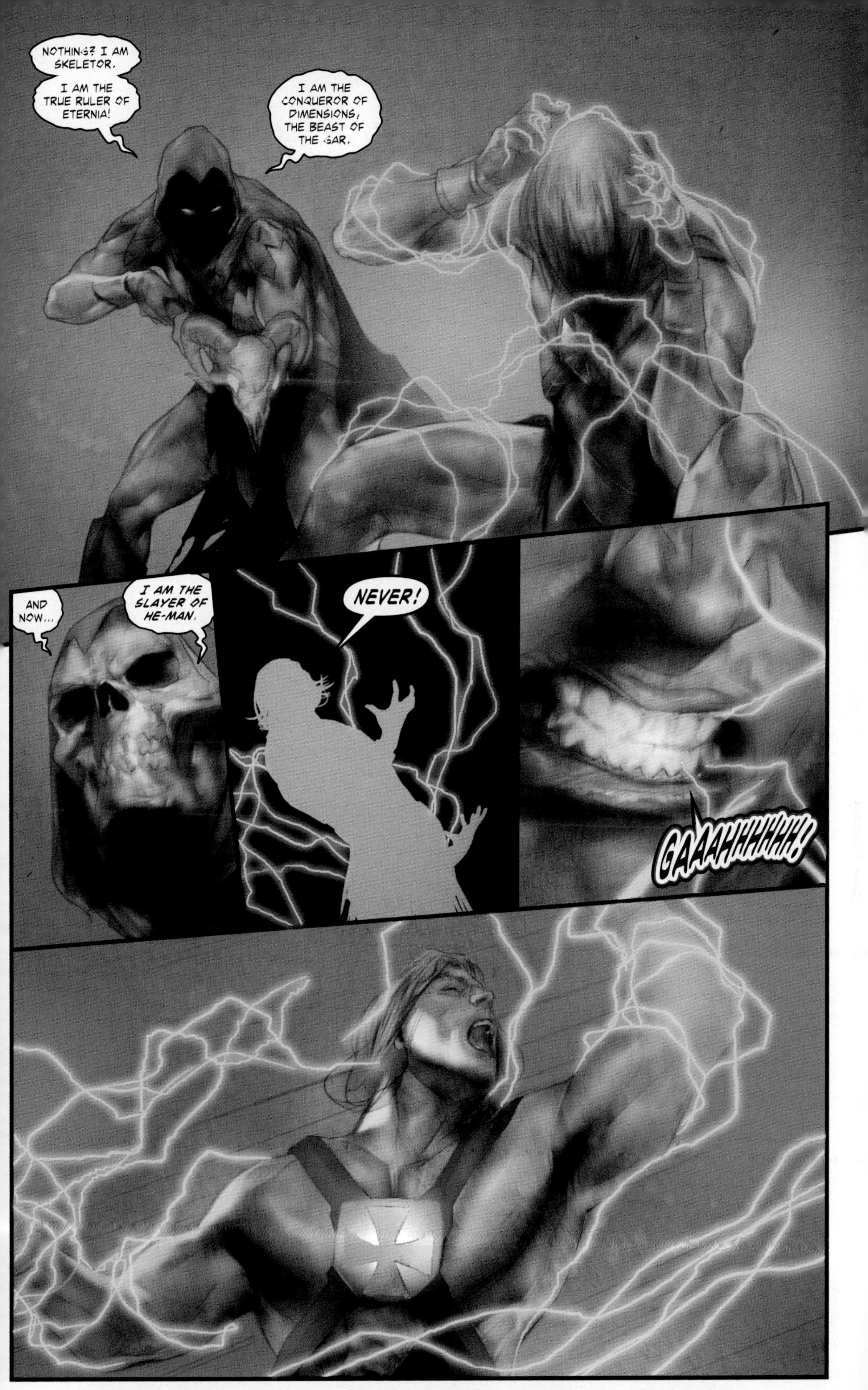
NOTHING? I AM SKELETOR.
I AM THE TRUE RULER OF ETERNIA!
I AM THE CONQUEROR OF DIMENSIONS, THE BEAST OF THE GAR.
AND NOW...
I AM THE SLAYER OF HE-MAN.
NEVER!
GAAAHHHHHH!

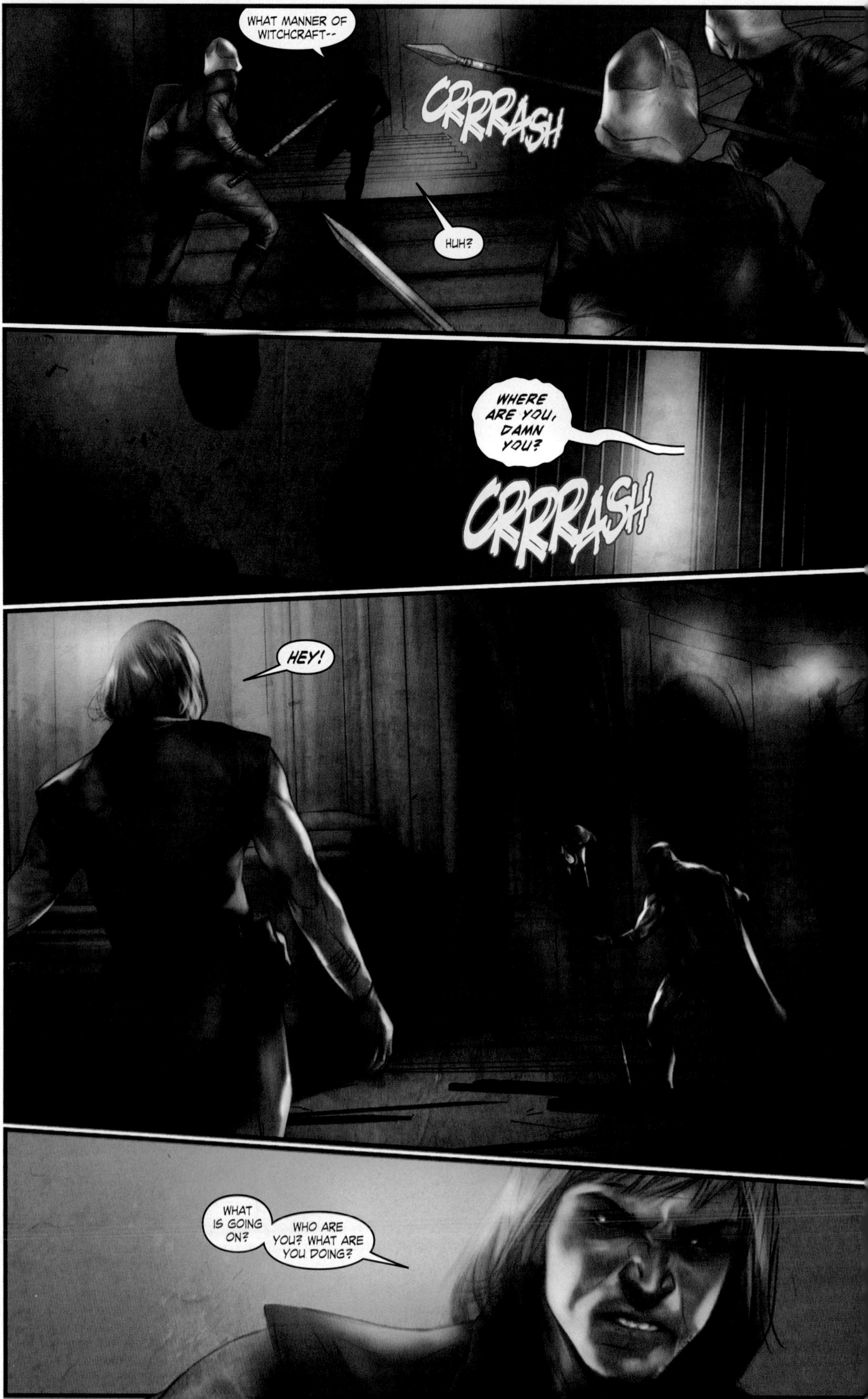
WHAT MANNER OF WITCHCRAFT--
CRRRASH
HUH?
WHERE ARE YOU, DAMN YOU?
CRRRASH
HEY!
WHAT IS GOING ON?
WHO ARE YOU? WHAT ARE YOU DOING?

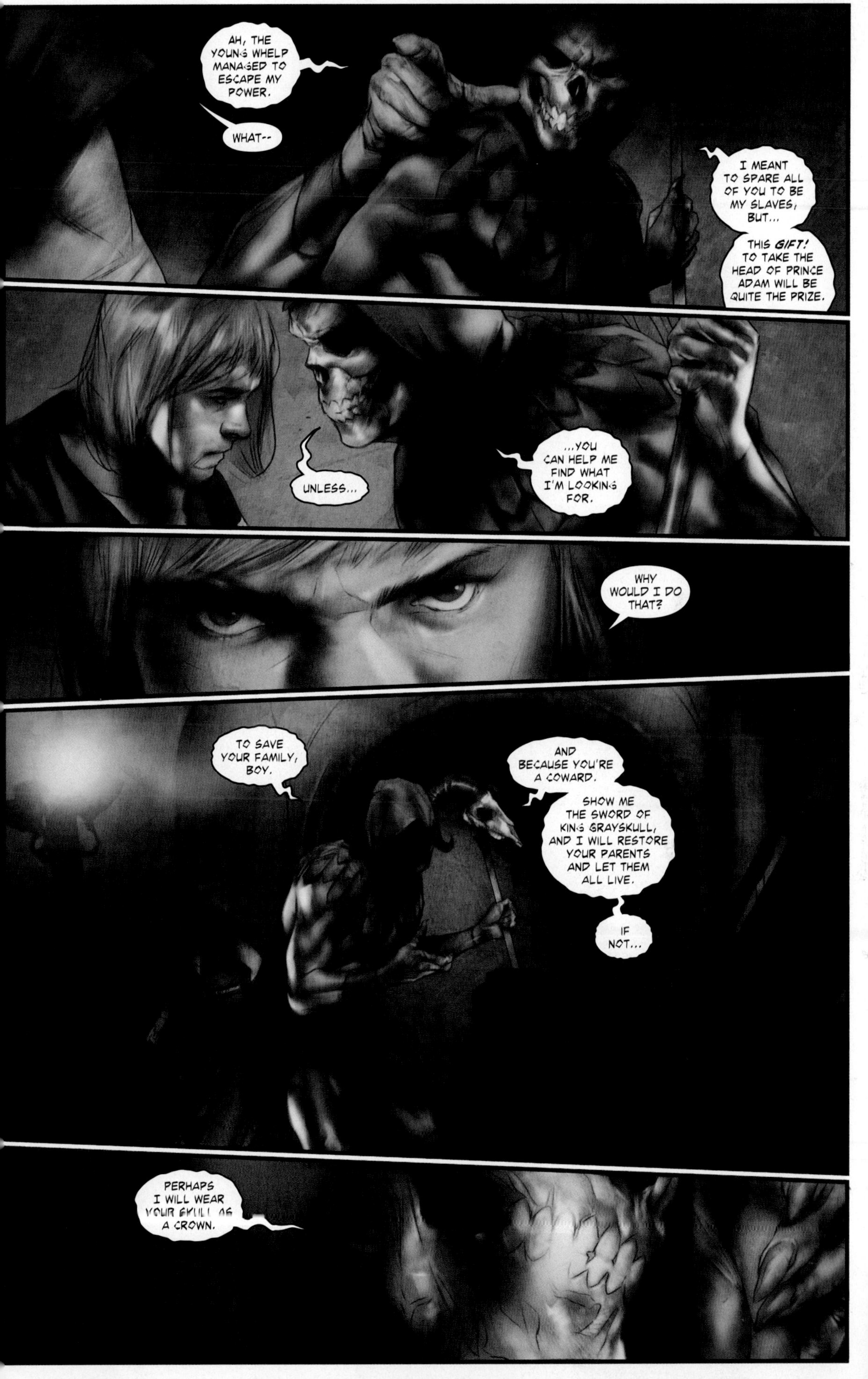
AH, THE YOUNG WHELP MANAGED TO ESCAPE MY POWER.
WHAT--
I MEANT TO SPARE ALL OF YOU TO BE MY SLAVES, BUT...
THIS GIFT! TO TAKE THE HEAD OF PRINCE ADAM WILL BE QUITE THE PRIZE.
UNLESS...
...YOU CAN HELP ME FIND WHAT I'M LOOKING FOR.
WHY WOULD I DO THAT?
TO SAVE YOUR FAMILY, BOY.
AND BECAUSE YOU'RE A COWARD.
SHOW ME THE SWORD OF KING GRAYSKULL, AND I WILL RESTORE YOUR PARENTS AND LET THEM ALL LIVE.
IF NOT...
PERHAPS I WILL WEAR YOUR SKULL AS A CROWN.

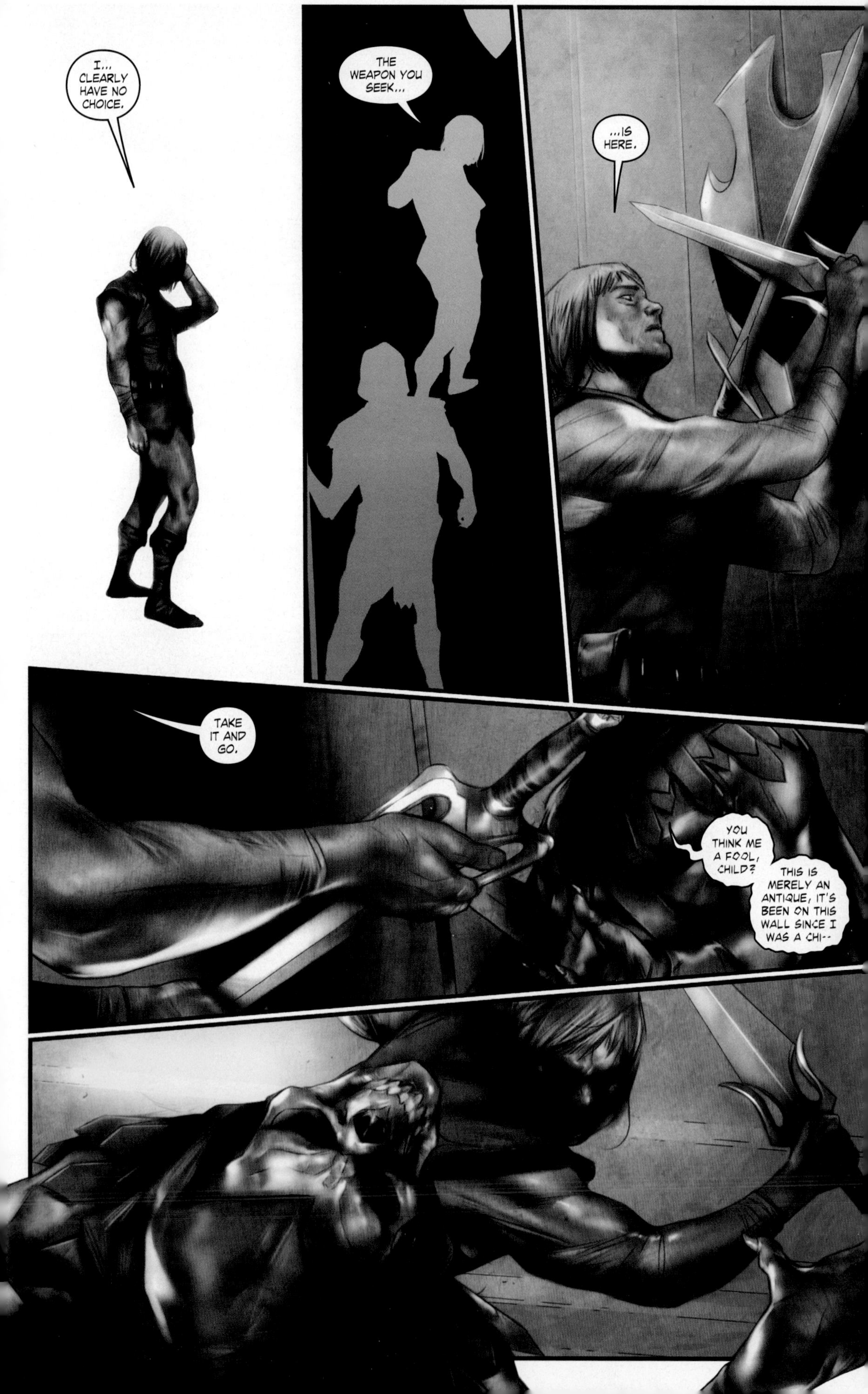
I... CLEARLY HAVE NO CHOICE.
THE WEAPON YOU SEEK...
...IS HERE.
TAKE IT AND GO.
YOU THINK ME A FOOL, CHILD?
THIS IS MERELY AN ANTIQUE, IT'S BEEN ON THIS WALL SINCE I WAS A CHI--

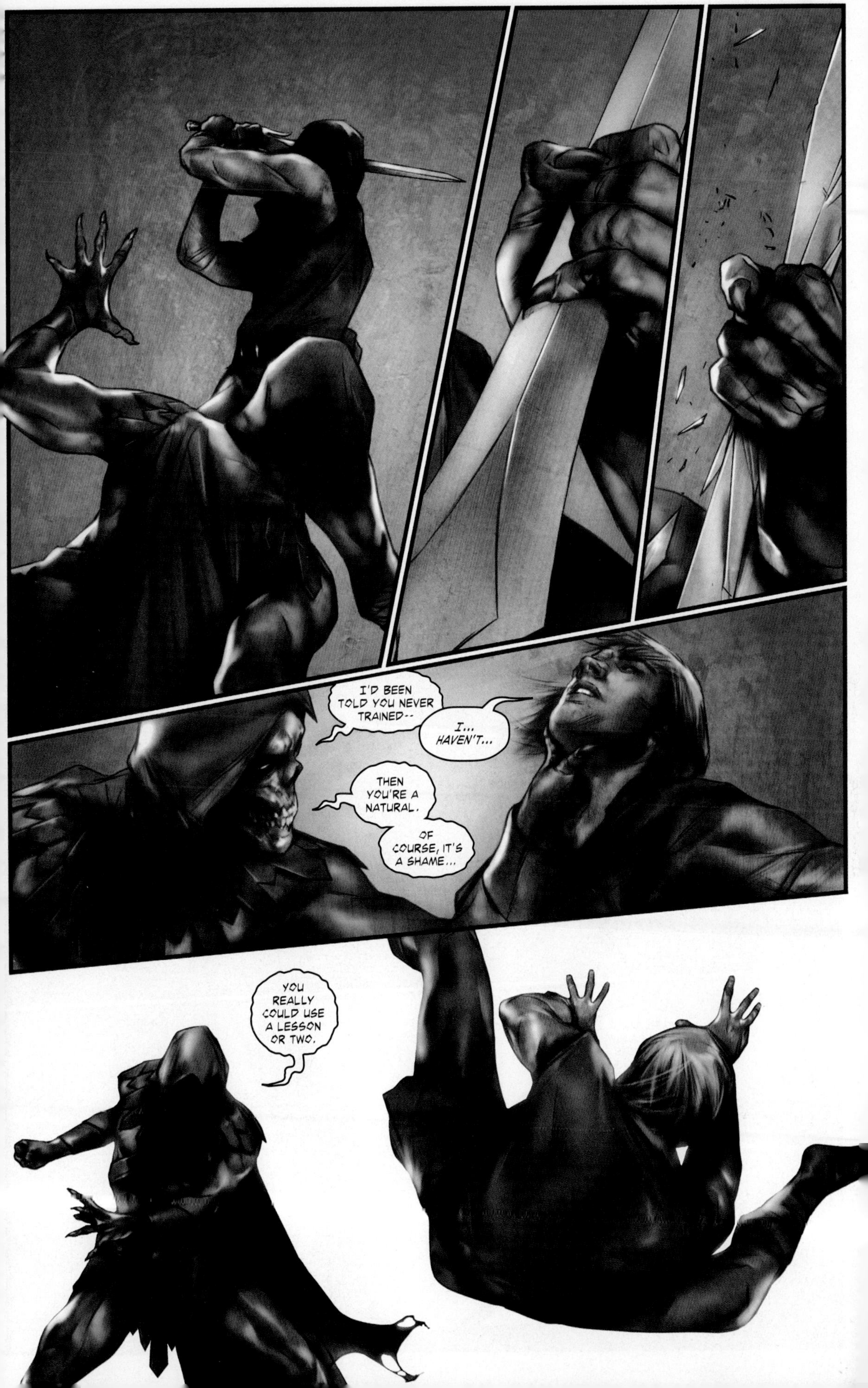
I'D BEEN TOLD YOU NEVER TRAINED--
I... HAVEN'T...
THEN YOU'RE A NATURAL.
OF COURSE, IT'S A SHAME...
YOU REALLY COULD USE A LESSON OR TWO.

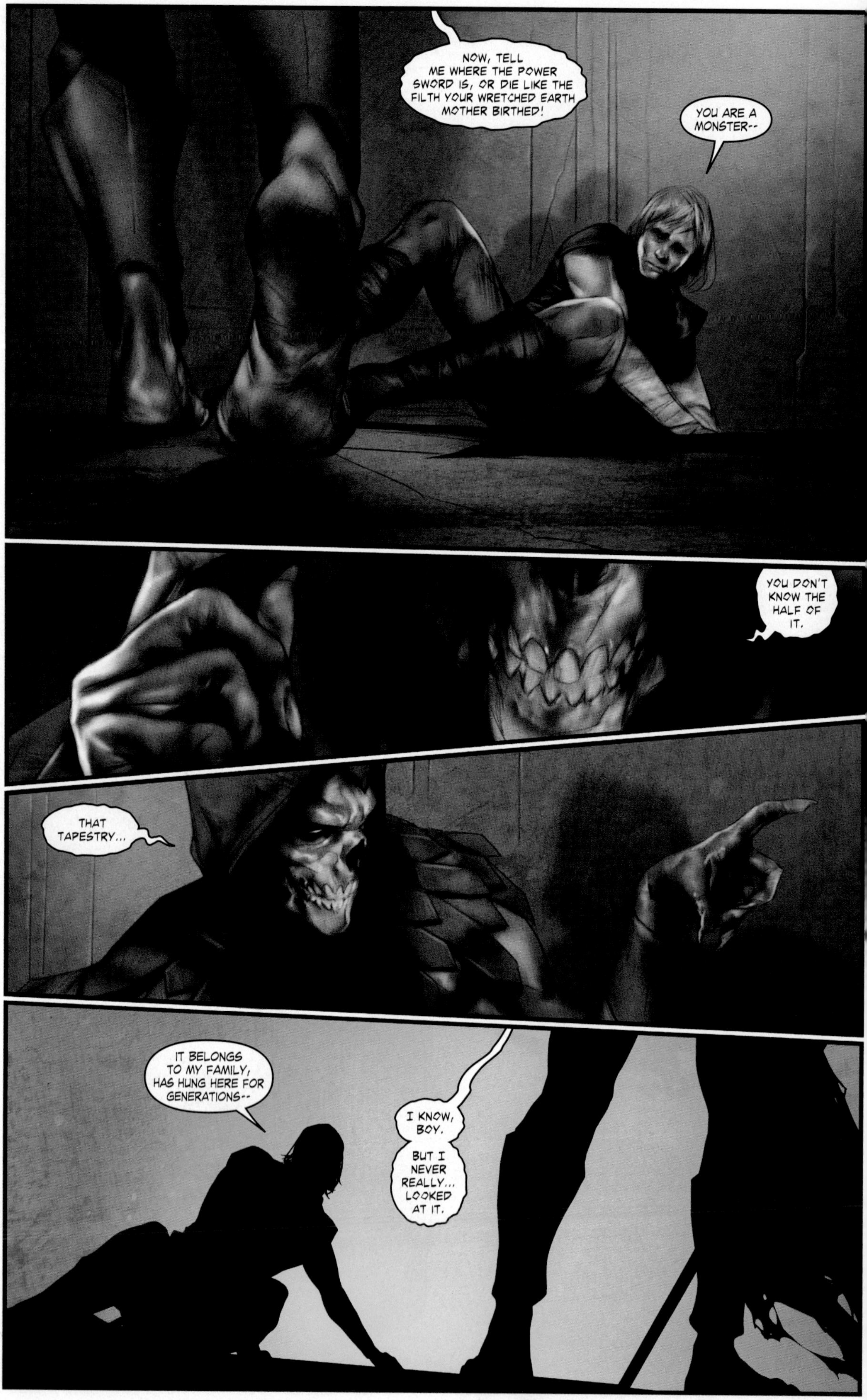
NOW, TELL ME WHERE THE POWER SWORD IS, OR DIE LIKE THE FILTH YOUR WRETCHED EARTH MOTHER BIRTHED!
YOU ARE A MONSTER--
YOU DON'T KNOW THE HALF OF IT.
THAT TAPESTRY...
IT BELONGS TO MY FAMILY, HAS HUNG HERE FOR GENERATIONS--
I KNOW, BOY.
BUT I NEVER REALLY... LOOKED AT IT.

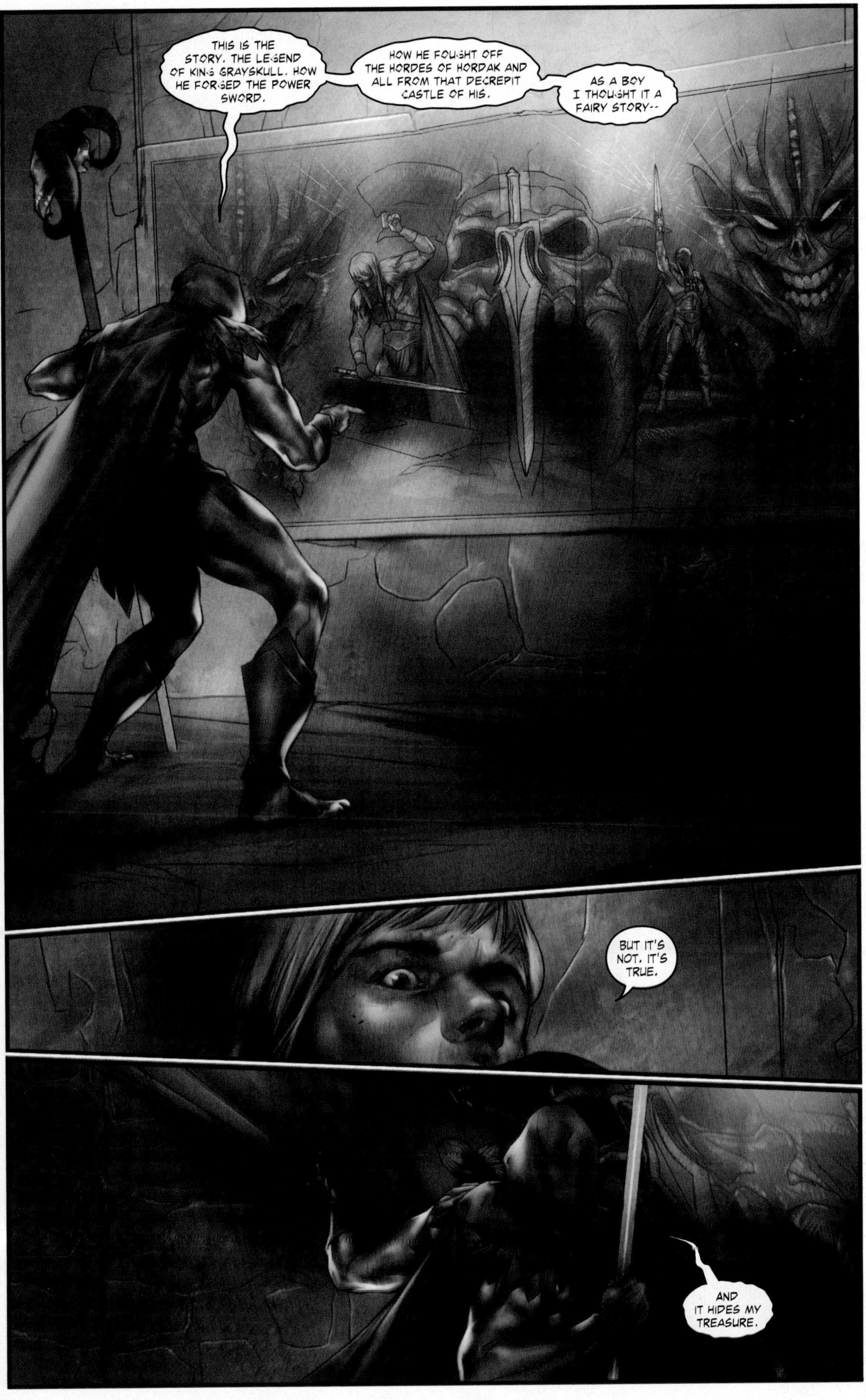
THIS IS THE STORY. THE LEGEND OF KING GRAYSKULL. HOW HE FORGED THE POWER SWORD.
HOW HE FOUGHT OFF THE HORDES OF HORDAK AND ALL FROM THAT DECREPIT CASTLE OF HIS.
AS A BOY I THOUGHT IT A FAIRY STORY--
BUT IT'S NOT. IT'S TRUE.
AND IT HIDES MY TREASURE.

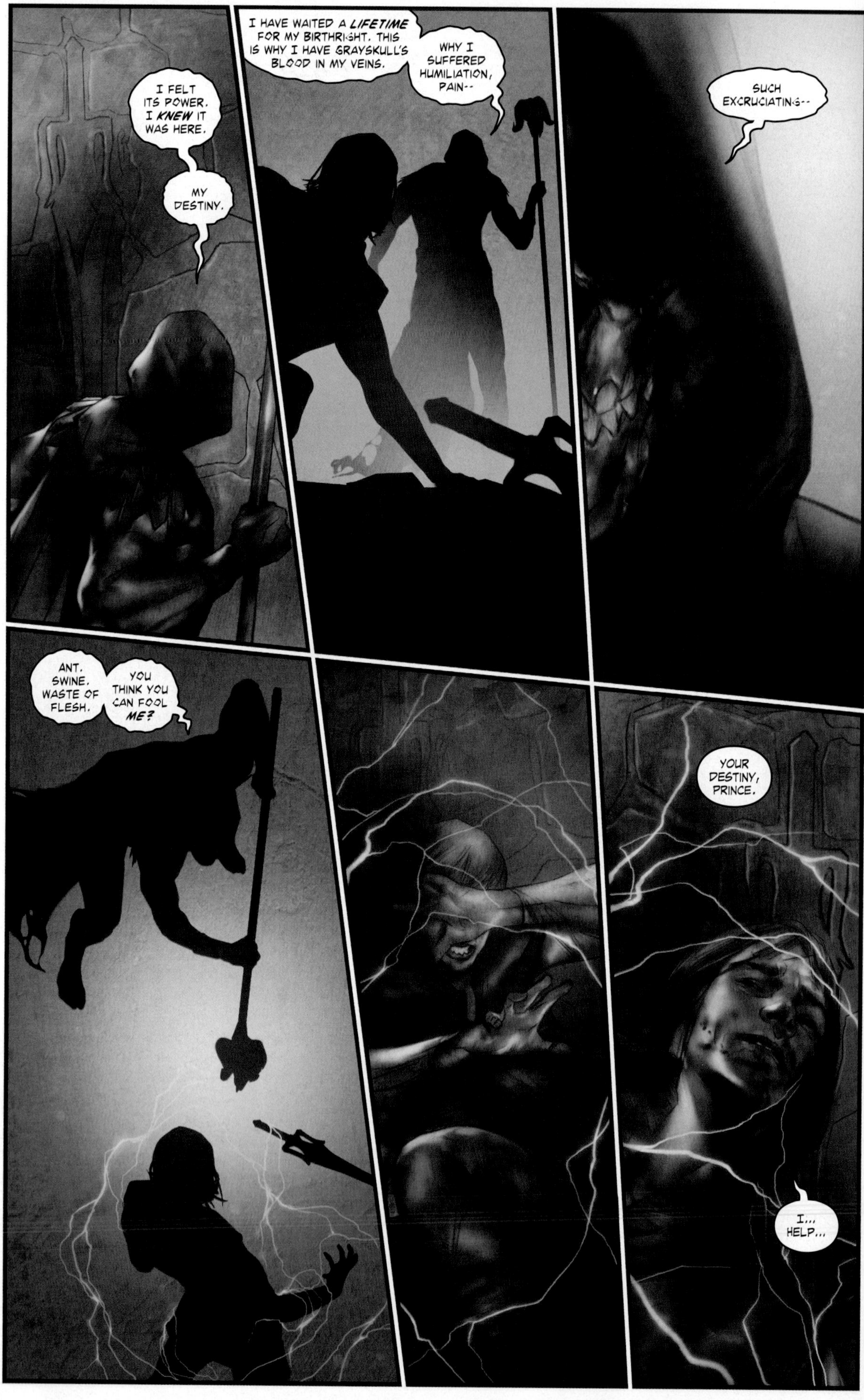
I FELT ITS POWER. I *KNEW* IT WAS HERE.
MY DESTINY.
I HAVE WAITED A *LIFETIME* FOR MY BIRTHRIGHT. THIS IS WHY I HAVE GRAYSKULL'S BLOOD IN MY VEINS.
WHY I SUFFERED HUMILIATION, PAIN--
SUCH EXCRUCIATING--
ANT. SWINE. WASTE OF FLESH.
YOU THINK YOU CAN FOOL *ME?*
YOUR DESTINY, PRINCE.
I... HELP...

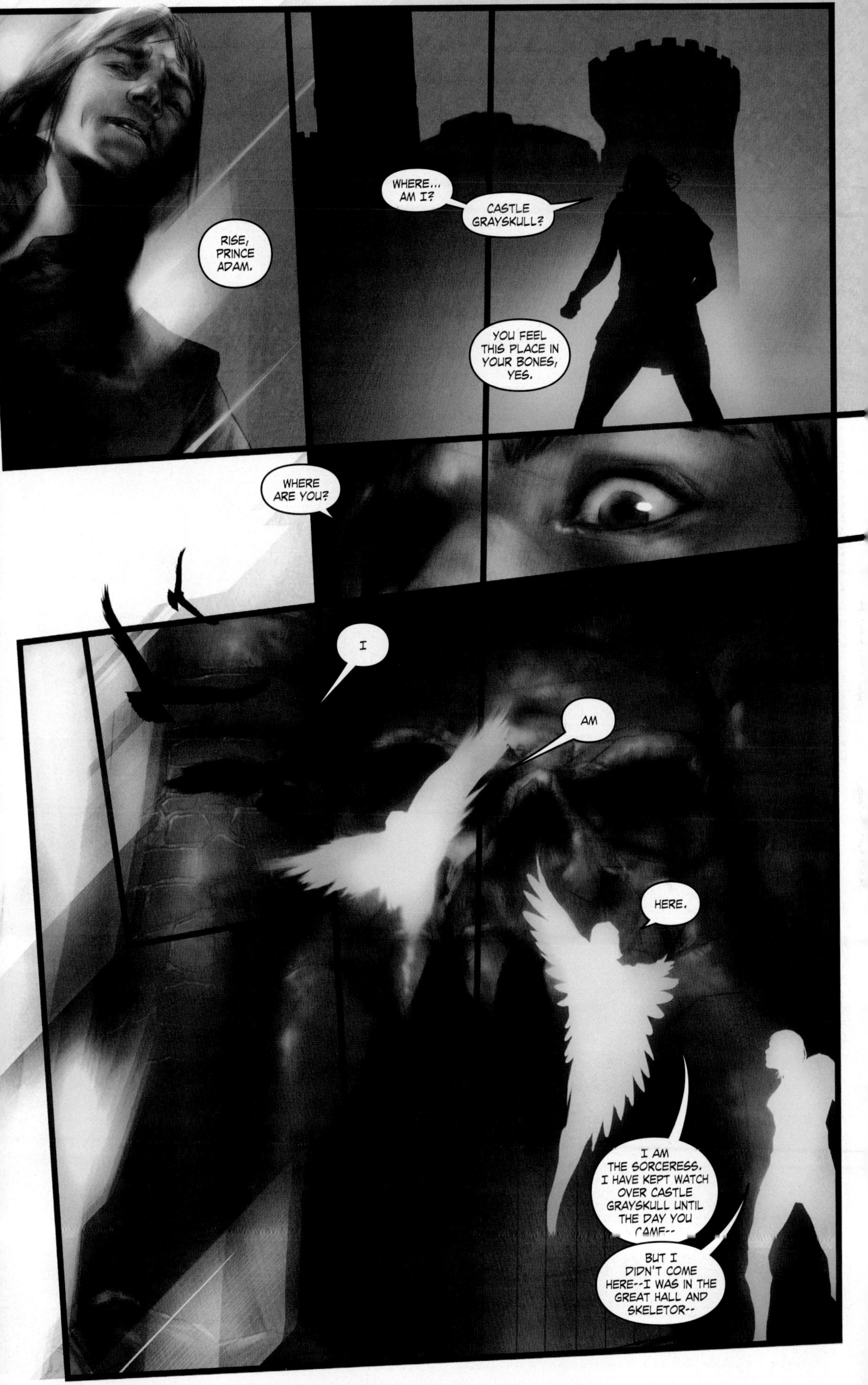
RISE, PRINCE ADAM.
WHERE... AM I?
CASTLE GRAYSKULL?
YOU FEEL THIS PLACE IN YOUR BONES, YES.
WHERE ARE YOU?
I
AM
HERE.
I AM THE SORCERESS. I HAVE KEPT WATCH OVER CASTLE GRAYSKULL UNTIL THE DAY YOU CAME--
BUT I DIDN'T COME HERE--I WAS IN THE GREAT HALL AND SKELETOR--

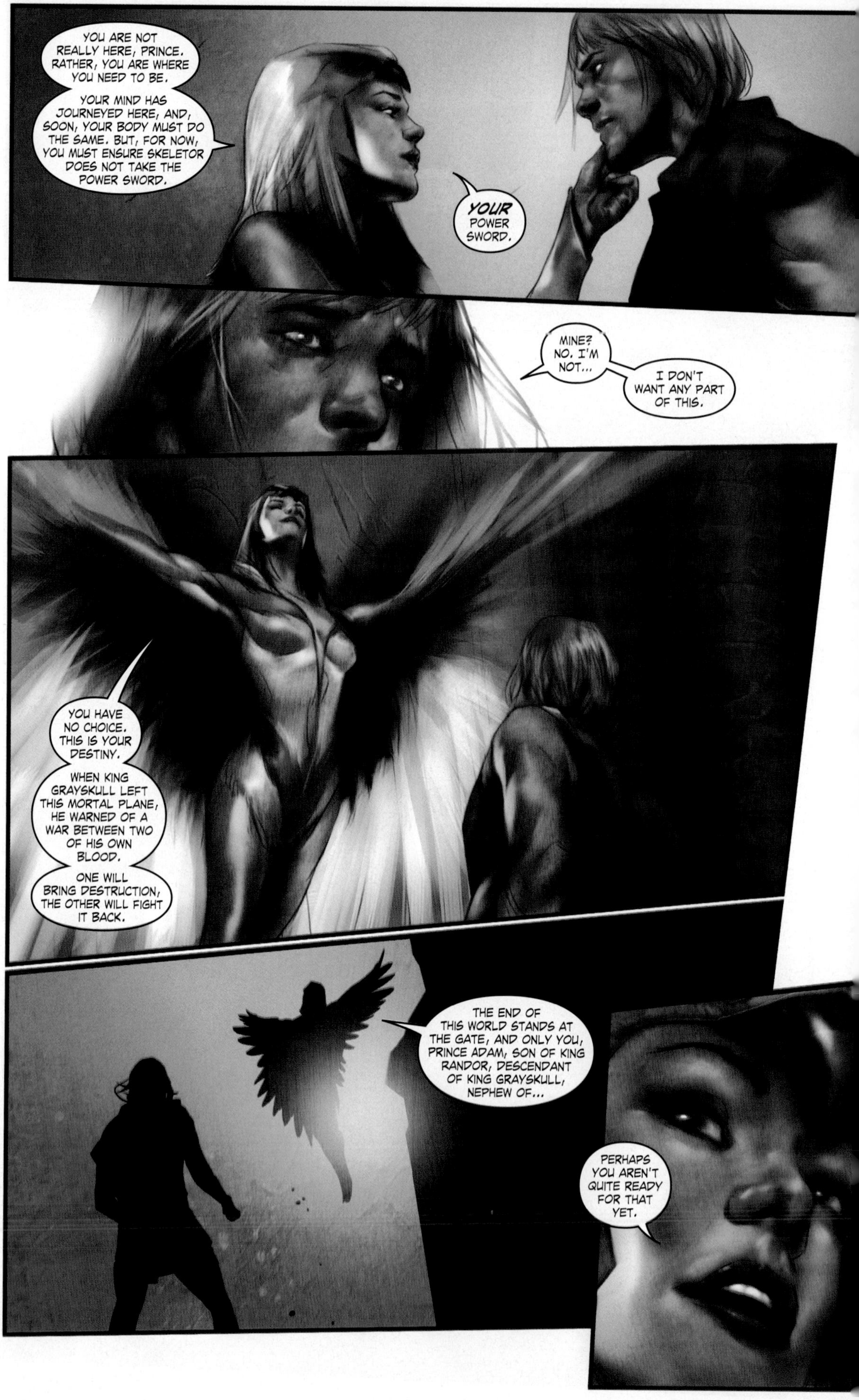
YOU ARE NOT REALLY HERE, PRINCE. RATHER, YOU ARE WHERE YOU NEED TO BE.
YOUR MIND HAS JOURNEYED HERE, AND, SOON, YOUR BODY MUST DO THE SAME. BUT, FOR NOW, YOU MUST ENSURE SKELETOR DOES NOT TAKE THE POWER SWORD.
YOUR POWER SWORD.
MINE? NO. I'M NOT...
I DON'T WANT ANY PART OF THIS.
YOU HAVE NO CHOICE. THIS IS YOUR DESTINY.
WHEN KING GRAYSKULL LEFT THIS MORTAL PLANE, HE WARNED OF A WAR BETWEEN TWO OF HIS OWN BLOOD.
ONE WILL BRING DESTRUCTION, THE OTHER WILL FIGHT IT BACK.
THE END OF THIS WORLD STANDS AT THE GATE, AND ONLY YOU, PRINCE ADAM, SON OF KING RANDOR, DESCENDANT OF KING GRAYSKULL, NEPHEW OF...
PERHAPS YOU AREN'T QUITE READY FOR THAT YET.

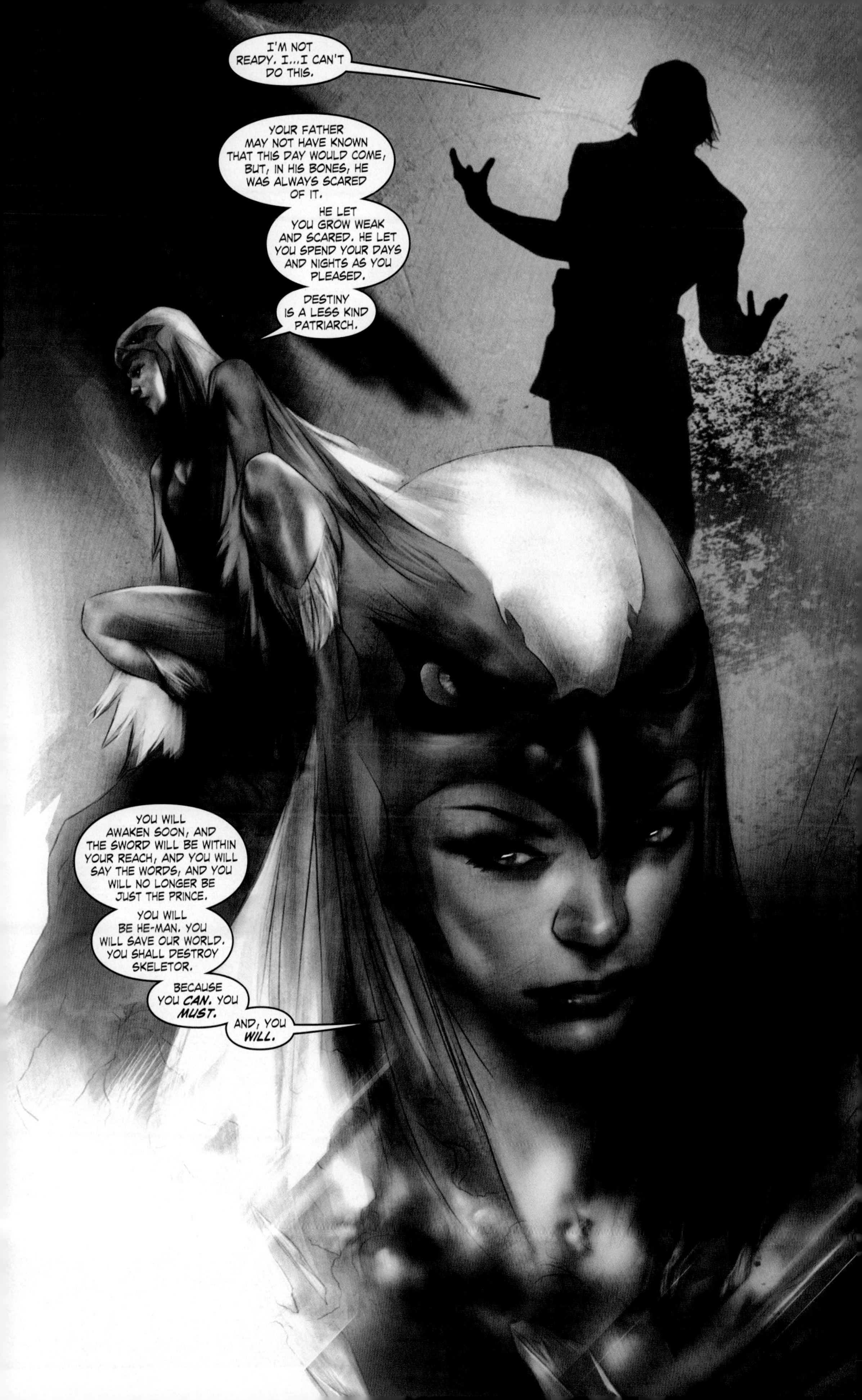
I'M NOT READY. I...I CAN'T DO THIS.
YOUR FATHER MAY NOT HAVE KNOWN THAT THIS DAY WOULD COME, BUT, IN HIS BONES, HE WAS ALWAYS SCARED OF IT.
HE LET YOU GROW WEAK AND SCARED. HE LET YOU SPEND YOUR DAYS AND NIGHTS AS YOU PLEASED.
DESTINY IS A LESS KIND PATRIARCH.
YOU WILL AWAKEN SOON, AND THE SWORD WILL BE WITHIN YOUR REACH, AND YOU WILL SAY THE WORDS, AND YOU WILL NO LONGER BE JUST THE PRINCE.
YOU WILL BE HE-MAN. YOU WILL SAVE OUR WORLD. YOU SHALL DESTROY SKELETOR.
BECAUSE YOU ***CAN***. YOU ***MUST***.
AND, YOU ***WILL***.

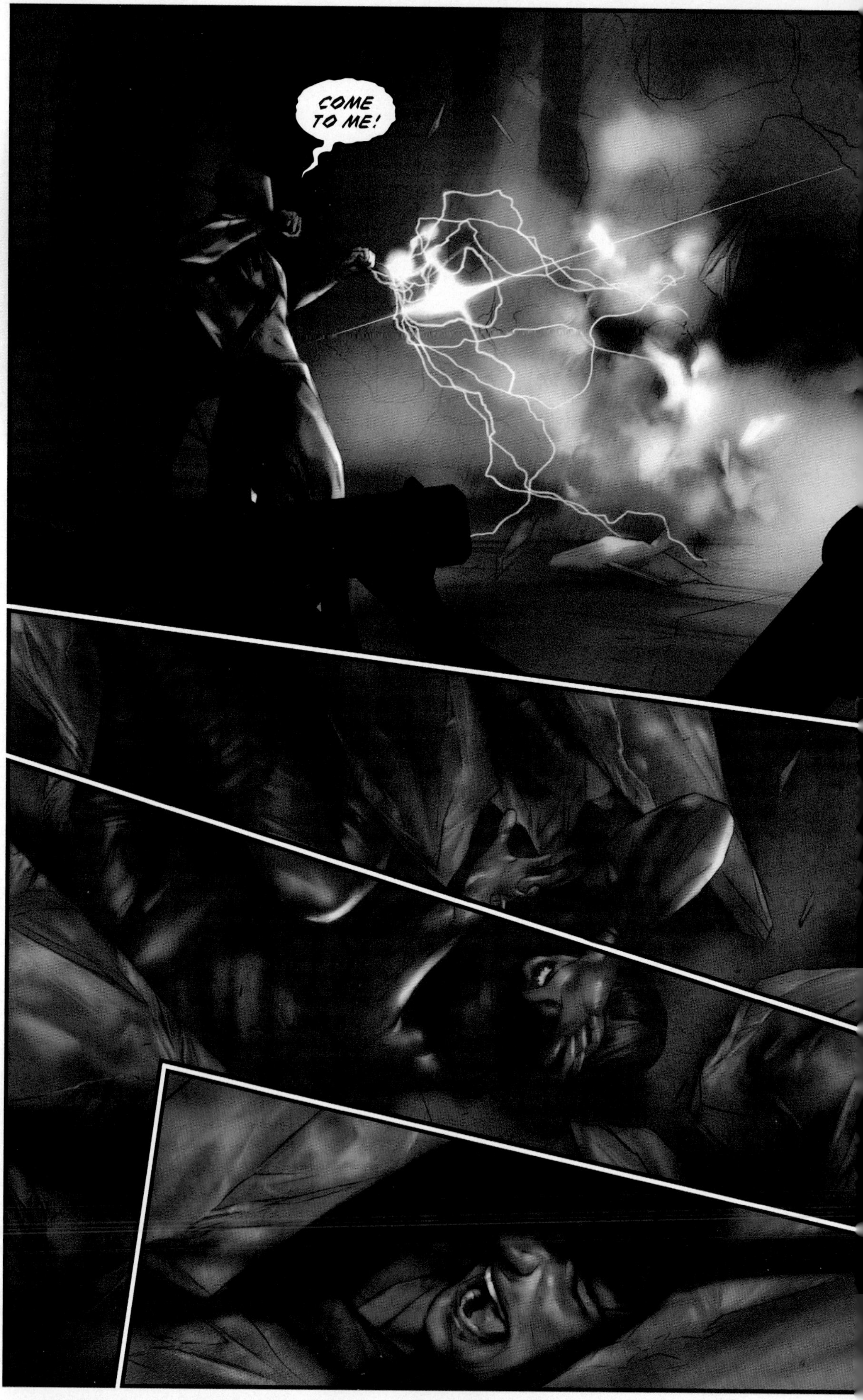
COME TO ME!

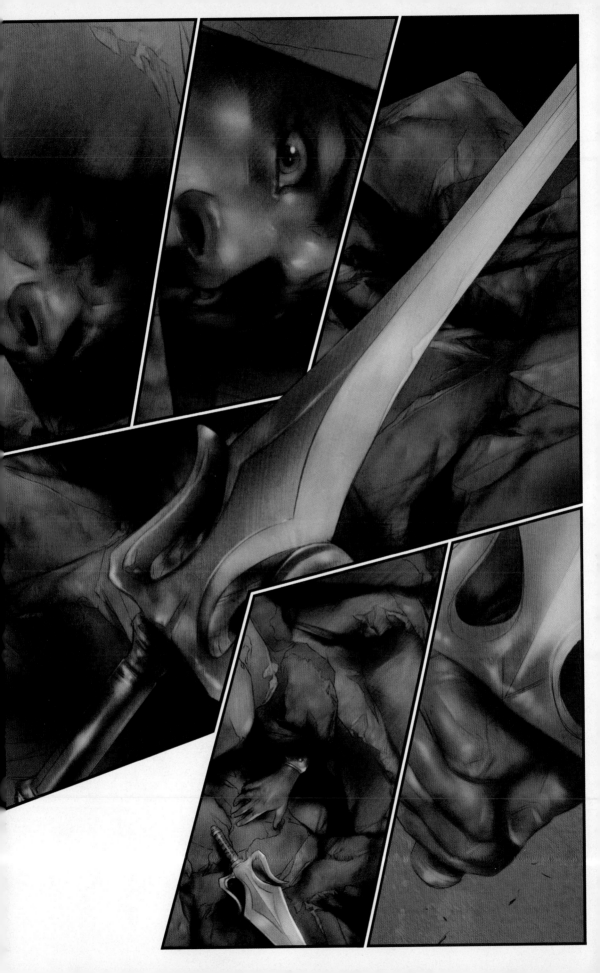

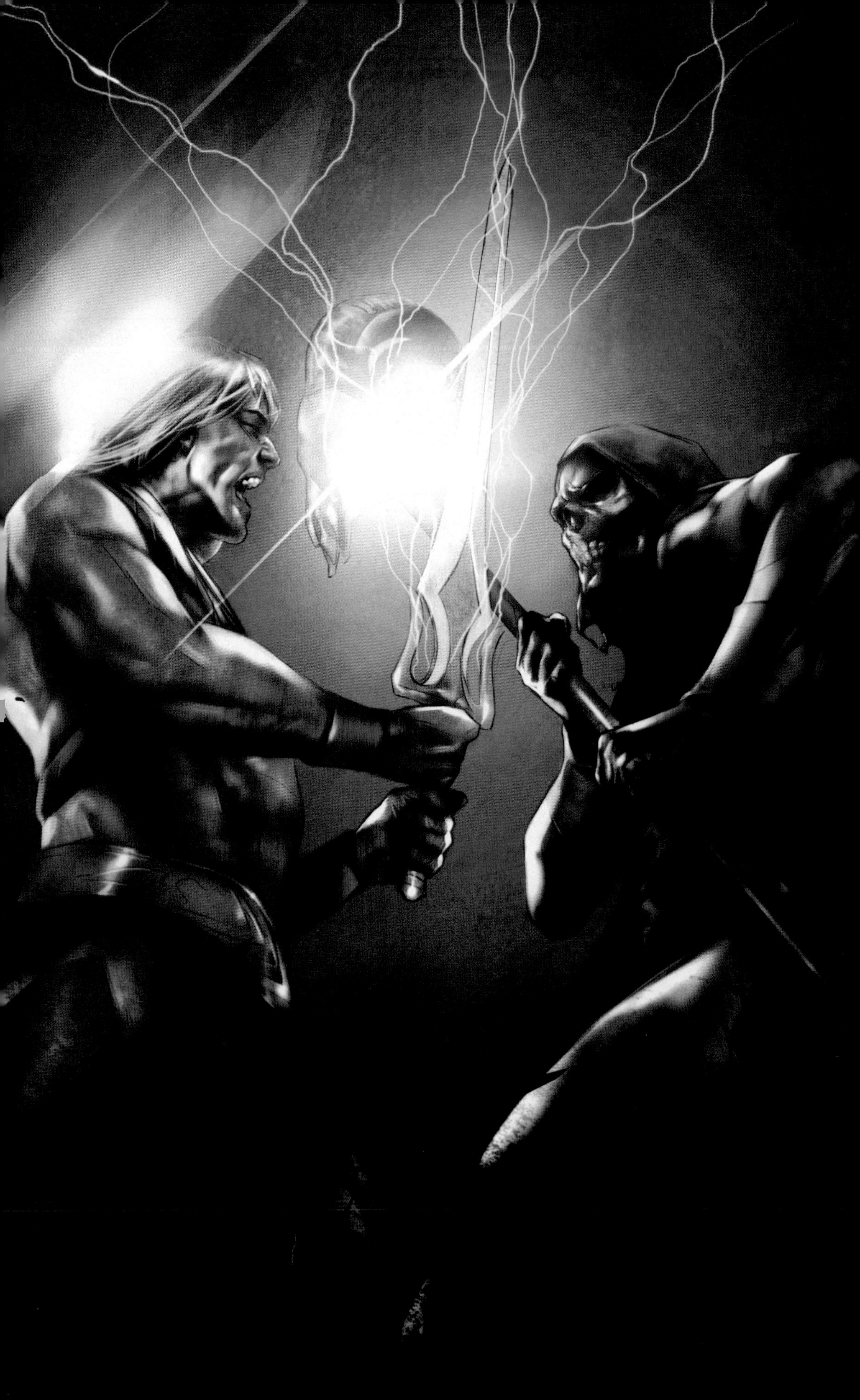

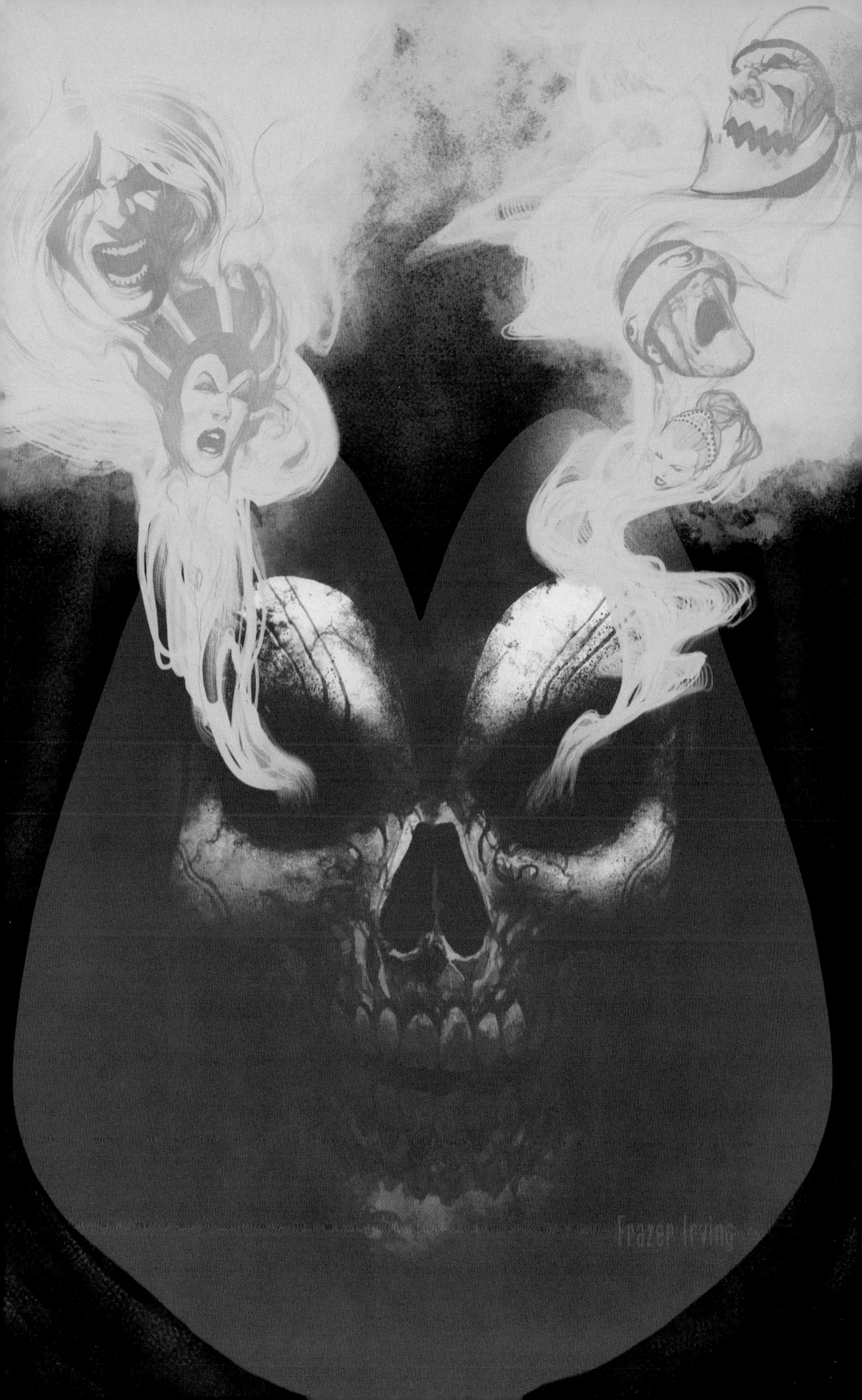
Frazer Irving

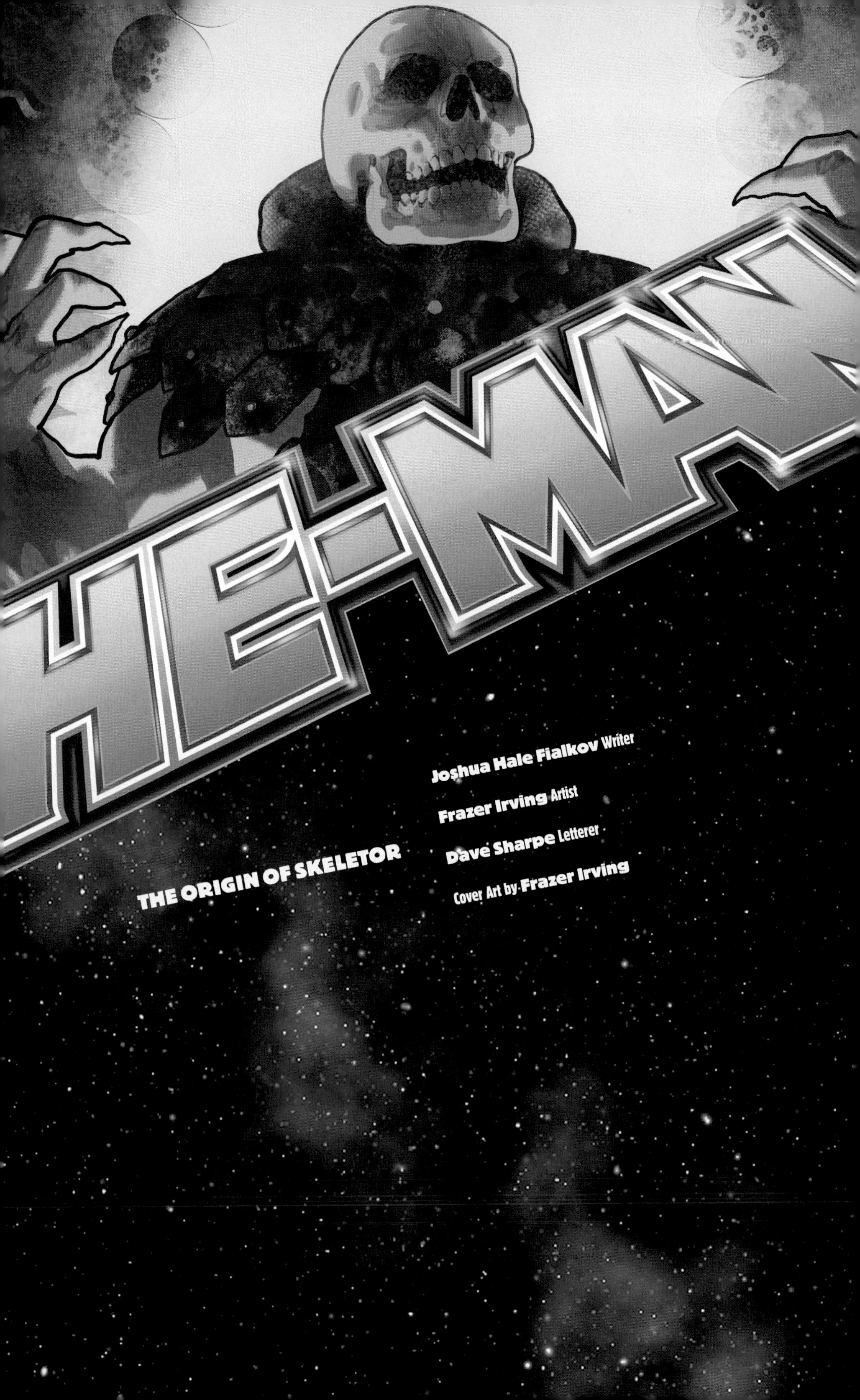
HE-MAN
THE ORIGIN OF SKELETOR
Joshua Hale Fialkov Writer
Frazer Irving Artist
Dave Sharpe Letterer
Cover Art by Frazer Irving

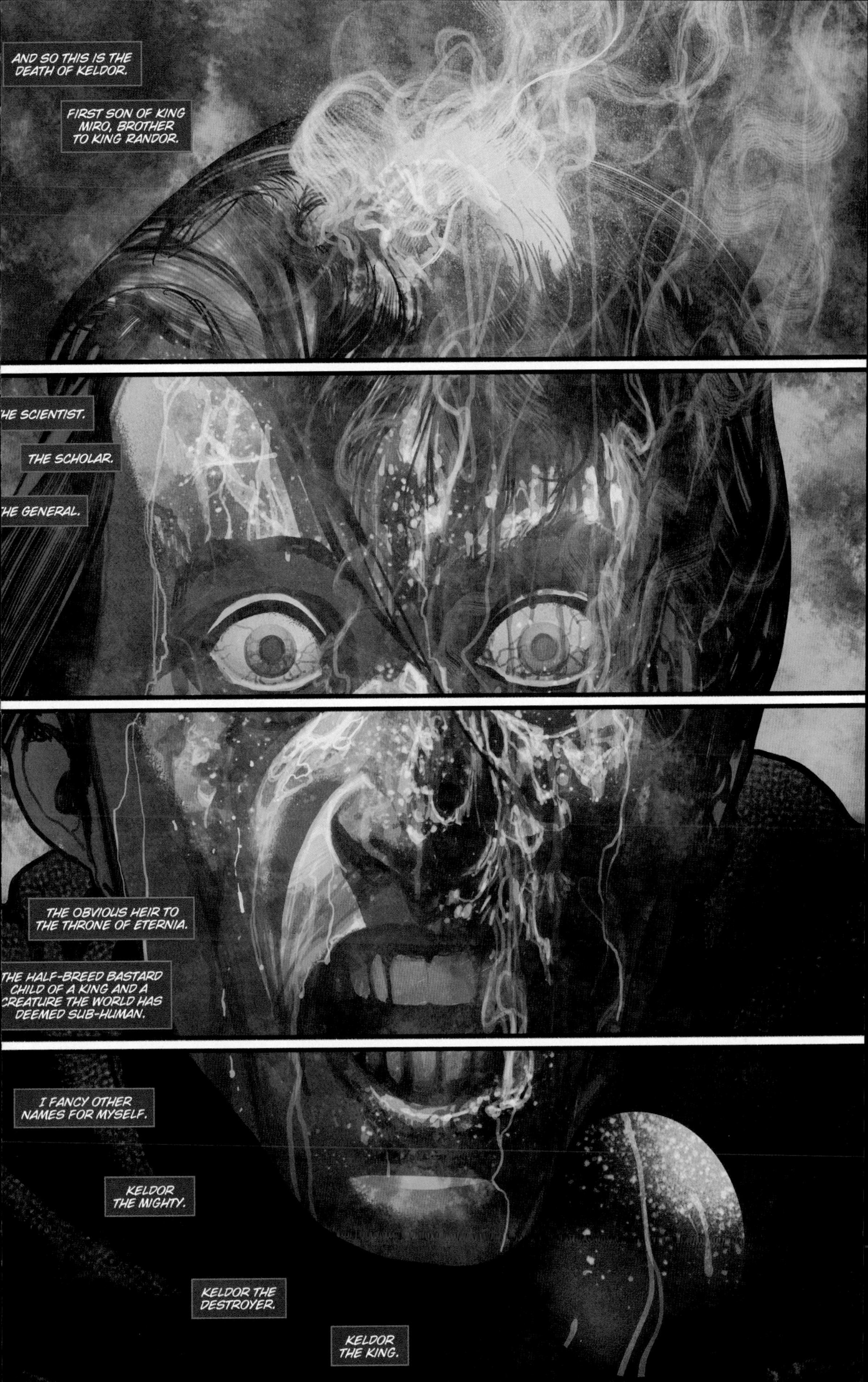
AND SO THIS IS THE DEATH OF KELDOR.
FIRST SON OF KING MIRO, BROTHER TO KING RANDOR.
THE SCIENTIST.
THE SCHOLAR.
THE GENERAL.
THE OBVIOUS HEIR TO THE THRONE OF ETERNIA.
THE HALF-BREED BASTARD CHILD OF A KING AND A CREATURE THE WORLD HAS DEEMED SUB-HUMAN.
I FANCY OTHER NAMES FOR MYSELF.
KELDOR THE MIGHTY.
KELDOR THE DESTROYER.
KELDOR THE KING.

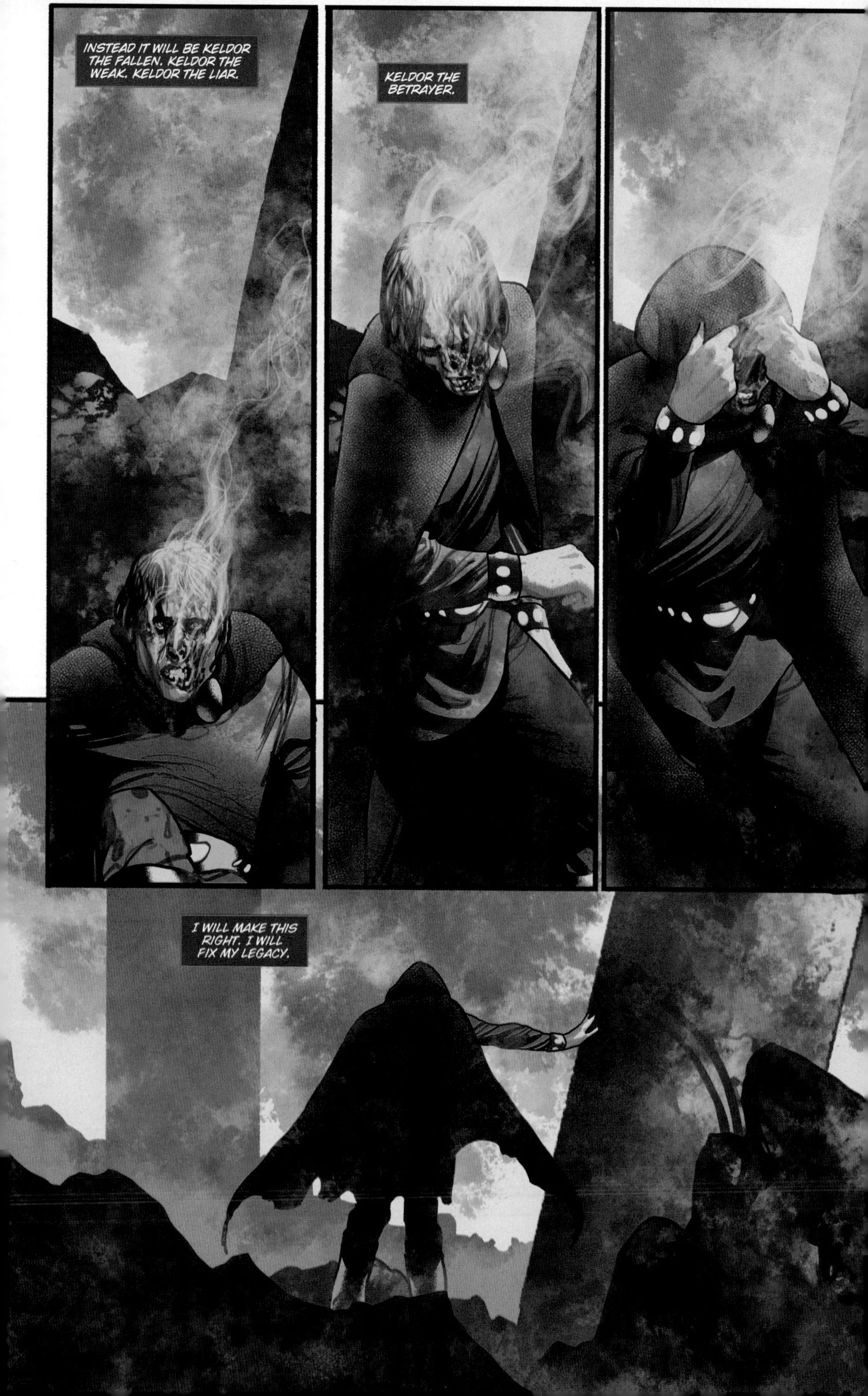
INSTEAD IT WILL BE KELDOR THE FALLEN. KELDOR THE WEAK. KELDOR THE LIAR.
KELDOR THE BETRAYER.
I WILL MAKE THIS RIGHT. I WILL FIX MY LEGACY.

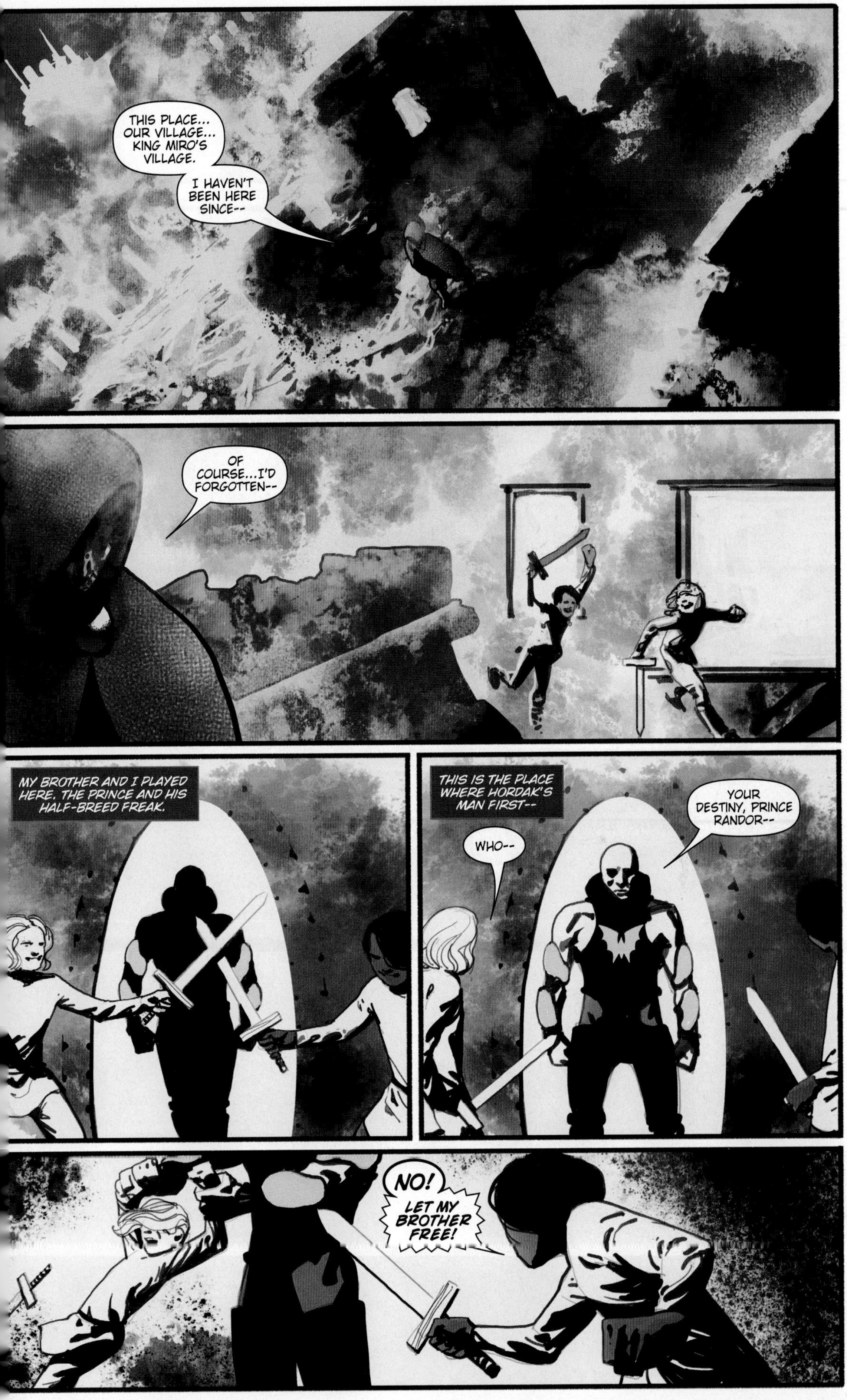
THIS PLACE... OUR VILLAGE... KING MIRO'S VILLAGE.
I HAVEN'T BEEN HERE SINCE--
OF COURSE...I'D FORGOTTEN--
MY BROTHER AND I PLAYED HERE. THE PRINCE AND HIS HALF-BREED FREAK.
THIS IS THE PLACE WHERE HORDAK'S MAN FIRST--
WHO--
YOUR DESTINY, PRINCE RANDOR--
NO!
LET MY BROTHER FREE!

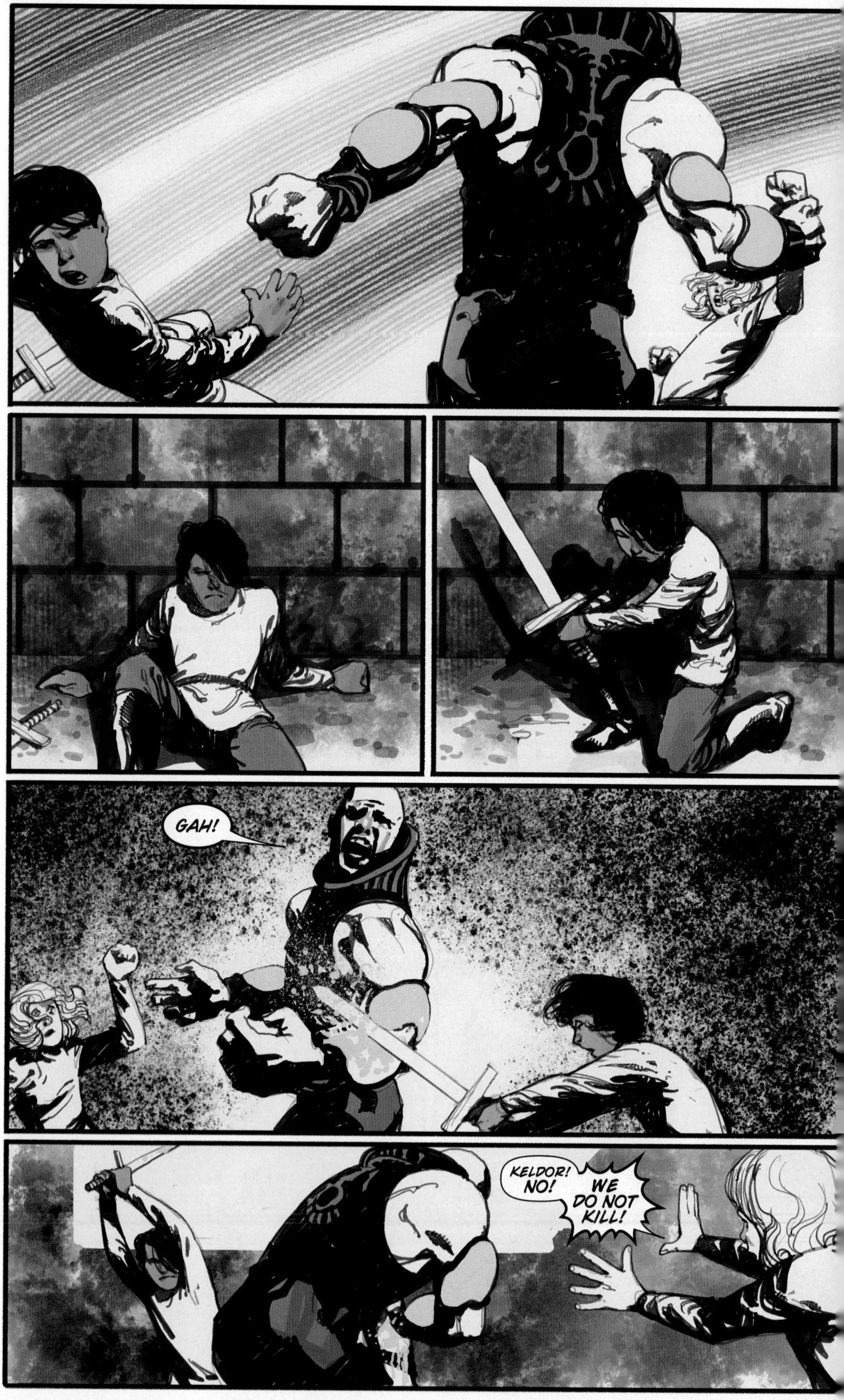
GAH!
KELDOR! NO!
WE DO NOT KILL!

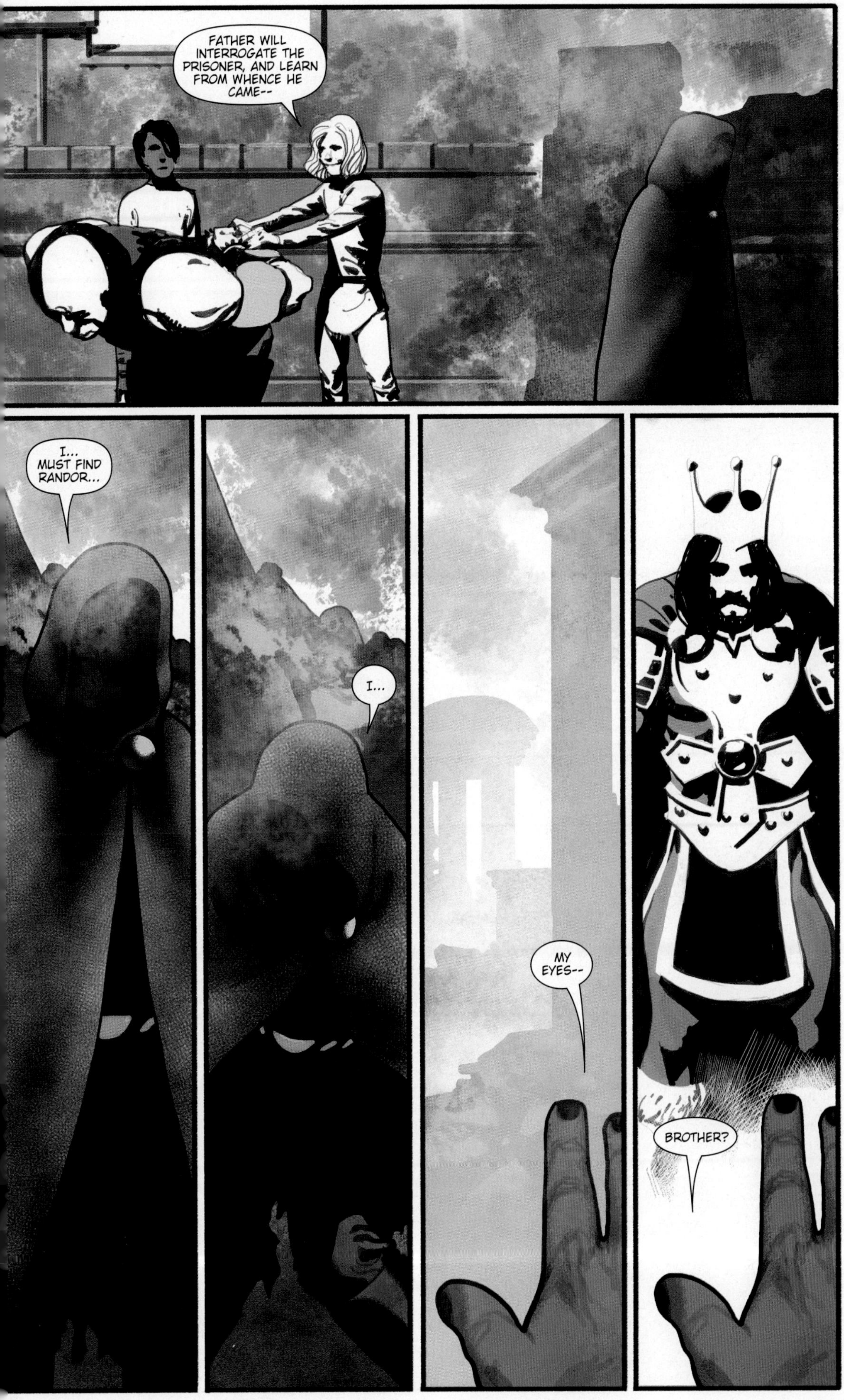
FATHER WILL INTERROGATE THE PRISONER, AND LEARN FROM WHENCE HE CAME--
I... MUST FIND RANDOR...
I...
MY EYES--
BROTHER?

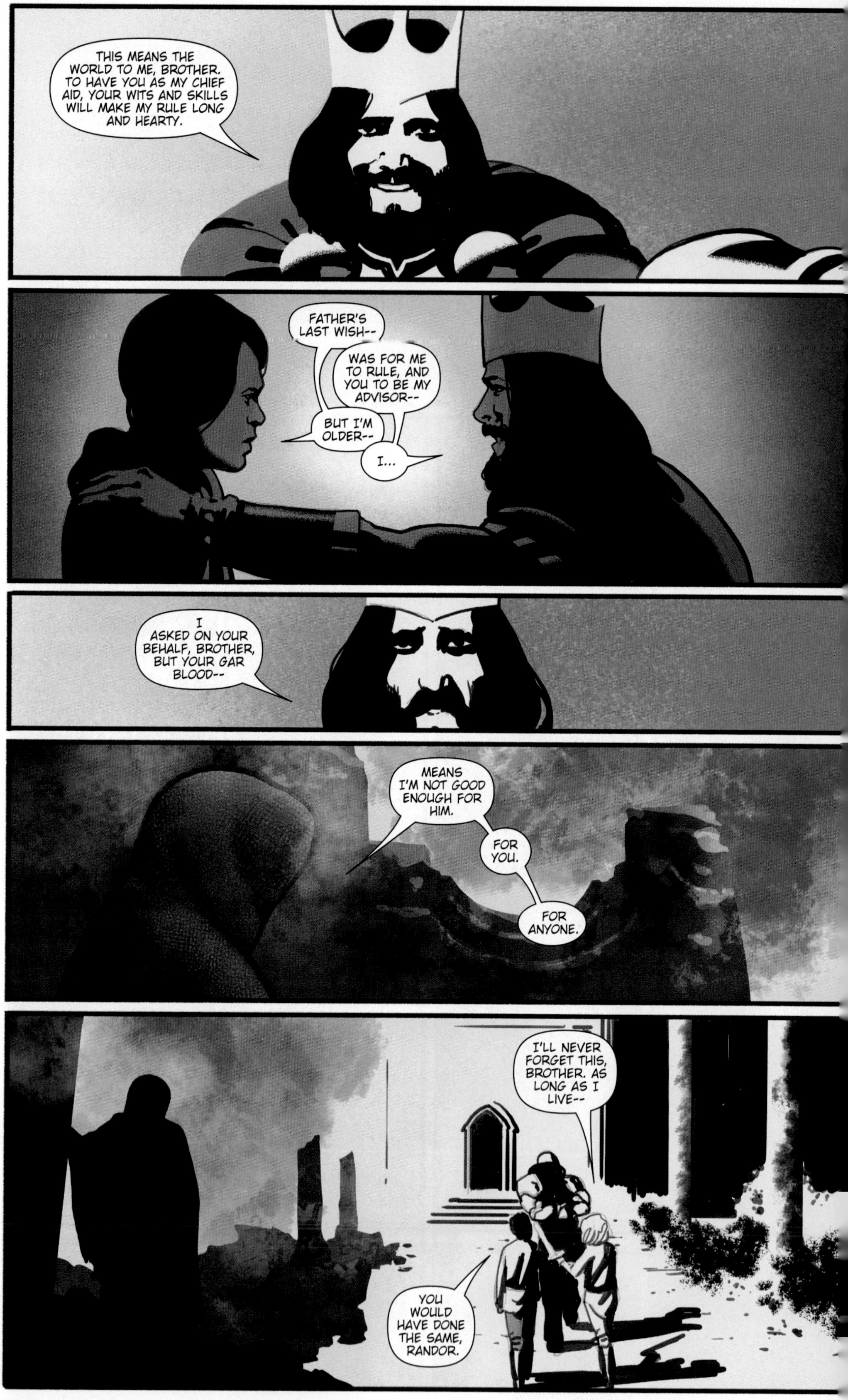
THIS MEANS THE WORLD TO ME, BROTHER. TO HAVE YOU AS MY CHIEF AID, YOUR WITS AND SKILLS WILL MAKE MY RULE LONG AND HEARTY.
FATHER'S LAST WISH--
WAS FOR ME TO RULE, AND YOU TO BE MY ADVISOR--
BUT I'M OLDER--
I...
I ASKED ON YOUR BEHALF, BROTHER, BUT YOUR GAR BLOOD--
MEANS I'M NOT GOOD ENOUGH FOR HIM.
FOR YOU.
FOR ANYONE.
I'LL NEVER FORGET THIS, BROTHER. AS LONG AS I LIVE--
YOU WOULD HAVE DONE THE SAME, RANDOR.

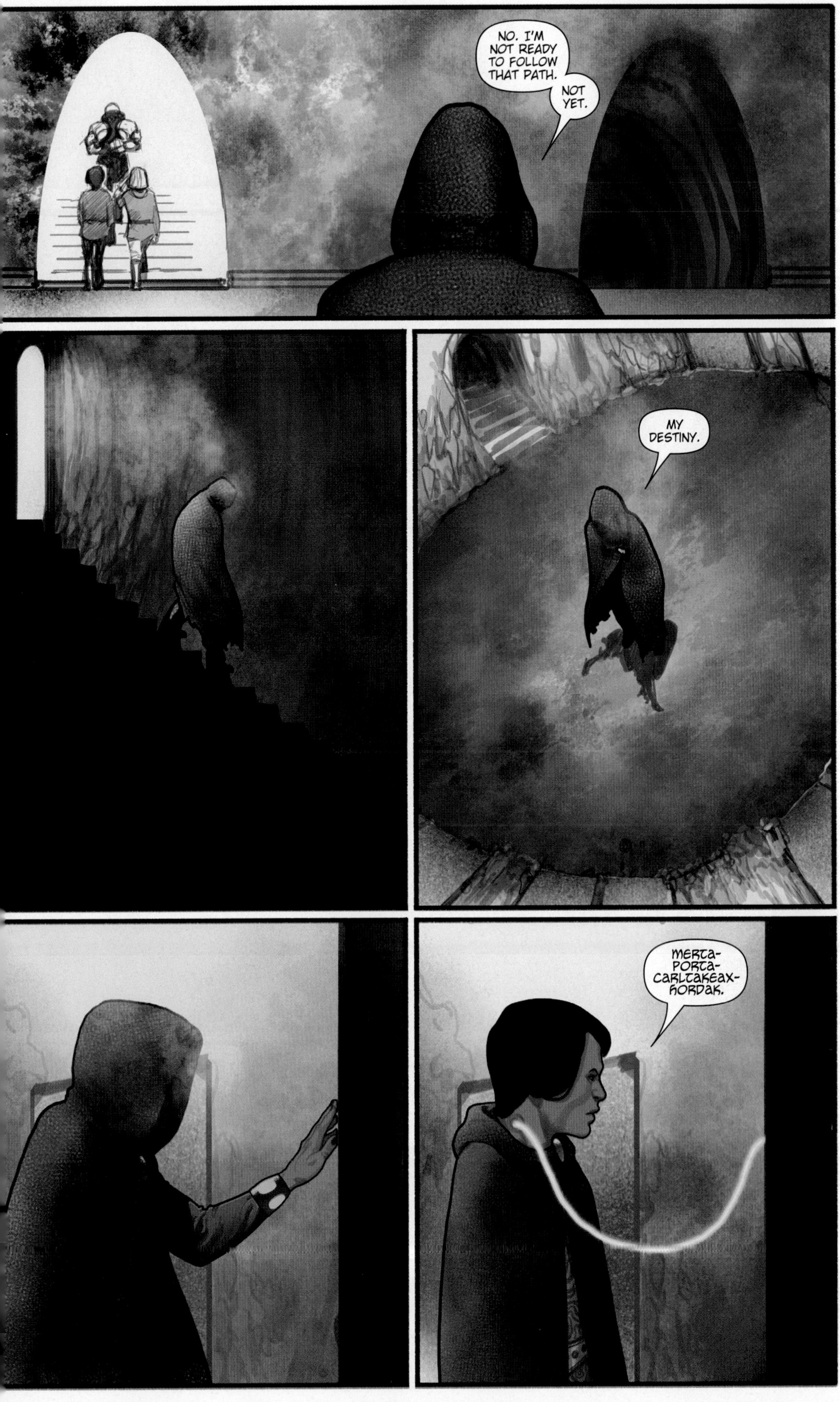
NO. I'M NOT READY TO FOLLOW THAT PATH.
NOT YET.
MY DESTINY.
MERTA-PORTA-CARLTAKEAX-KORDAK.

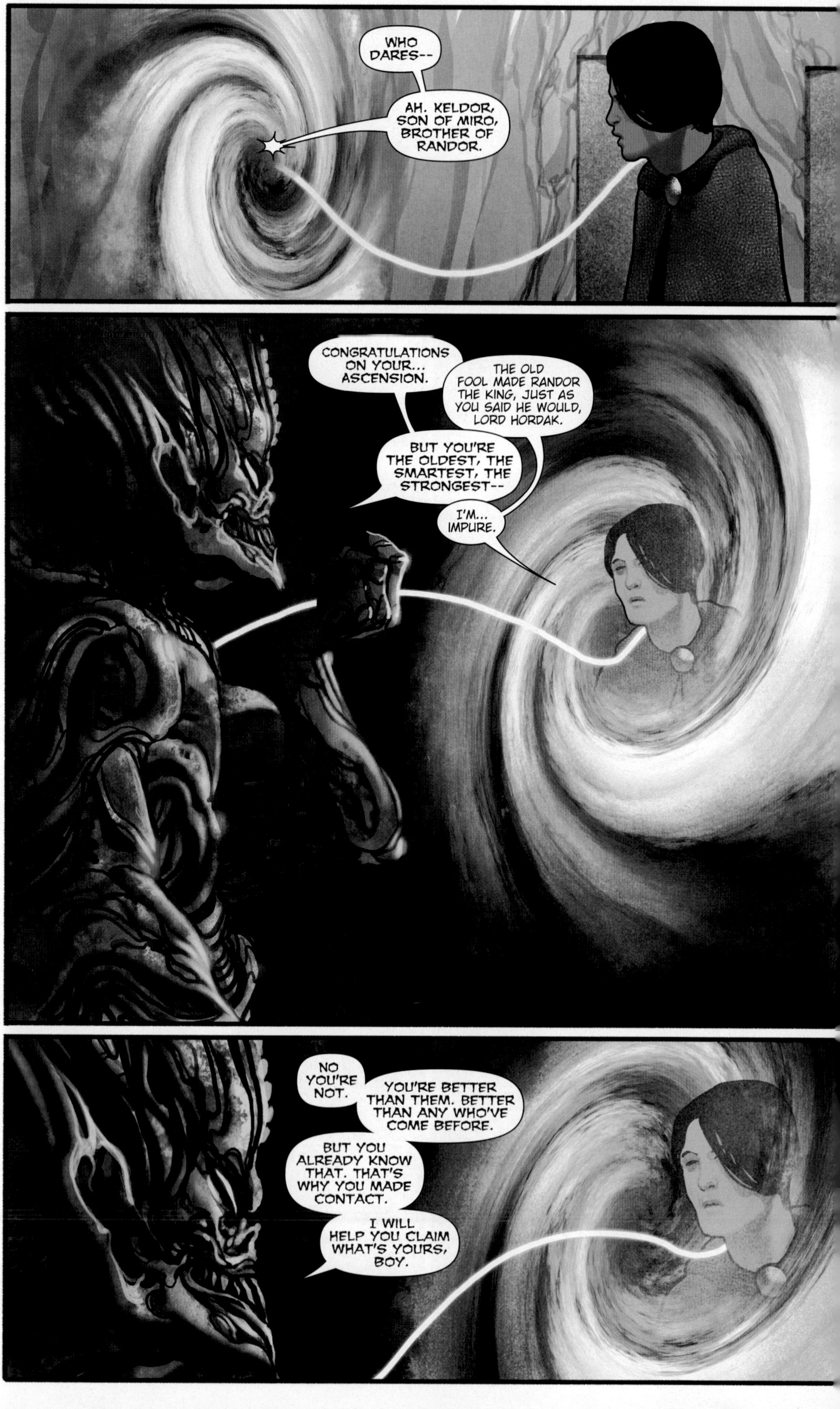
WHO DARES--
AH. KELDOR, SON OF MIRO, BROTHER OF RANDOR.
CONGRATULATIONS ON YOUR... ASCENSION.
THE OLD FOOL MADE RANDOR THE KING, JUST AS YOU SAID HE WOULD, LORD HORDAK.
BUT YOU'RE THE OLDEST, THE SMARTEST, THE STRONGEST--
I'M... IMPURE.
NO YOU'RE NOT.
YOU'RE BETTER THAN THEM. BETTER THAN ANY WHO'VE COME BEFORE.
BUT YOU ALREADY KNOW THAT. THAT'S WHY YOU MADE CONTACT.
I WILL HELP YOU CLAIM WHAT'S YOURS, BOY.

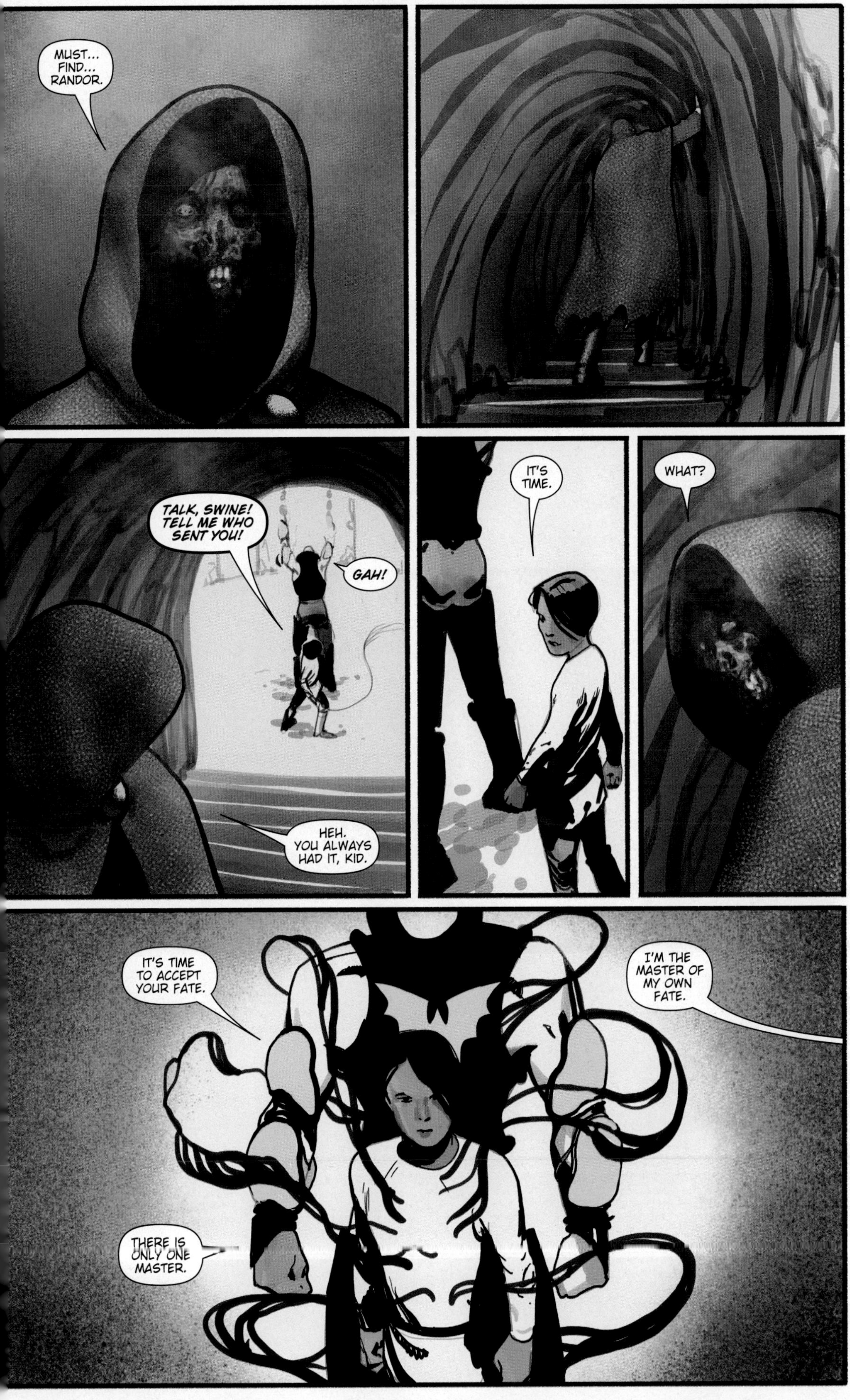
MUST... FIND... RANDOR.
TALK, SWINE! TELL ME WHO SENT YOU!
GAH!
HEH. YOU ALWAYS HAD IT, KID.
IT'S TIME.
WHAT?
IT'S TIME TO ACCEPT YOUR FATE.
I'M THE MASTER OF MY OWN FATE.
THERE IS ONLY ONE MASTER.

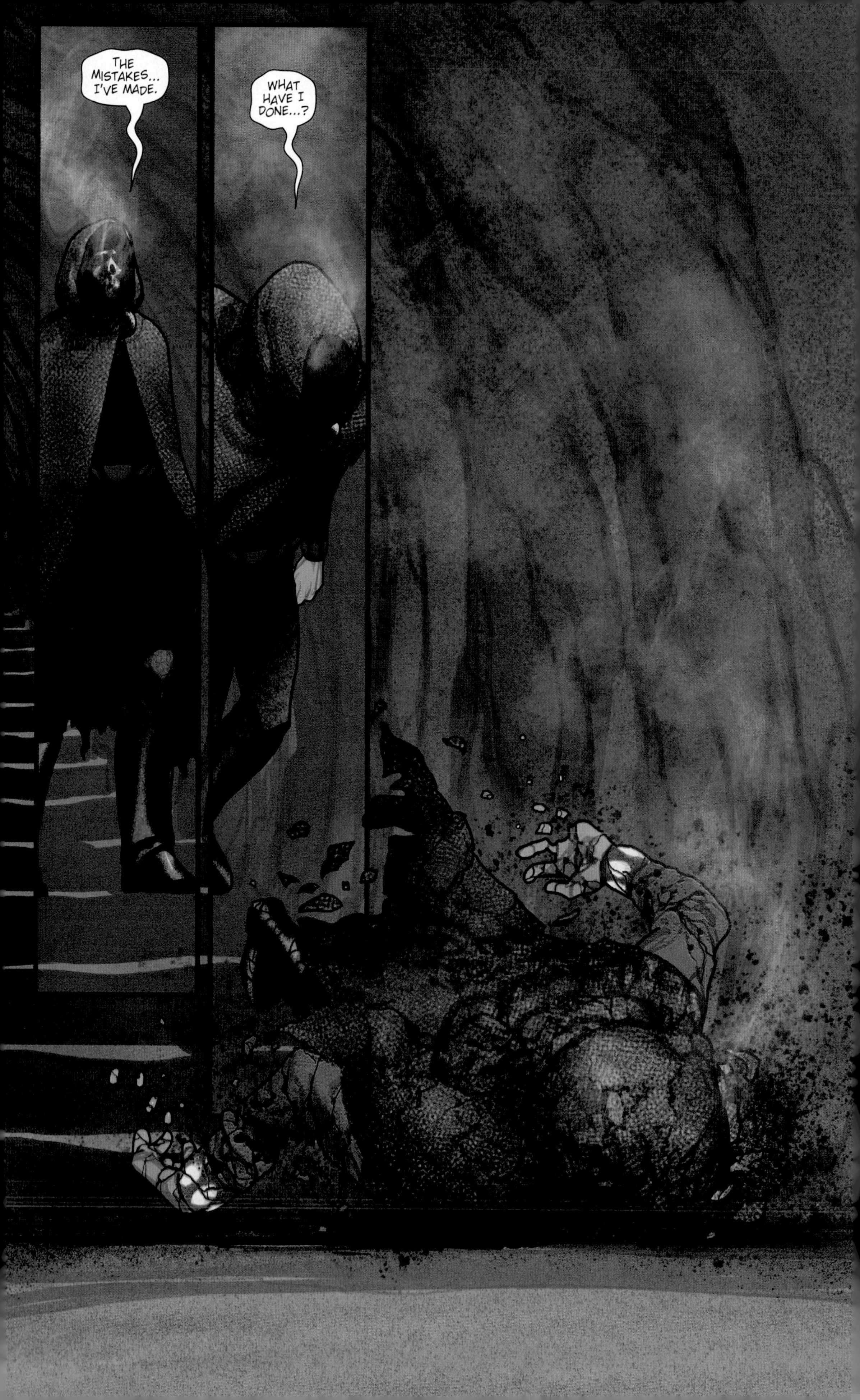
THE MISTAKES... I'VE MADE.
WHAT HAVE I DONE...?

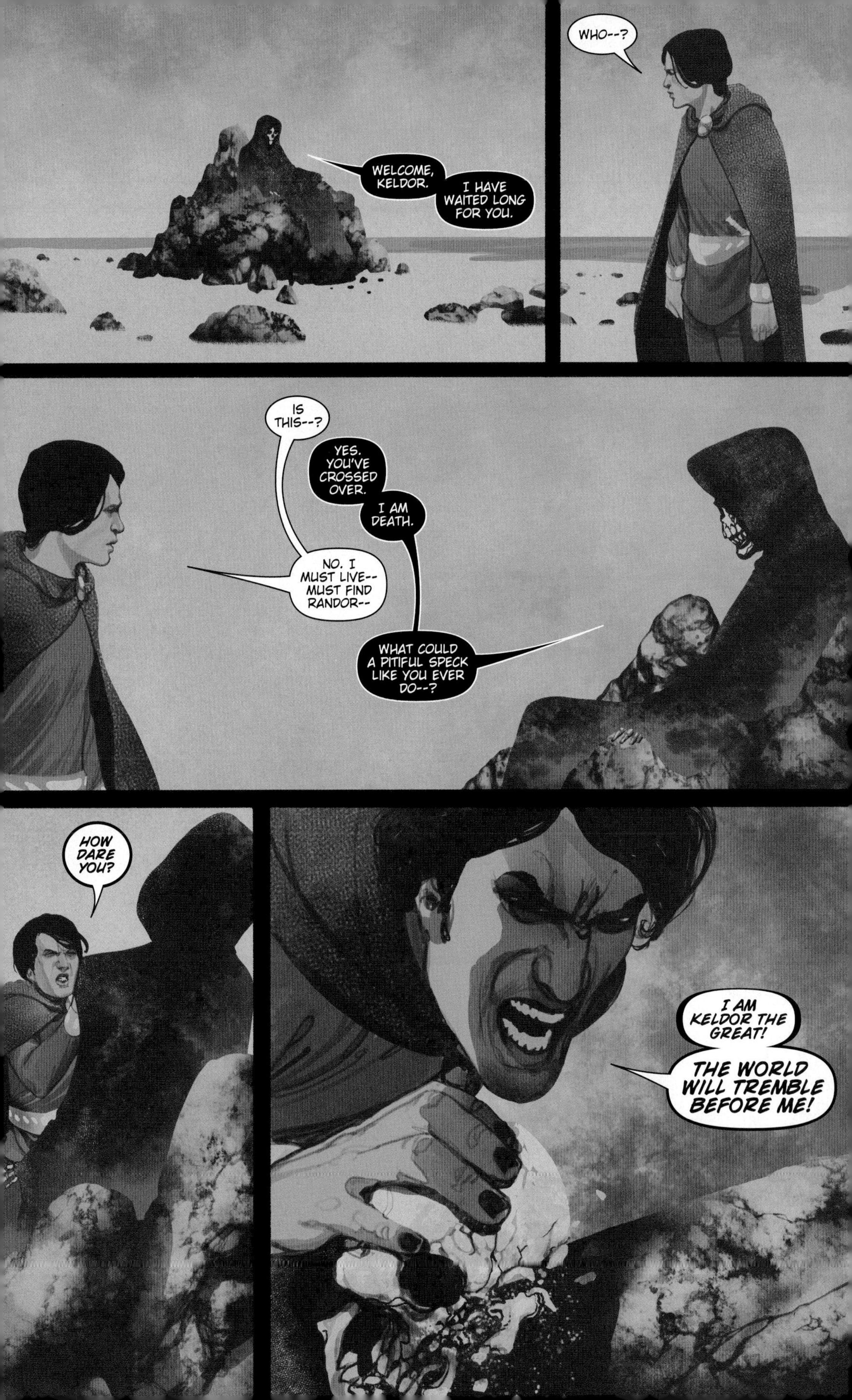
WELCOME, KELDOR.
I HAVE WAITED LONG FOR YOU.
WHO--?
IS THIS--?
YES. YOU'VE CROSSED OVER.
I AM DEATH.
NO. I MUST LIVE-- MUST FIND RANDOR--
WHAT COULD A PITIFUL SPECK LIKE YOU EVER DO--?
HOW DARE YOU?
I AM KELDOR THE GREAT!
THE WORLD WILL TREMBLE BEFORE ME!

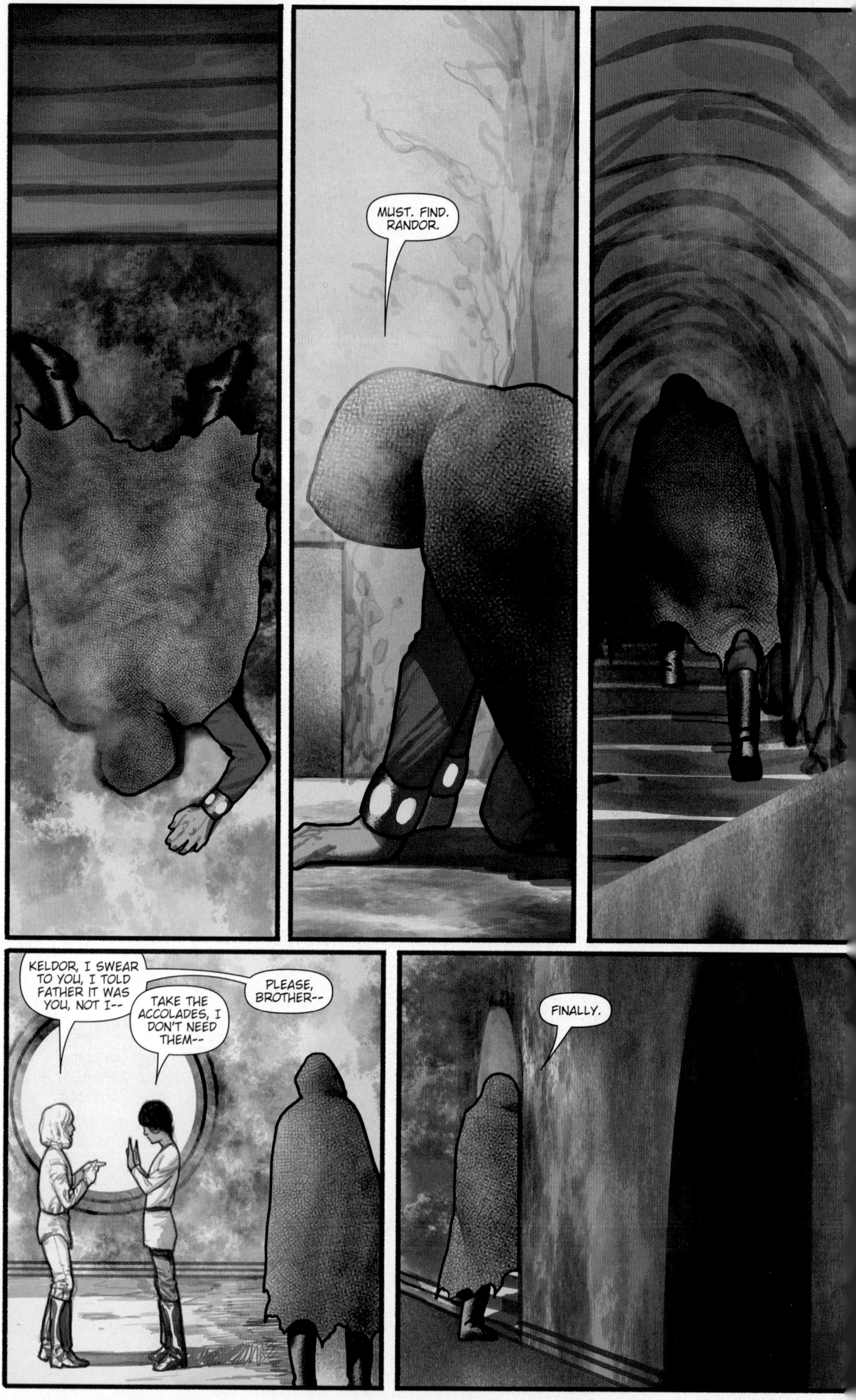
MUST. FIND. RANDOR.
KELDOR, I SWEAR TO YOU, I TOLD FATHER IT WAS YOU, NOT I--
TAKE THE ACCOLADES, I DON'T NEED THEM--
PLEASE, BROTHER--
FINALLY.

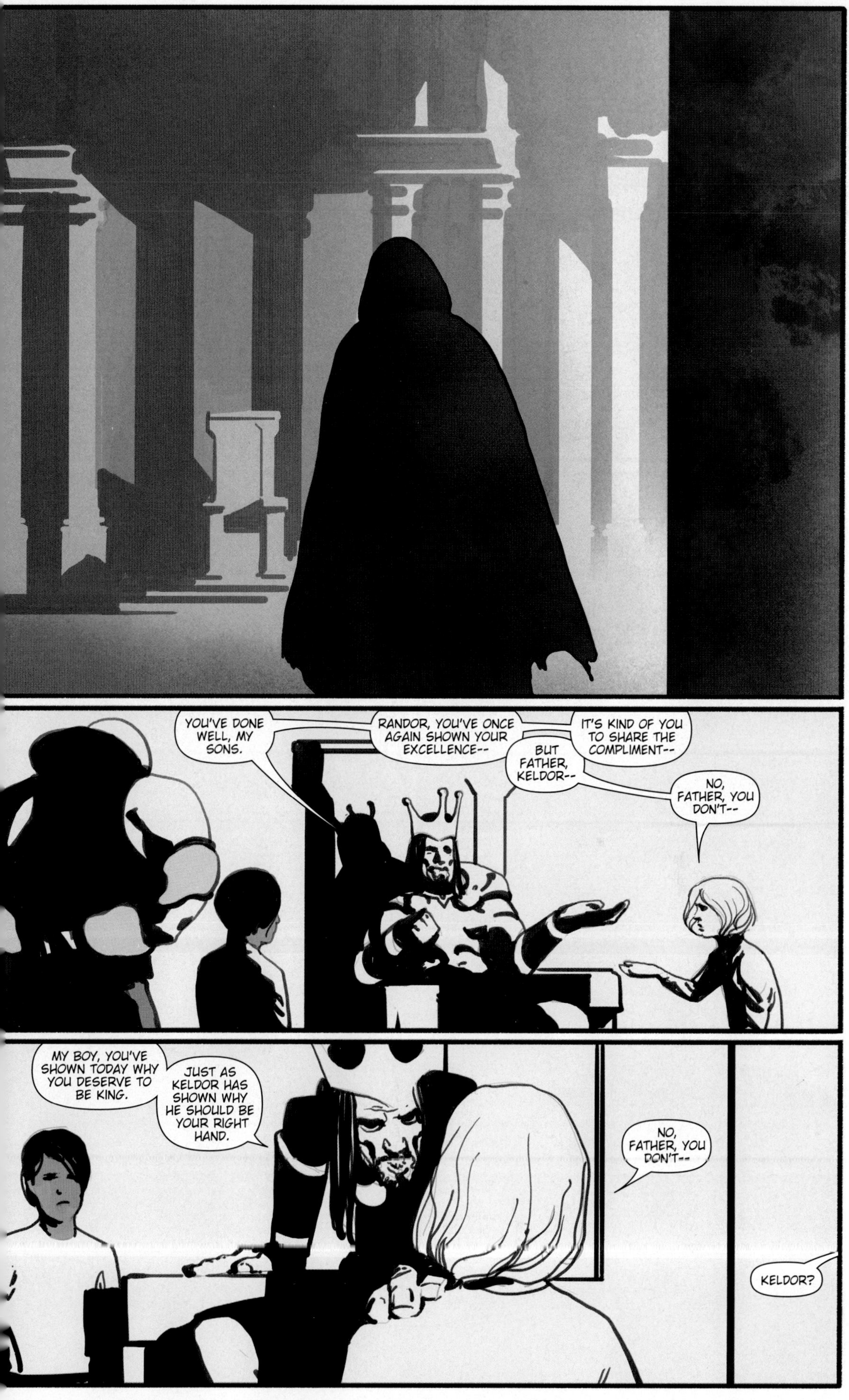

YOU'VE DONE WELL, MY SONS.
RANDOR, YOU'VE ONCE AGAIN SHOWN YOUR EXCELLENCE--
IT'S KIND OF YOU TO SHARE THE COMPLIMENT--
BUT FATHER, KELDOR--
NO, FATHER, YOU DON'T--
MY BOY, YOU'VE SHOWN TODAY WHY YOU DESERVE TO BE KING.
JUST AS KELDOR HAS SHOWN WHY HE SHOULD BE YOUR RIGHT HAND.
NO, FATHER, YOU DON'T--
KELDOR?

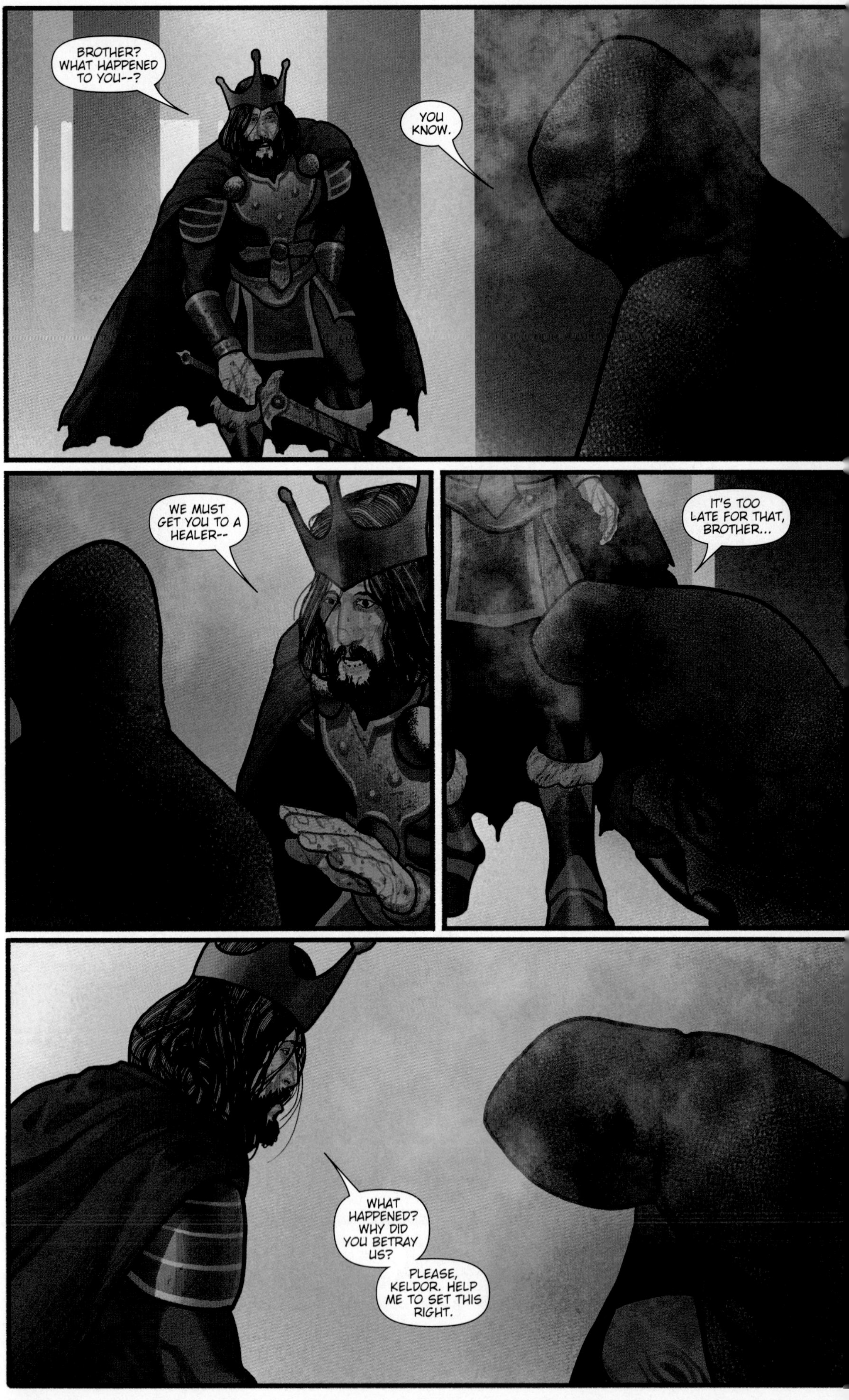
BROTHER? WHAT HAPPENED TO YOU--?
YOU KNOW.
WE MUST GET YOU TO A HEALER--
IT'S TOO LATE FOR THAT, BROTHER...
WHAT HAPPENED? WHY DID YOU BETRAY US?
PLEASE, KELDOR. HELP ME TO SET THIS RIGHT.

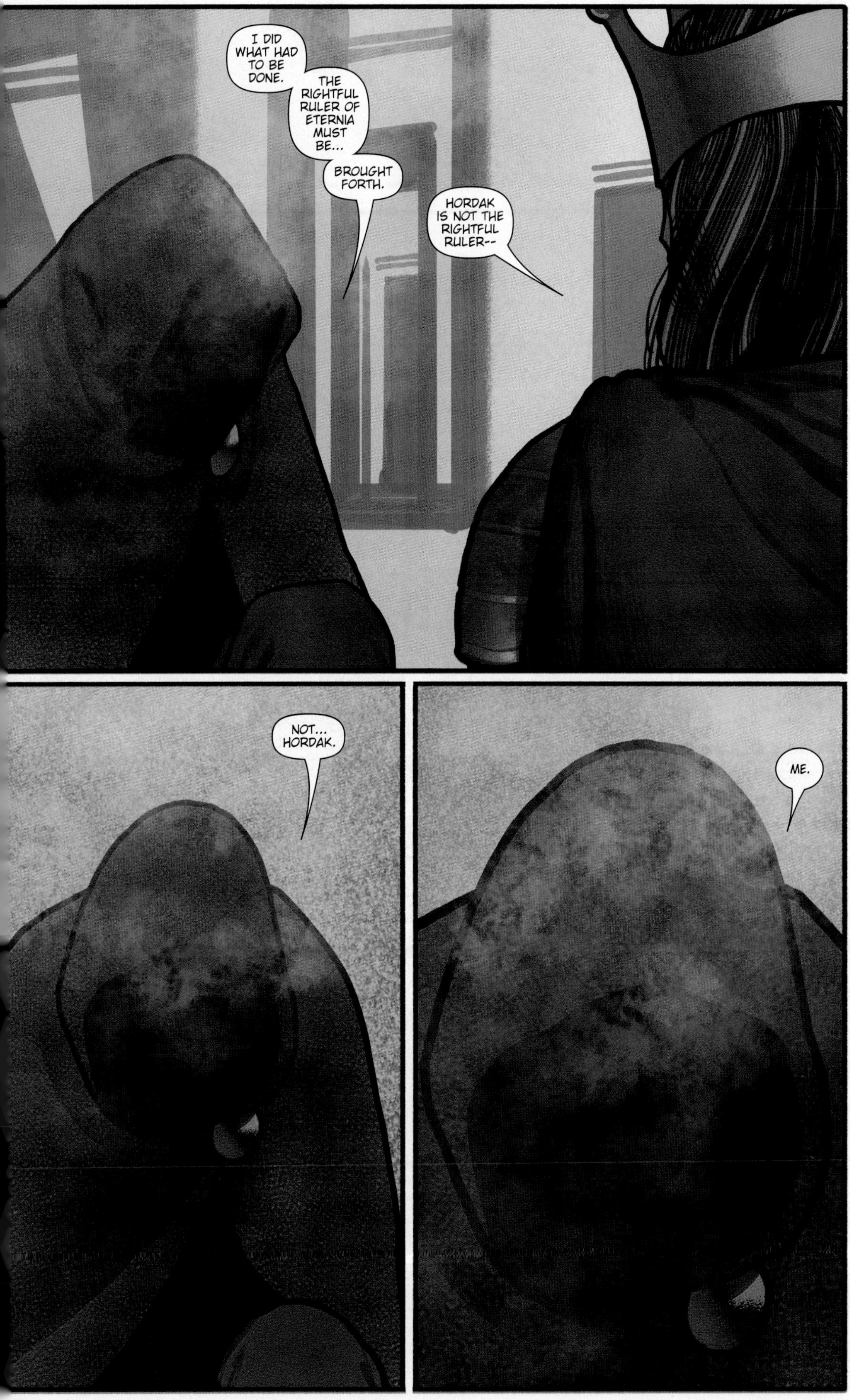
I DID WHAT HAD TO BE DONE.
THE RIGHTFUL RULER OF ETERNIA MUST BE...
BROUGHT FORTH.
HORDAK IS NOT THE RIGHTFUL RULER--
NOT... HORDAK.
ME.

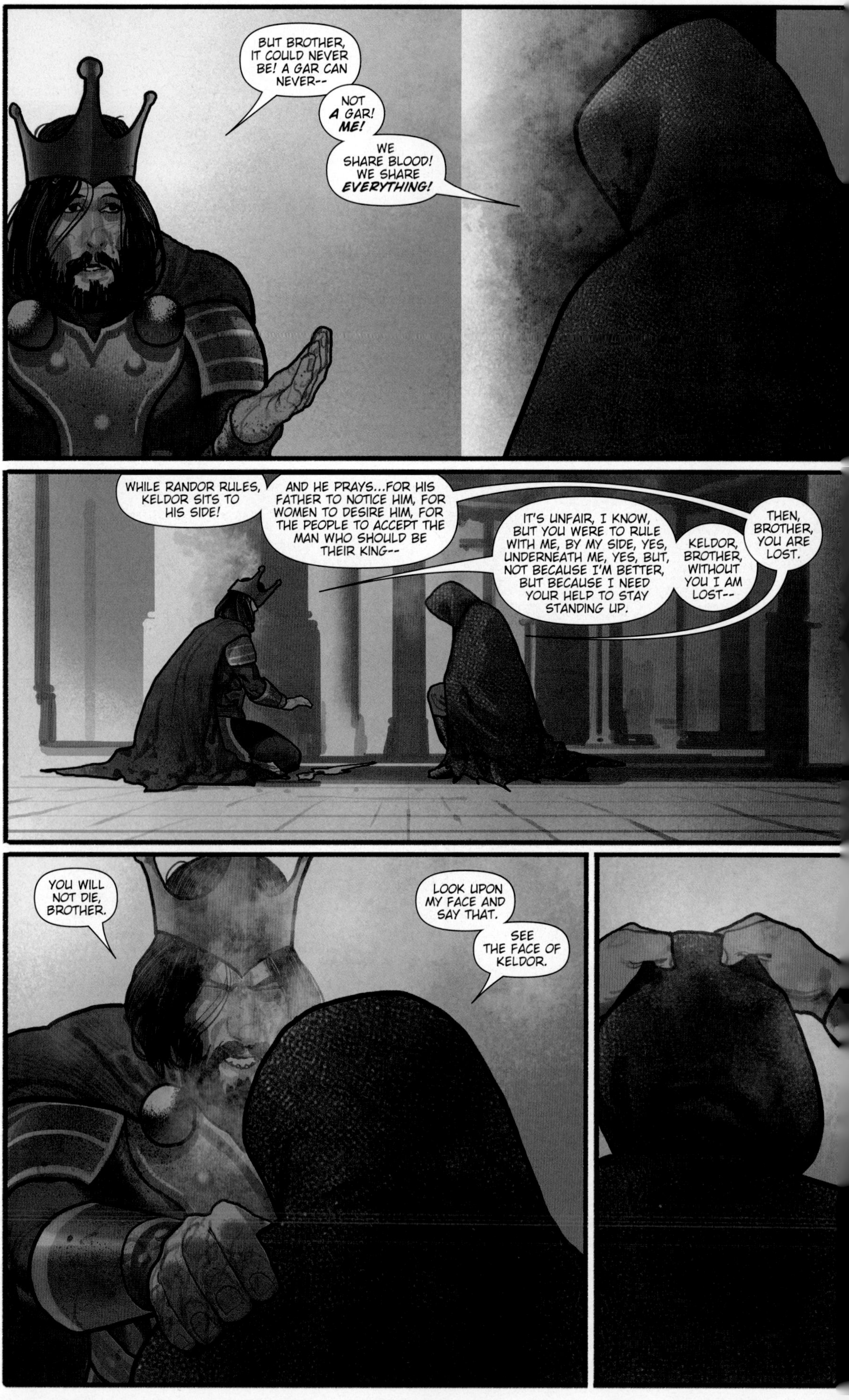
BUT BROTHER, IT COULD NEVER BE! A GAR CAN NEVER--
NOT A GAR! ME!
WE SHARE BLOOD! WE SHARE EVERYTHING!
WHILE RANDOR RULES, KELDOR SITS TO HIS SIDE!
AND HE PRAYS...FOR HIS FATHER TO NOTICE HIM, FOR WOMEN TO DESIRE HIM, FOR THE PEOPLE TO ACCEPT THE MAN WHO SHOULD BE THEIR KING--
IT'S UNFAIR, I KNOW, BUT YOU WERE TO RULE WITH ME, BY MY SIDE, YES, UNDERNEATH ME, YES, BUT, NOT BECAUSE I'M BETTER, BUT BECAUSE I NEED YOUR HELP TO STAY STANDING UP.
KELDOR, BROTHER, WITHOUT YOU I AM LOST--
THEN, BROTHER, YOU ARE LOST.
YOU WILL NOT DIE, BROTHER.
LOOK UPON MY FACE AND SAY THAT.
SEE THE FACE OF KELDOR.

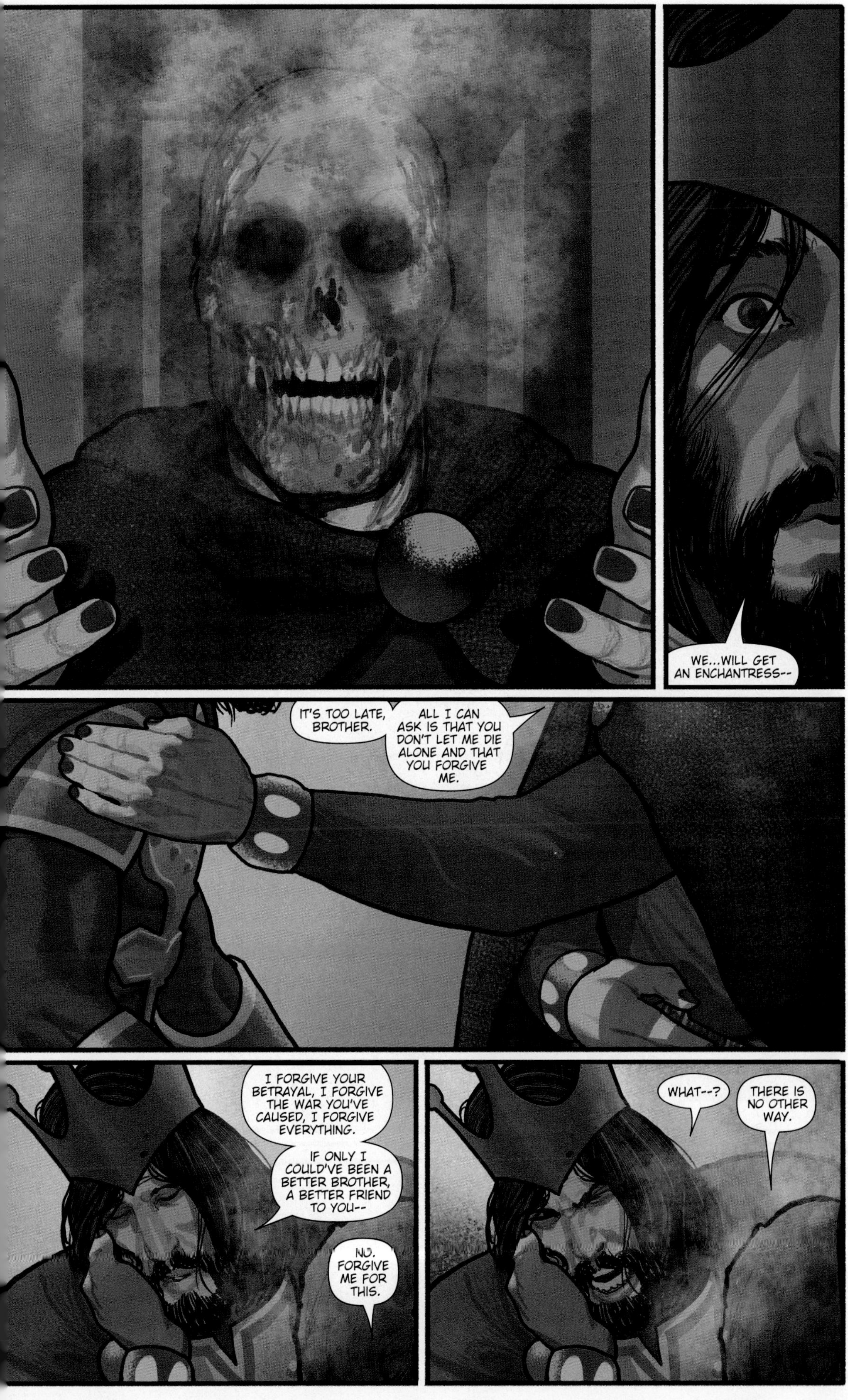
WE...WILL GET AN ENCHANTRESS--
IT'S TOO LATE, BROTHER.
ALL I CAN ASK IS THAT YOU DON'T LET ME DIE ALONE AND THAT YOU FORGIVE ME.
I FORGIVE YOUR BETRAYAL, I FORGIVE THE WAR YOU'VE CAUSED, I FORGIVE EVERYTHING.
IF ONLY I COULD'VE BEEN A BETTER BROTHER, A BETTER FRIEND TO YOU--
NO. FORGIVE ME FOR THIS.
WHAT--?
THERE IS NO OTHER WAY.

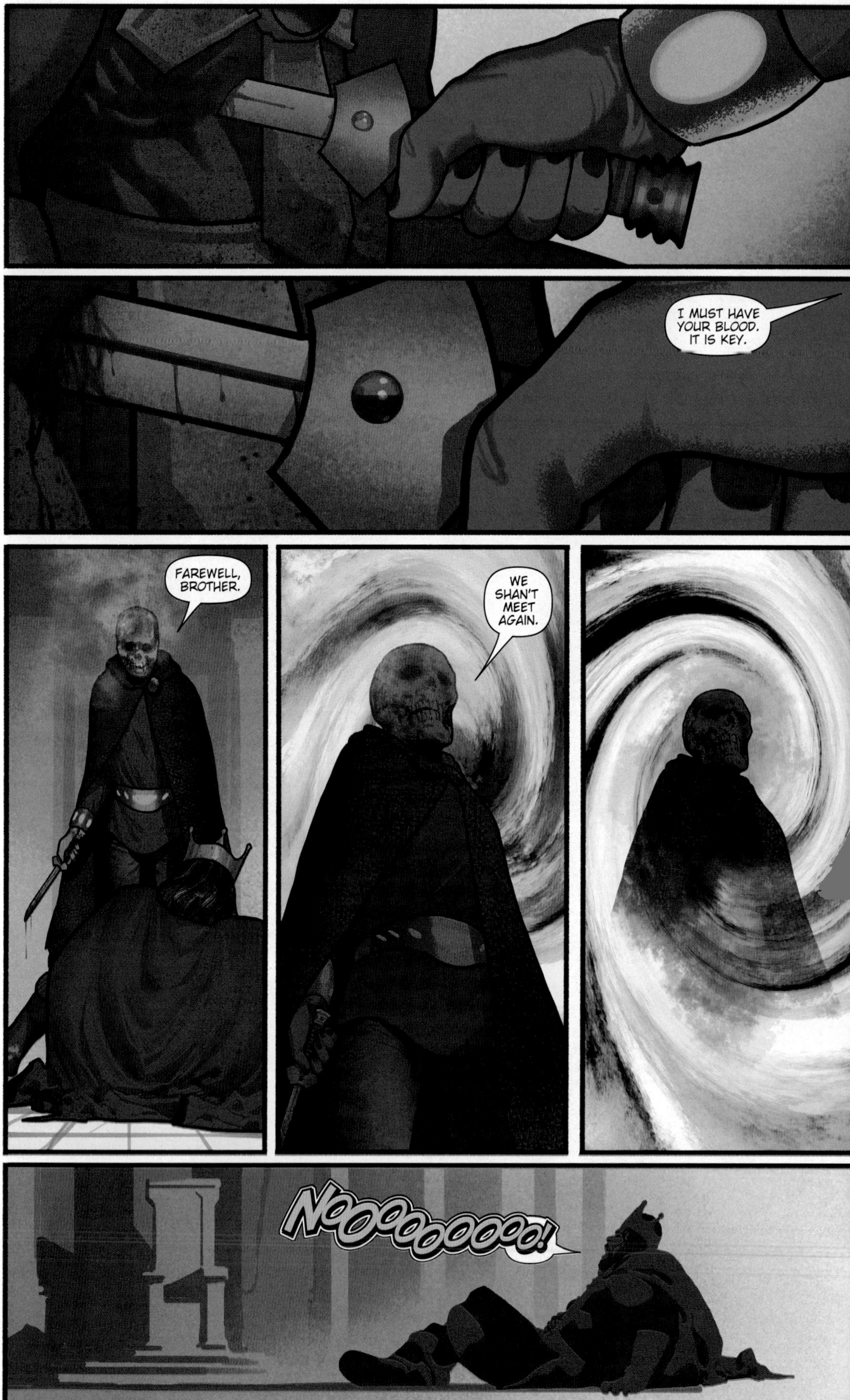
I MUST HAVE YOUR BLOOD. IT IS KEY.
FAREWELL, BROTHER.
WE SHAN'T MEET AGAIN.
NOOOOOOOOOO!

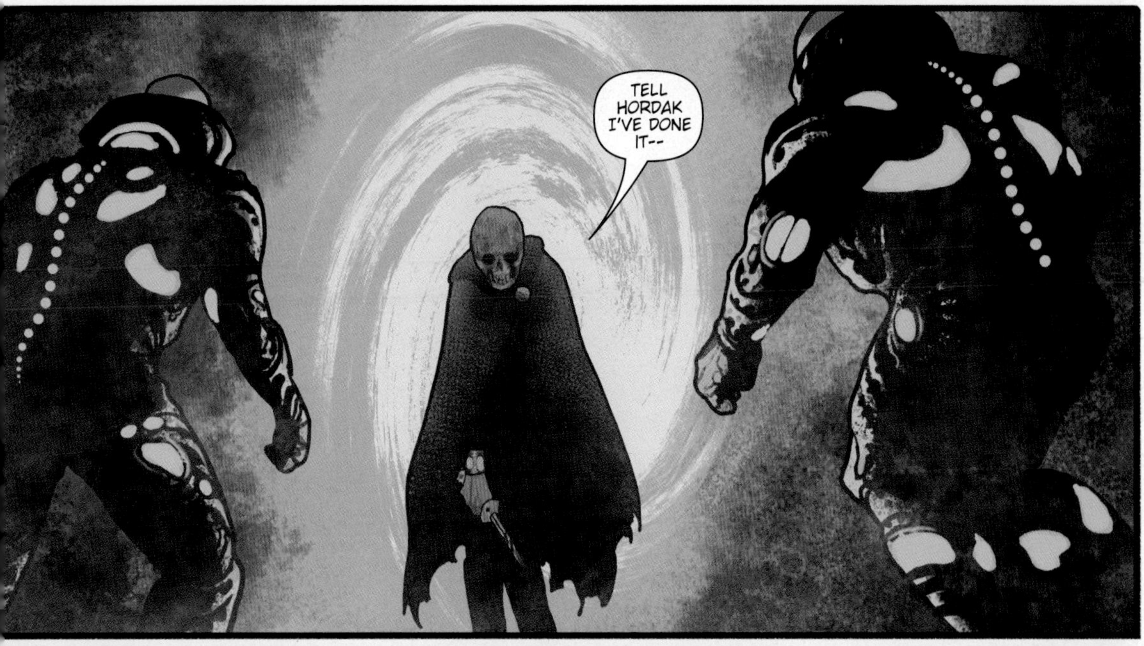
TELL HORDAK I'VE DONE IT--

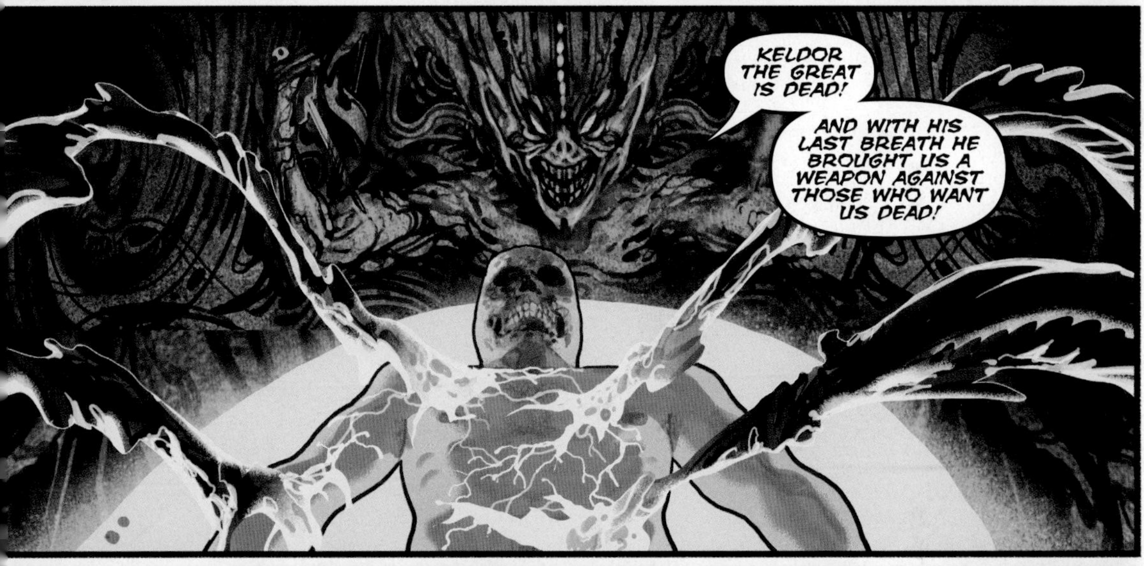
KELDOR THE GREAT IS DEAD!
AND WITH HIS LAST BREATH HE BROUGHT US A WEAPON AGAINST THOSE WHO WANT US DEAD!

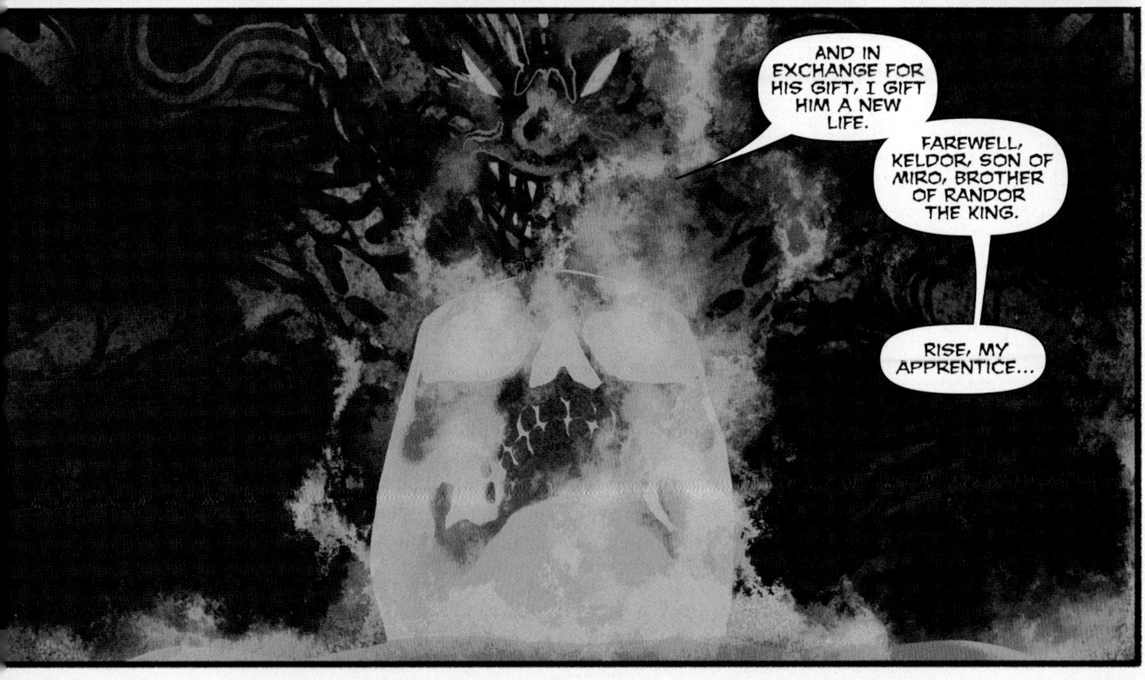
AND IN EXCHANGE FOR HIS GIFT, I GIFT HIM A NEW LIFE.
FAREWELL, KELDOR, SON OF MIRO, BROTHER OF RANDOR THE KING.
RISE, MY APPRENTICE...

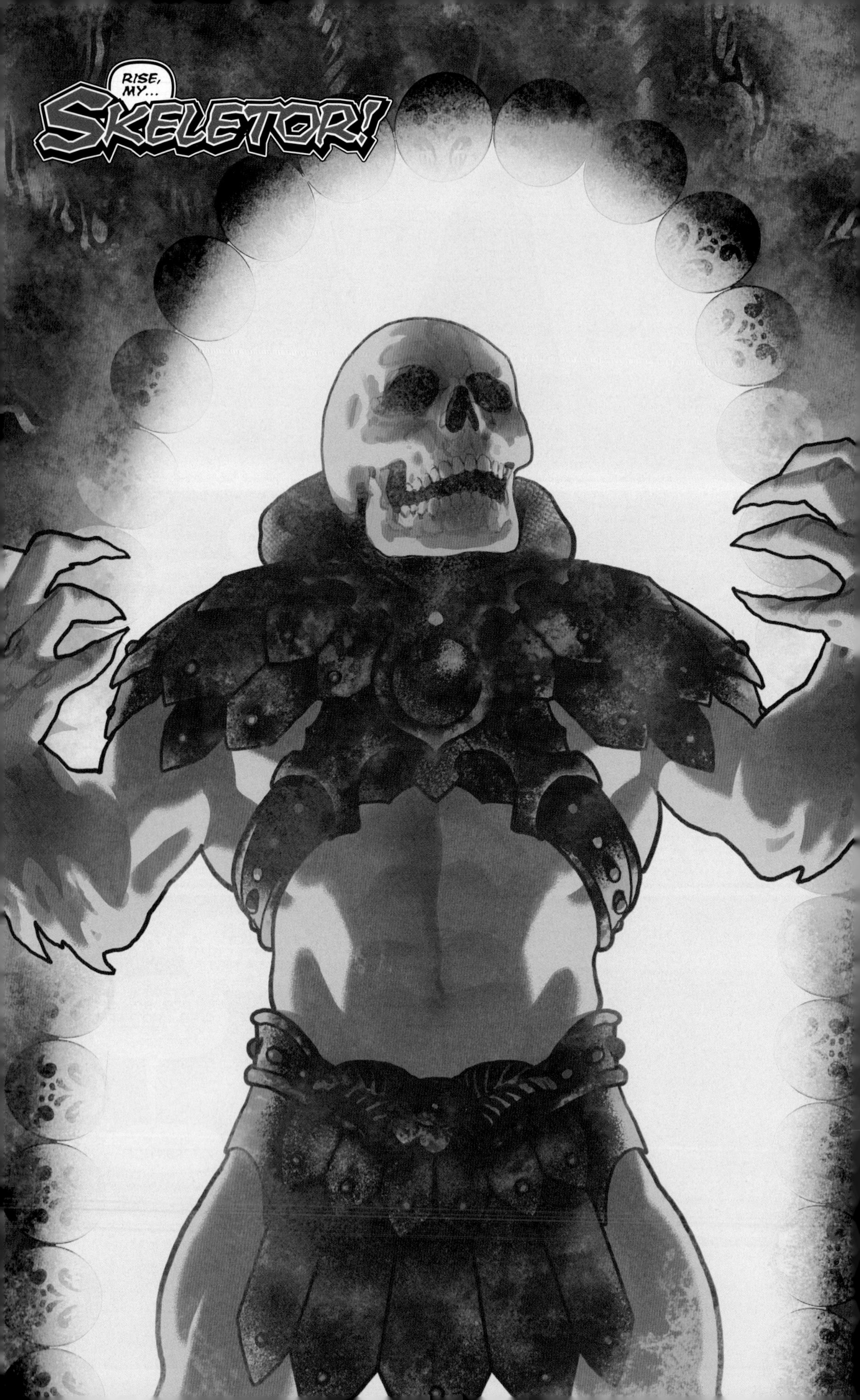
RISE, MY...
SKELETOR!

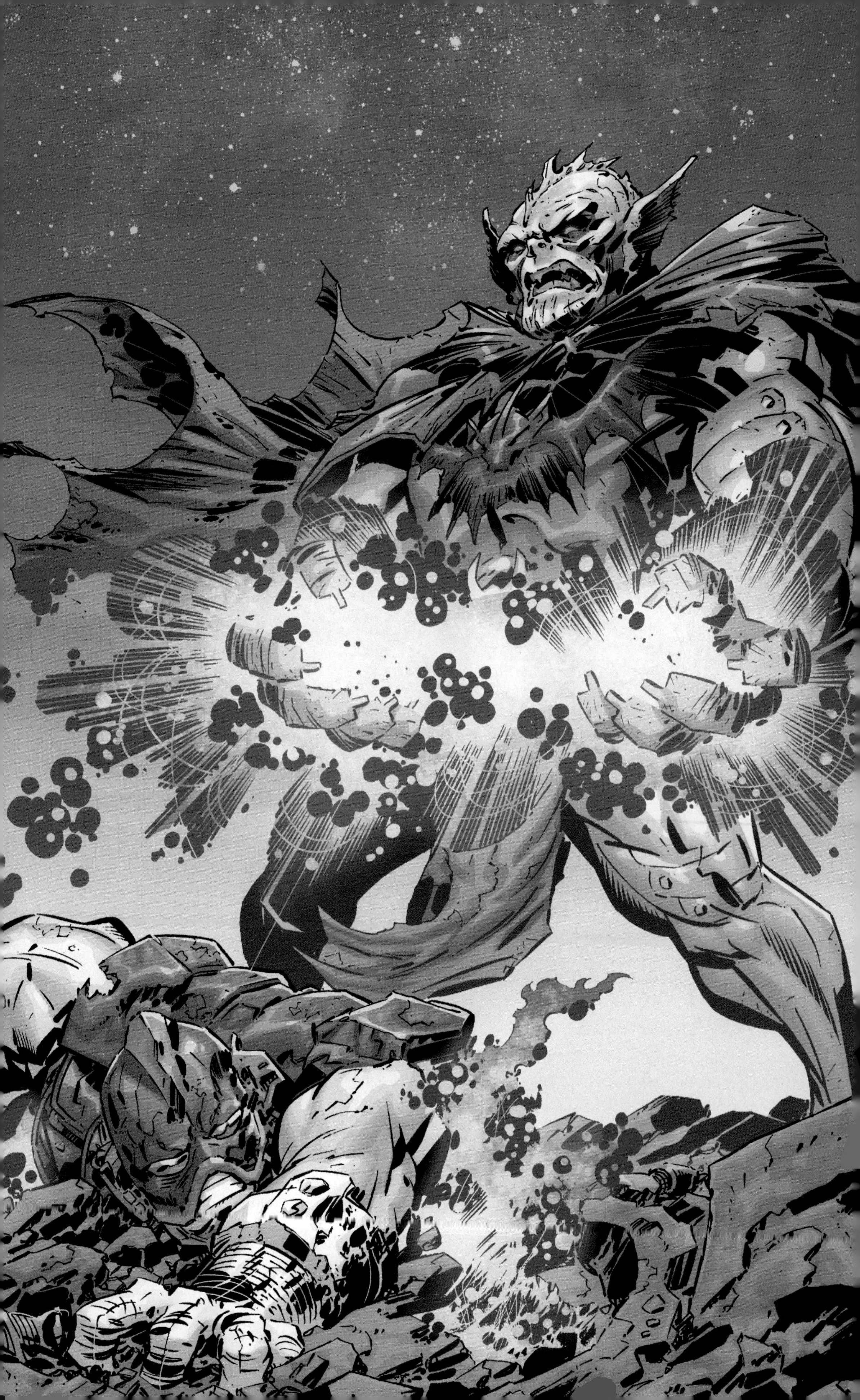

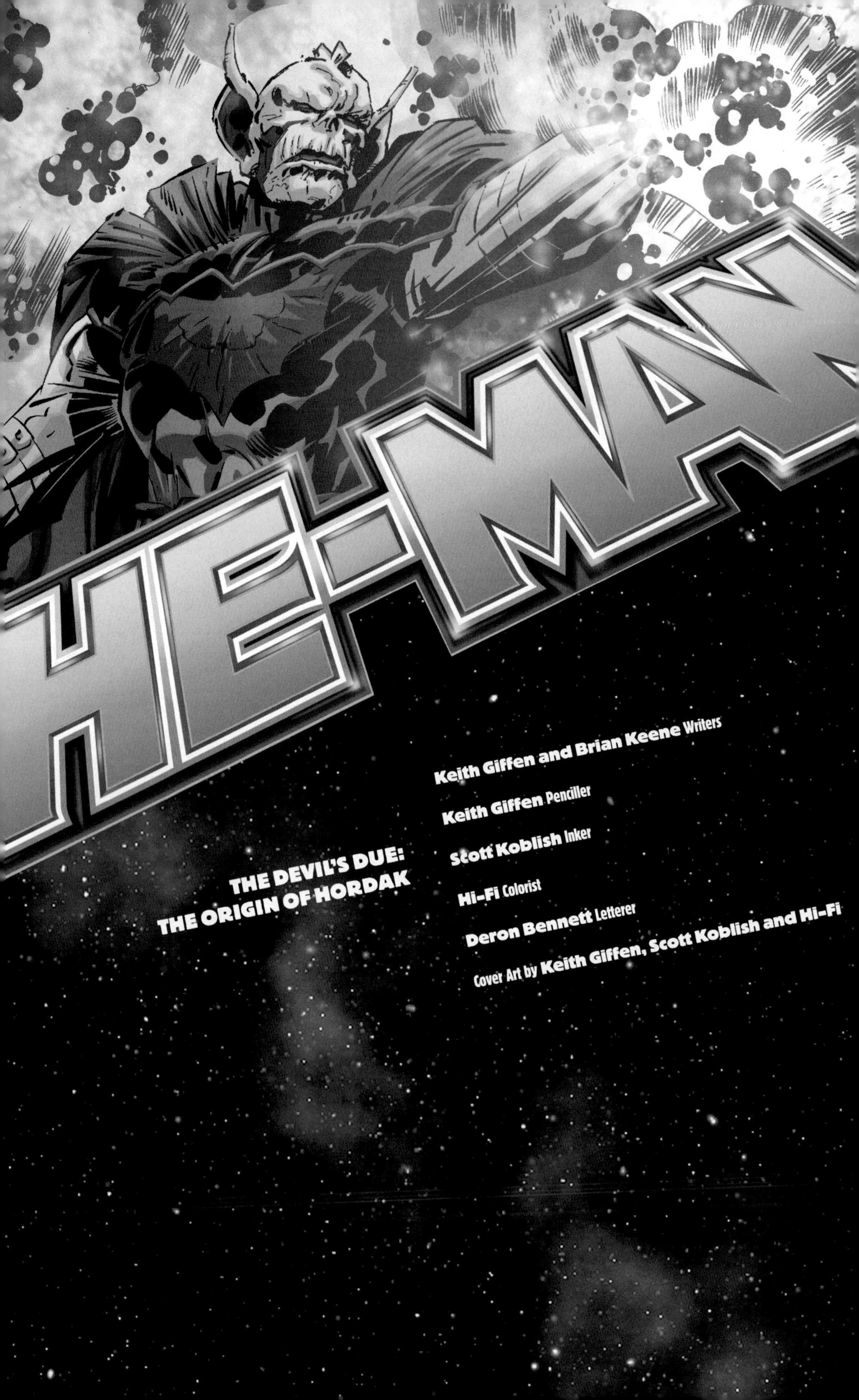

THE DEVIL'S DUE: THE ORIGIN OF HORDAK

Keith Giffen and Brian Keene Writers

Keith Giffen Penciller

Scott Koblish Inker

Hi-Fi Colorist

Deron Bennett Letterer

Cover Art by **Keith Giffen, Scott Koblish and Hi-Fi**

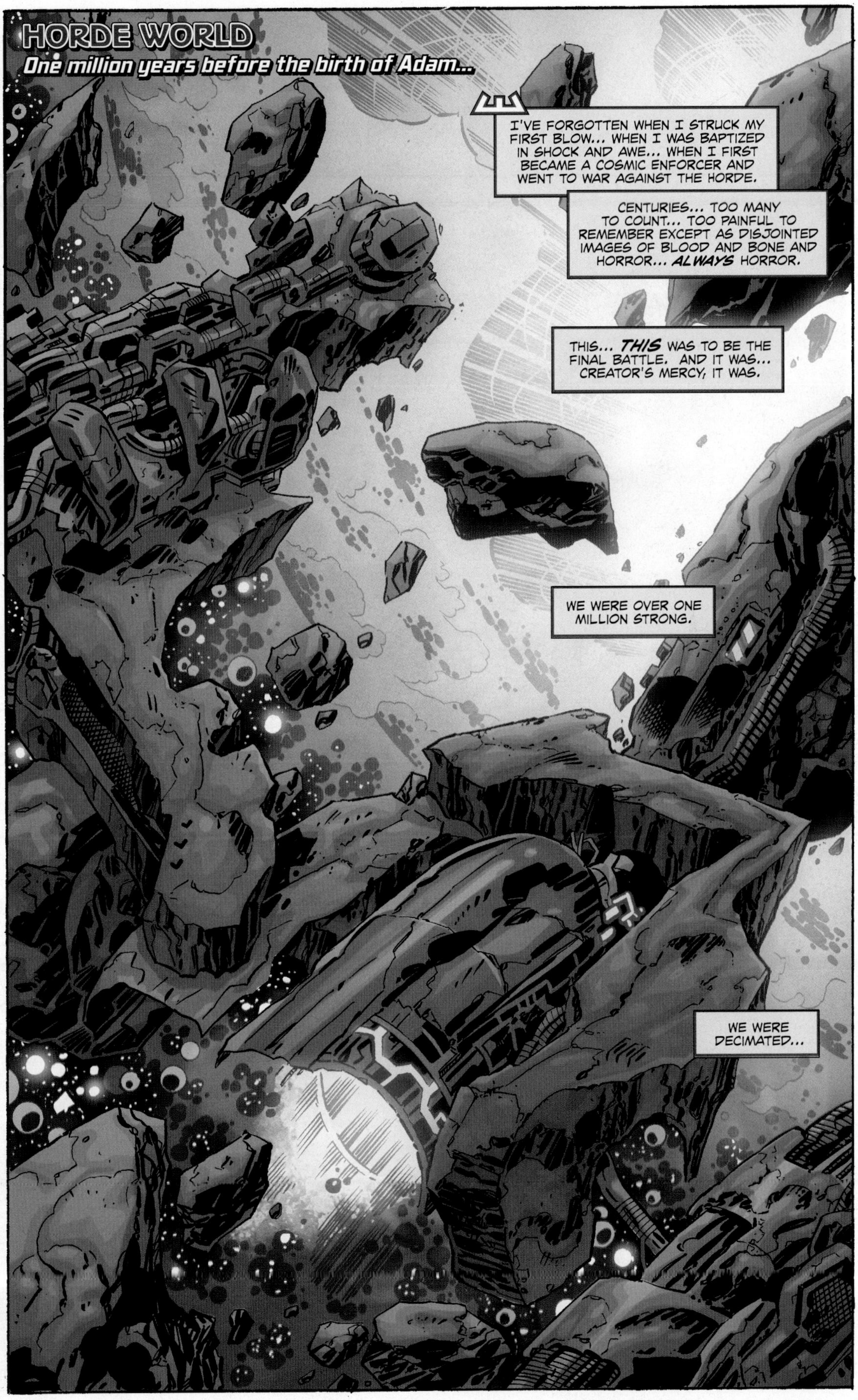
HORDE WORLD
One million years before the birth of Adam...
I'VE FORGOTTEN WHEN I STRUCK MY FIRST BLOW... WHEN I WAS BAPTIZED IN SHOCK AND AWE... WHEN I FIRST BECAME A COSMIC ENFORCER AND WENT TO WAR AGAINST THE HORDE.
CENTURIES... TOO MANY TO COUNT... TOO PAINFUL TO REMEMBER EXCEPT AS DISJOINTED IMAGES OF BLOOD AND BONE AND HORROR... ALWAYS HORROR.
THIS... THIS WAS TO BE THE FINAL BATTLE. AND IT WAS... CREATOR'S MERCY, IT WAS.
WE WERE OVER ONE MILLION STRONG.
WE WERE DECIMATED...

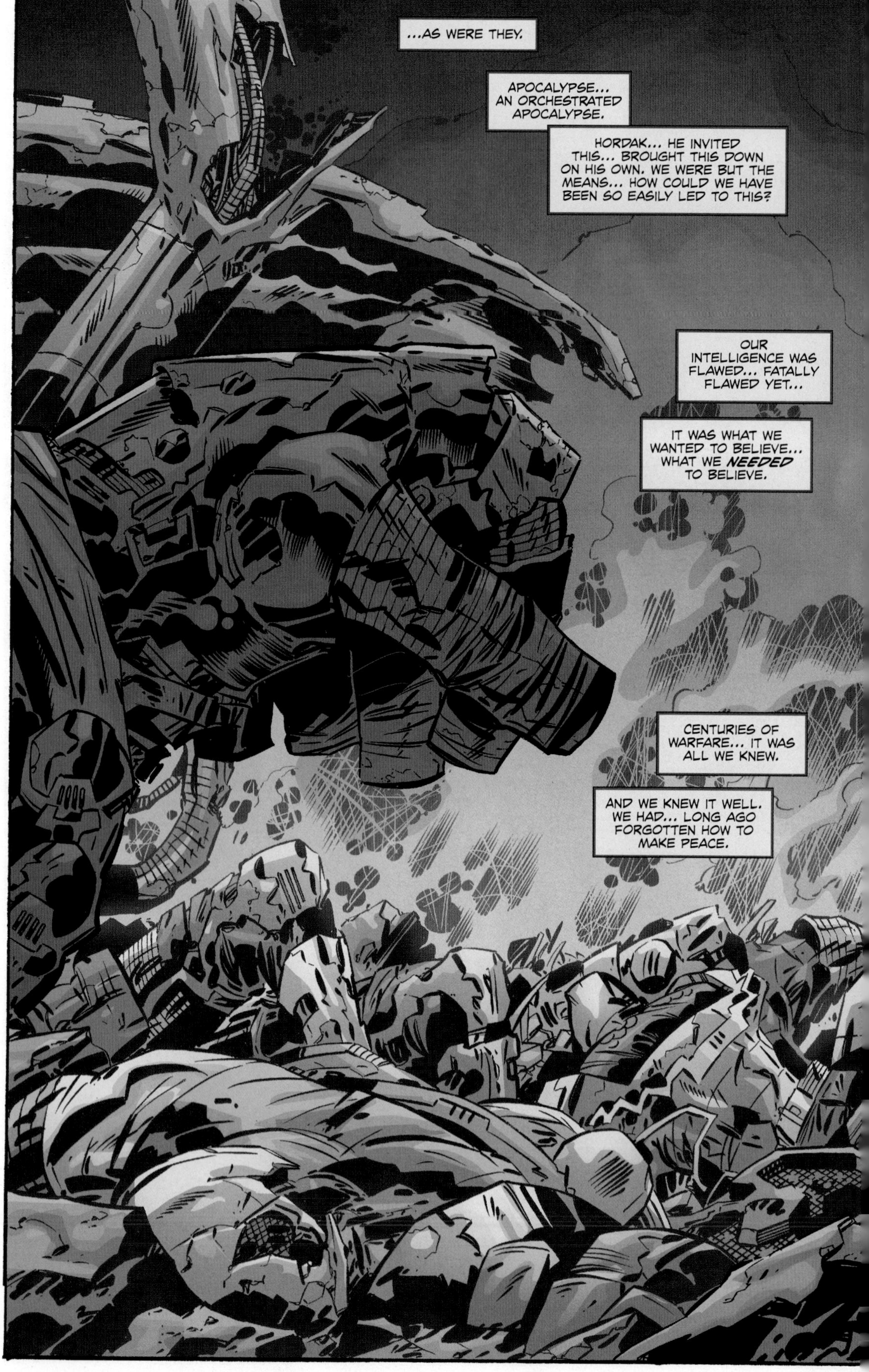
...AS WERE THEY.
APOCALYPSE... AN ORCHESTRATED APOCALYPSE.
HORDAK... HE INVITED THIS... BROUGHT THIS DOWN ON HIS OWN. WE WERE BUT THE MEANS... HOW COULD WE HAVE BEEN SO EASILY LED TO THIS?
OUR INTELLIGENCE WAS FLAWED... FATALLY FLAWED YET...
IT WAS WHAT WE WANTED TO BELIEVE... WHAT WE *NEEDED* TO BELIEVE.
CENTURIES OF WARFARE... IT WAS ALL WE KNEW.
AND WE KNEW IT WELL. WE HAD... LONG AGO FORGOTTEN HOW TO MAKE PEACE.

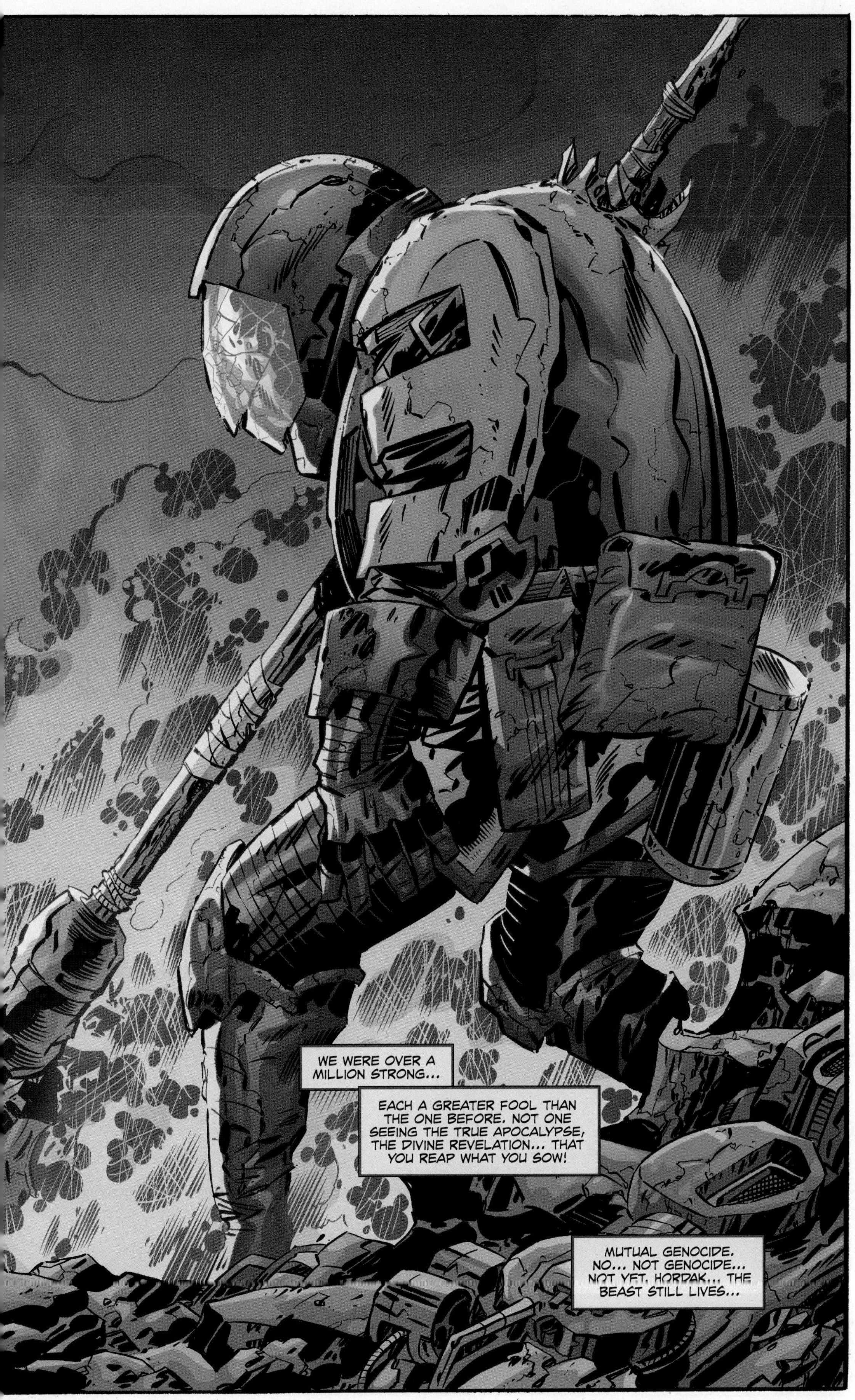
WE WERE OVER A MILLION STRONG...
EACH A GREATER FOOL THAN THE ONE BEFORE. NOT ONE SEEING THE TRUE APOCALYPSE, THE DIVINE REVELATION... THAT YOU REAP WHAT YOU SOW!
MUTUAL GENOCIDE. NO... NOT GENOCIDE... NOT YET, HORDAK... THE BEAST STILL LIVES...

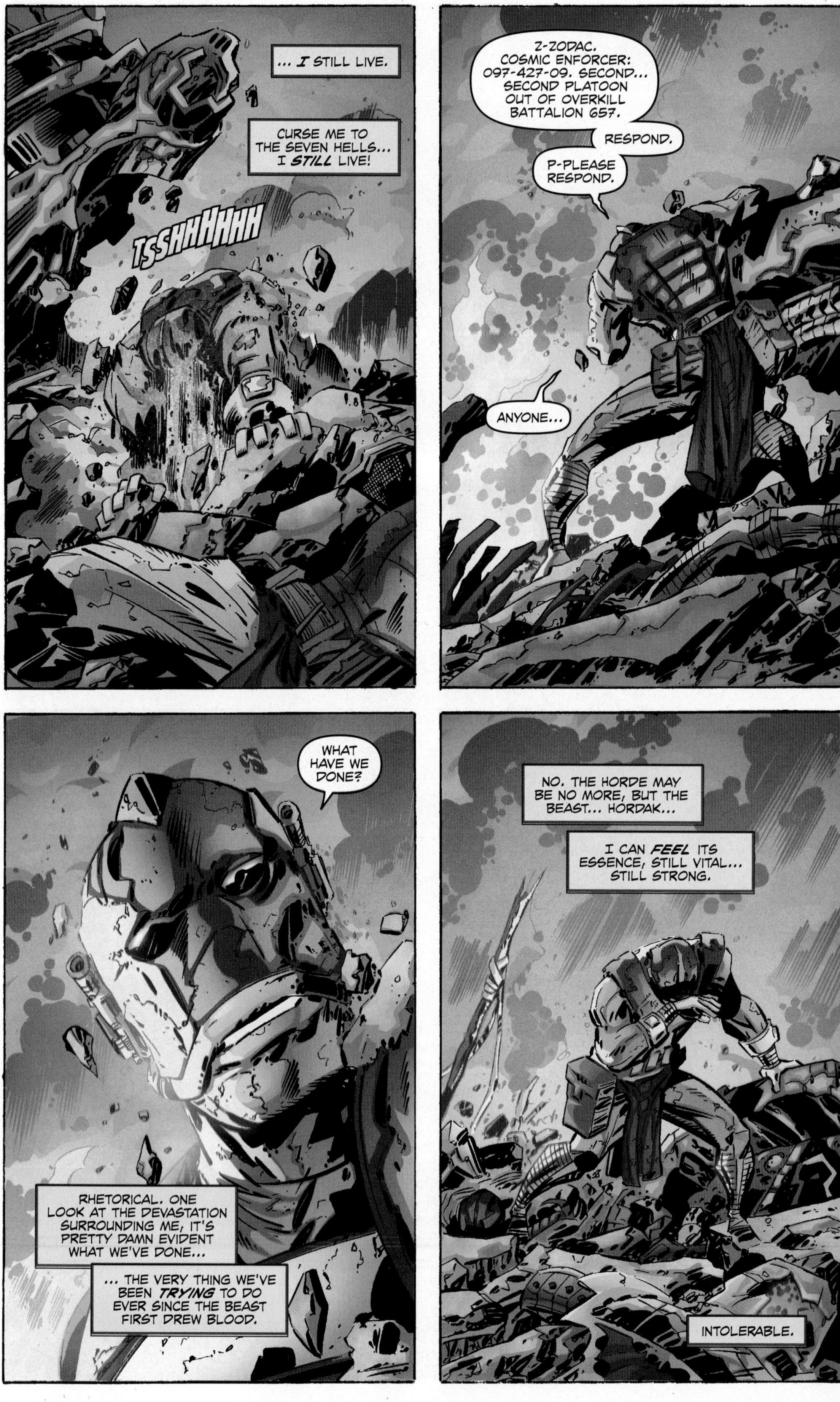

... I STILL LIVE.
CURSE ME TO THE SEVEN HELLS... I STILL LIVE!
TSSHHHHHH
Z-ZODAC. COSMIC ENFORCER: 097-427-09. SECOND... SECOND PLATOON OUT OF OVERKILL BATTALION 657.
RESPOND.
P-PLEASE RESPOND.
ANYONE...
WHAT HAVE WE DONE?
RHETORICAL. ONE LOOK AT THE DEVASTATION SURROUNDING ME, IT'S PRETTY DAMN EVIDENT WHAT WE'VE DONE...
... THE VERY THING WE'VE BEEN TRYING TO DO EVER SINCE THE BEAST FIRST DREW BLOOD.
NO. THE HORDE MAY BE NO MORE, BUT THE BEAST... HORDAK...
I CAN FEEL ITS ESSENCE, STILL VITAL... STILL STRONG.
INTOLERABLE.

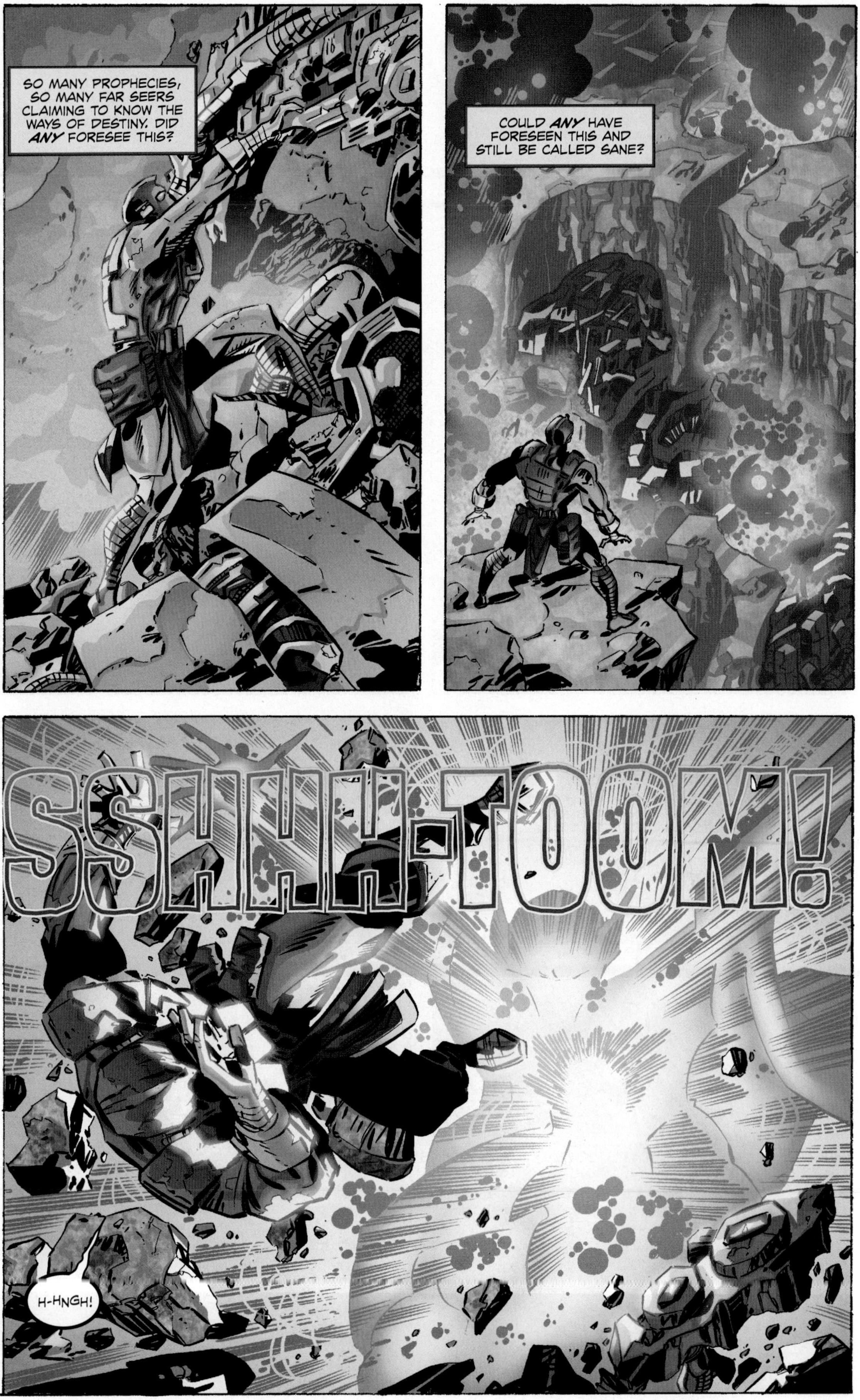
SO MANY PROPHECIES, SO MANY FAR SEERS CLAIMING TO KNOW THE WAYS OF DESTINY. DID ANY FORESEE THIS?
COULD ANY HAVE FORESEEN THIS AND STILL BE CALLED SANE?
SSHHH-TOOOM!
H-HNGH!

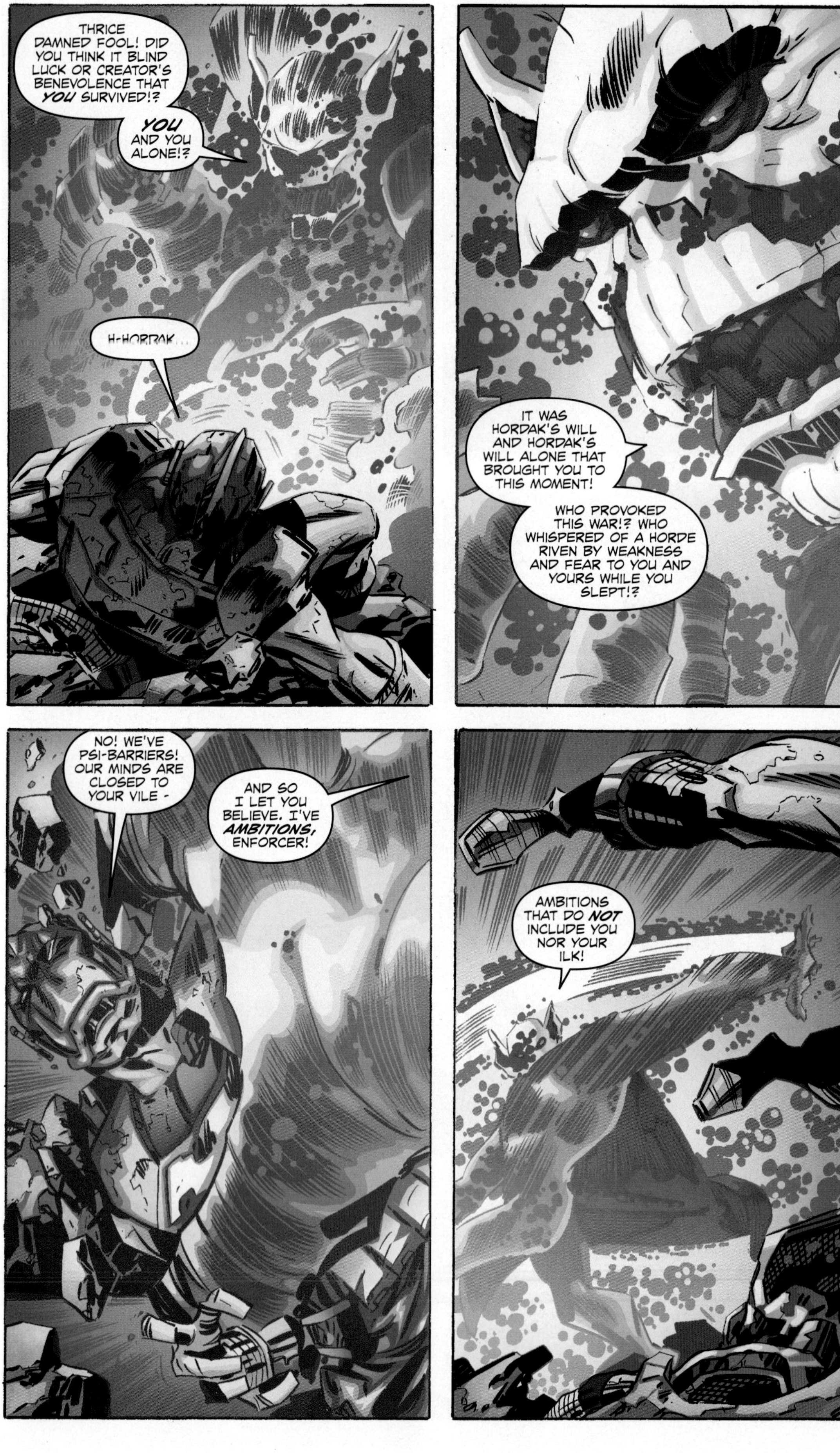
THRICE DAMNED FOOL! DID YOU THINK IT BLIND LUCK OR CREATOR'S BENEVOLENCE THAT YOU SURVIVED!?
YOU AND YOU ALONE!?
H-HORDAK...
IT WAS HORDAK'S WILL AND HORDAK'S WILL ALONE THAT BROUGHT YOU TO THIS MOMENT!
WHO PROVOKED THIS WAR!? WHO WHISPERED OF A HORDE RIVEN BY WEAKNESS AND FEAR TO YOU AND YOURS WHILE YOU SLEPT!?
NO! WE'VE PSI-BARRIERS! OUR MINDS ARE CLOSED TO YOUR VILE -
AND SO I LET YOU BELIEVE. I'VE AMBITIONS, ENFORCER!
AMBITIONS THAT DO NOT INCLUDE YOU NOR YOUR ILK!

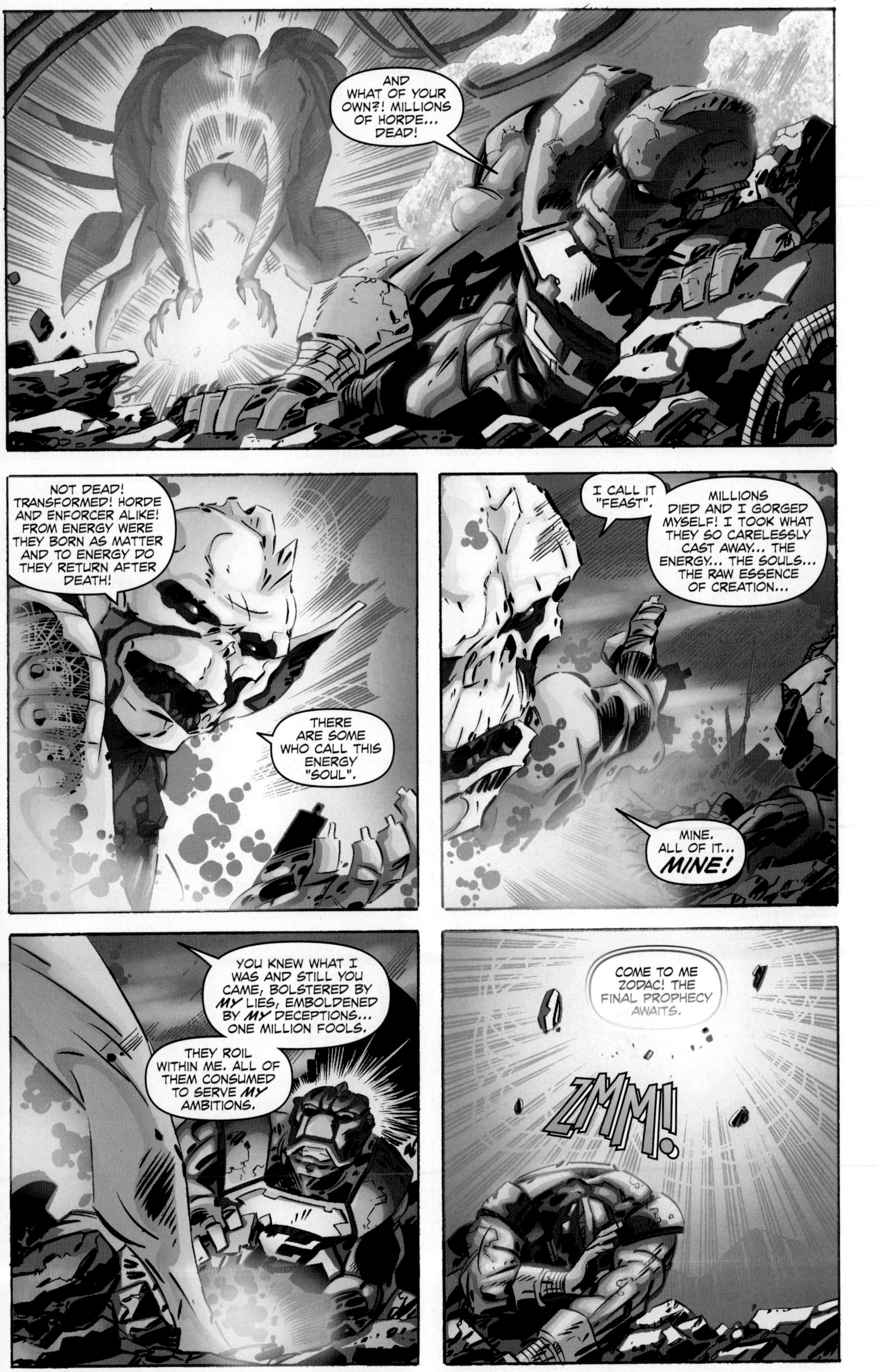
AND WHAT OF YOUR OWN?! MILLIONS OF HORDE... DEAD!
NOT DEAD! TRANSFORMED! HORDE AND ENFORCER ALIKE! FROM ENERGY WERE THEY BORN AS MATTER AND TO ENERGY DO THEY RETURN AFTER DEATH!
THERE ARE SOME WHO CALL THIS ENERGY "SOUL".
I CALL IT "FEAST".
MILLIONS DIED AND I GORGED MYSELF! I TOOK WHAT THEY SO CARELESSLY CAST AWAY... THE ENERGY... THE SOULS... THE RAW ESSENCE OF CREATION...
MINE. ALL OF IT... MINE!
YOU KNEW WHAT I WAS AND STILL YOU CAME, BOLSTERED BY MY LIES, EMBOLDENED BY MY DECEPTIONS... ONE MILLION FOOLS.
THEY ROIL WITHIN ME. ALL OF THEM CONSUMED TO SERVE MY AMBITIONS.
COME TO ME ZODAC! THE FINAL PROPHECY AWAITS.
ZMM!

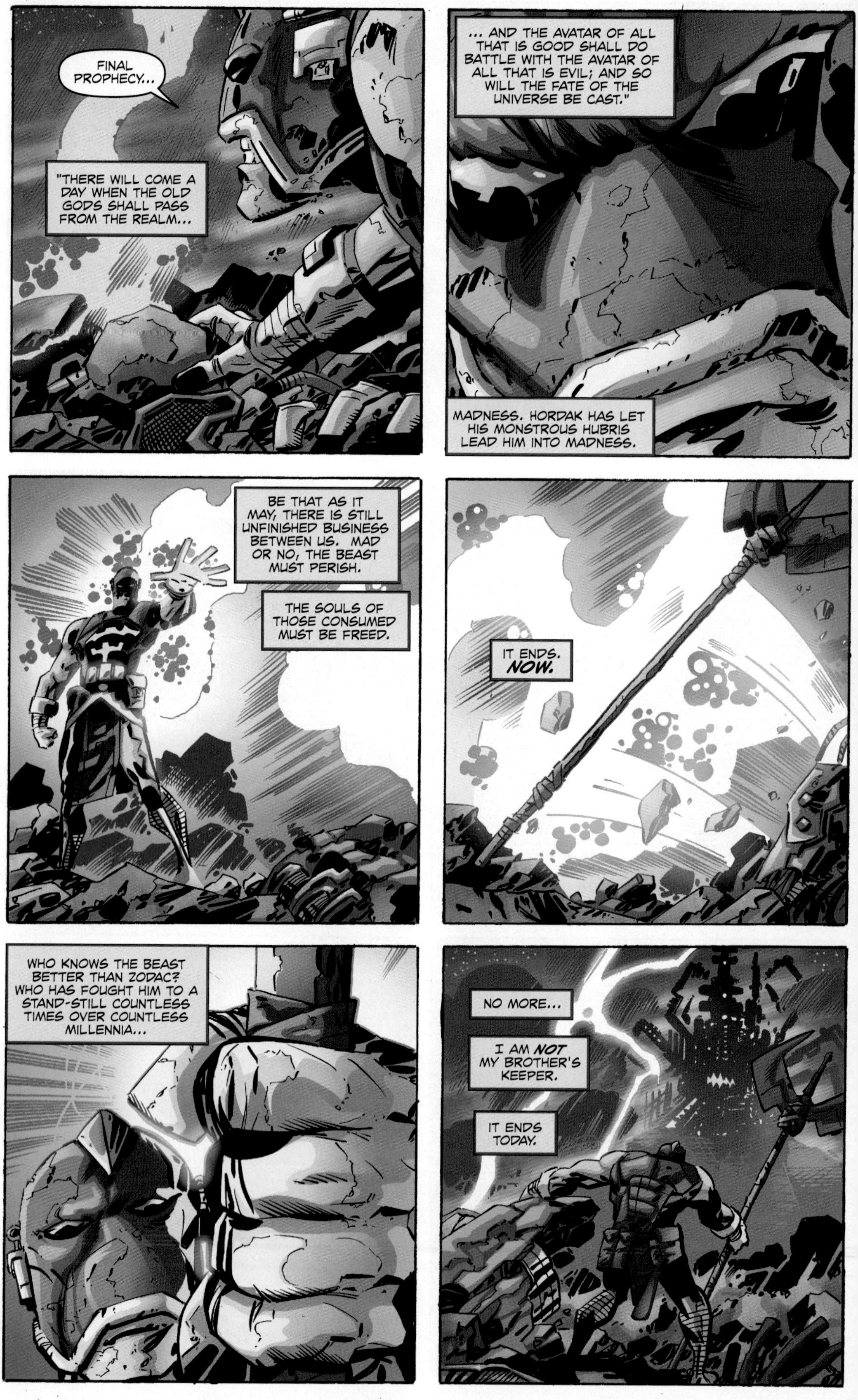
FINAL PROPHECY...
"THERE WILL COME A DAY WHEN THE OLD GODS SHALL PASS FROM THE REALM...
... AND THE AVATAR OF ALL THAT IS GOOD SHALL DO BATTLE WITH THE AVATAR OF ALL THAT IS EVIL; AND SO WILL THE FATE OF THE UNIVERSE BE CAST."
MADNESS. HORDAK HAS LET HIS MONSTROUS HUBRIS LEAD HIM INTO MADNESS.
BE THAT AS IT MAY, THERE IS STILL UNFINISHED BUSINESS BETWEEN US. MAD OR NO, THE BEAST MUST PERISH.
THE SOULS OF THOSE CONSUMED MUST BE FREED.
IT ENDS. ***NOW.***
WHO KNOWS THE BEAST BETTER THAN ZODAC? WHO HAS FOUGHT HIM TO A STAND-STILL COUNTLESS TIMES OVER COUNTLESS MILLENNIA...
NO MORE...
I AM ***NOT*** MY BROTHER'S KEEPER.
IT ENDS TODAY.

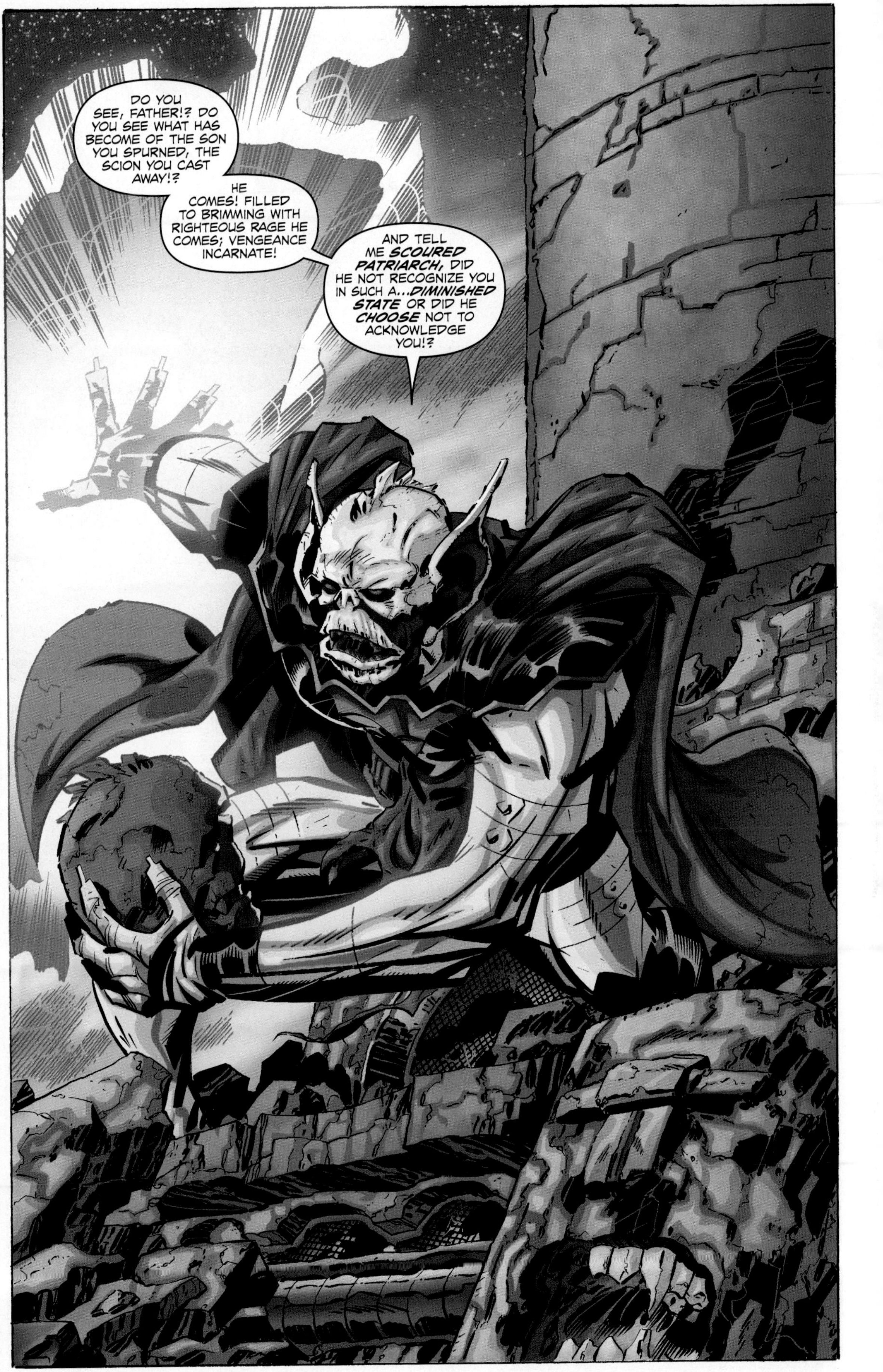
DO YOU SEE, FATHER!? DO YOU SEE WHAT HAS BECOME OF THE SON YOU SPURNED, THE SCION YOU CAST AWAY!?
HE COMES! FILLED TO BRIMMING WITH RIGHTEOUS RAGE HE COMES; VENGEANCE INCARNATE!
AND TELL ME ***SCOURED PATRIARCH,*** DID HE NOT RECOGNIZE YOU IN SUCH A...***DIMINISHED STATE*** OR DID HE ***CHOOSE*** NOT TO ACKNOWLEDGE YOU!?

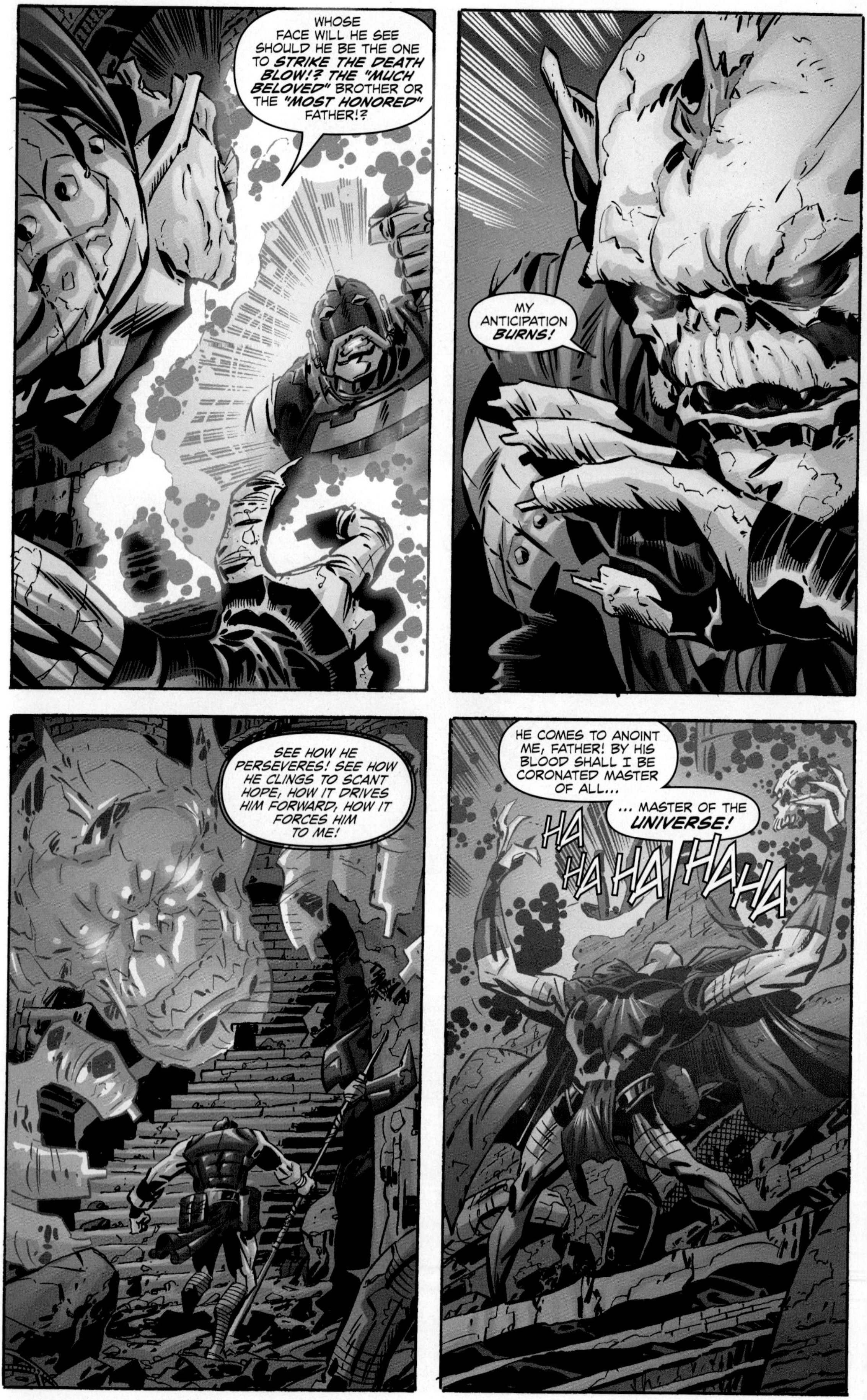
WHOSE FACE WILL HE SEE SHOULD HE BE THE ONE TO STRIKE THE DEATH BLOW!? THE "MUCH BELOVED" BROTHER OR THE "MOST HONORED" FATHER!?
MY ANTICIPATION BURNS!
SEE HOW HE PERSEVERES! SEE HOW HE CLINGS TO SCANT HOPE, HOW IT DRIVES HIM FORWARD, HOW IT FORCES HIM TO ME!
HE COMES TO ANOINT ME, FATHER! BY HIS BLOOD SHALL I BE CORONATED MASTER OF ALL...
... MASTER OF THE UNIVERSE!
HA HA HA HA HA HA

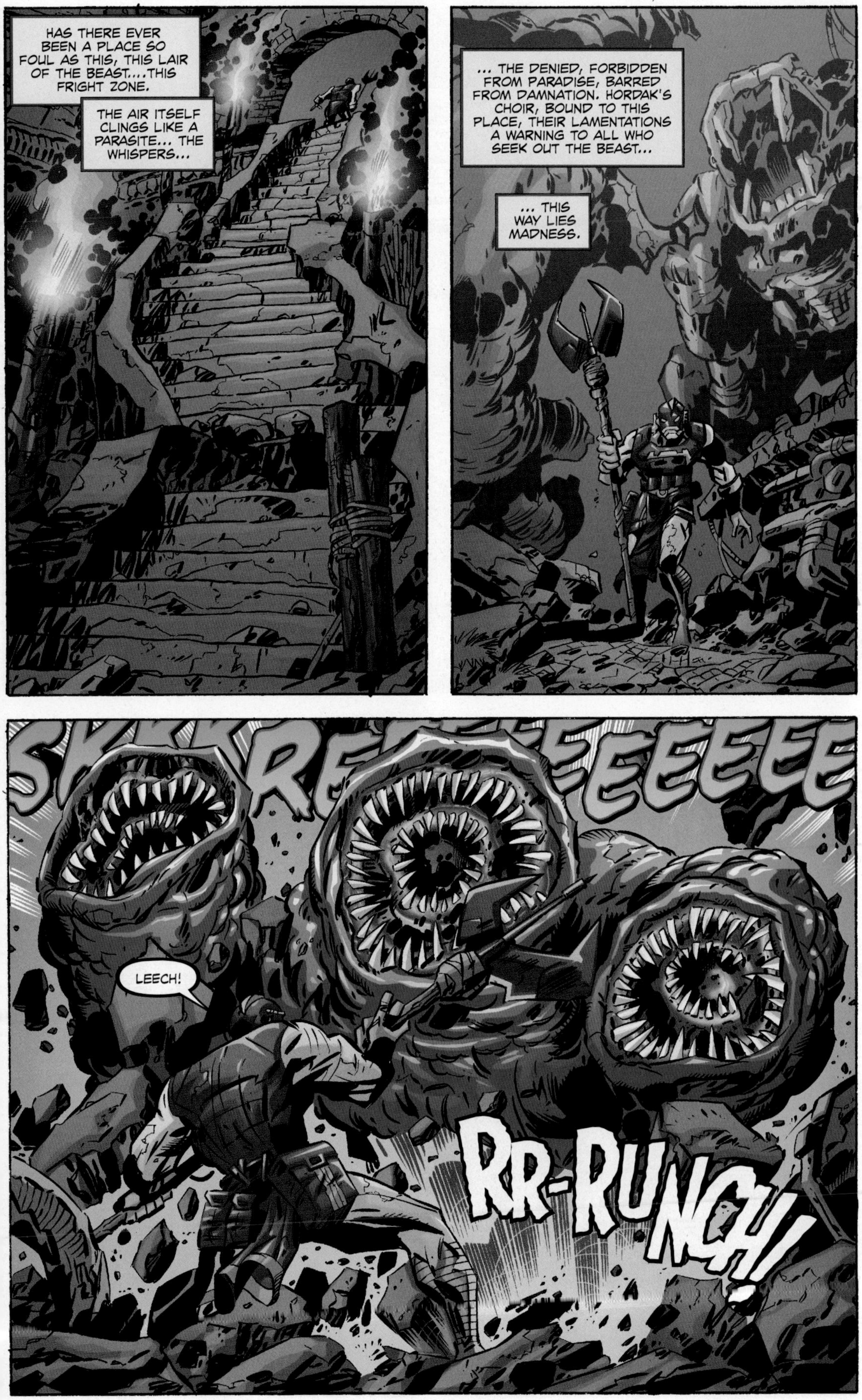
HAS THERE EVER BEEN A PLACE SO FOUL AS THIS, THIS LAIR OF THE BEAST....THIS FRIGHT ZONE.
THE AIR ITSELF CLINGS LIKE A PARASITE... THE WHISPERS...
... THE DENIED, FORBIDDEN FROM PARADISE, BARRED FROM DAMNATION. HORDAK'S CHOIR, BOUND TO THIS PLACE, THEIR LAMENTATIONS A WARNING TO ALL WHO SEEK OUT THE BEAST...
... THIS WAY LIES MADNESS.
LEECH!
RR-RUNCH!

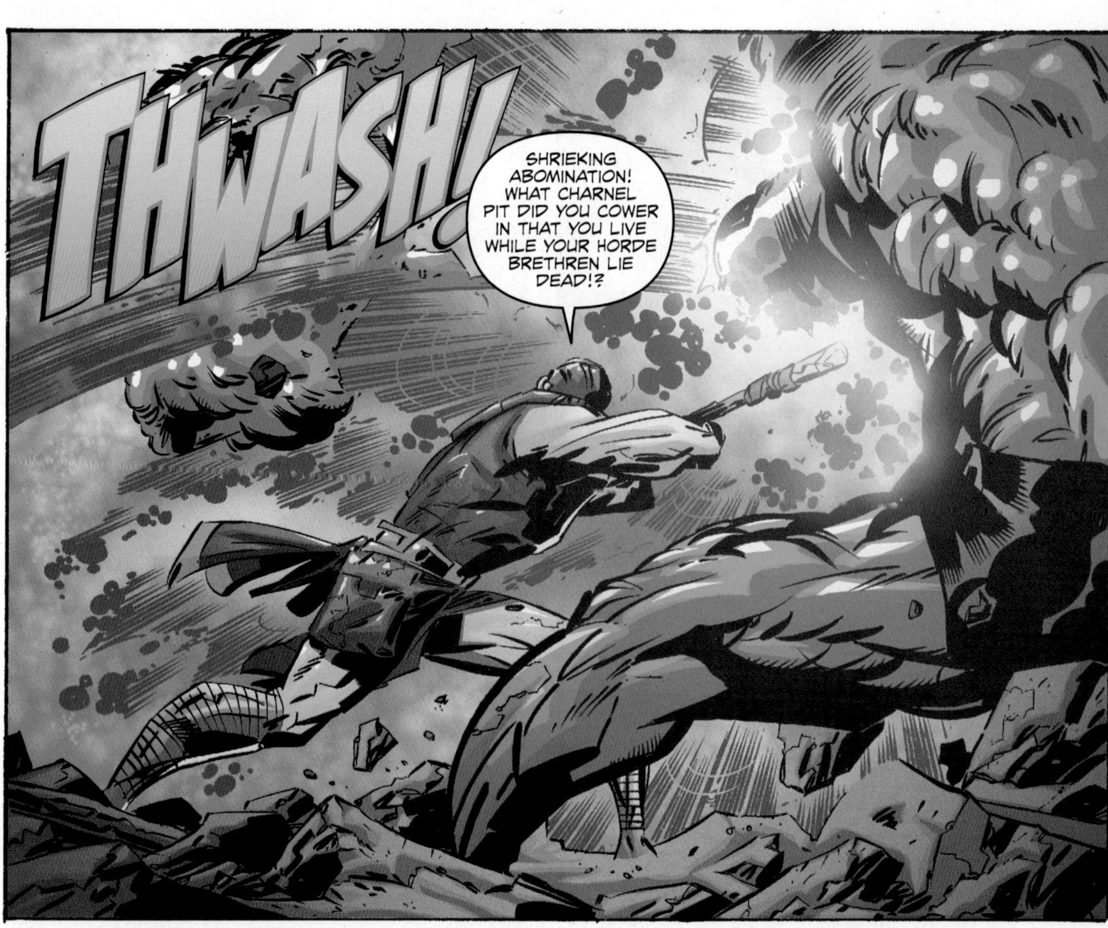
THWASH!
SHRIEKING ABOMINATION! WHAT CHARNEL PIT DID YOU COWER IN THAT YOU LIVE WHILE YOUR HORDE BRETHREN LIE DEAD!?

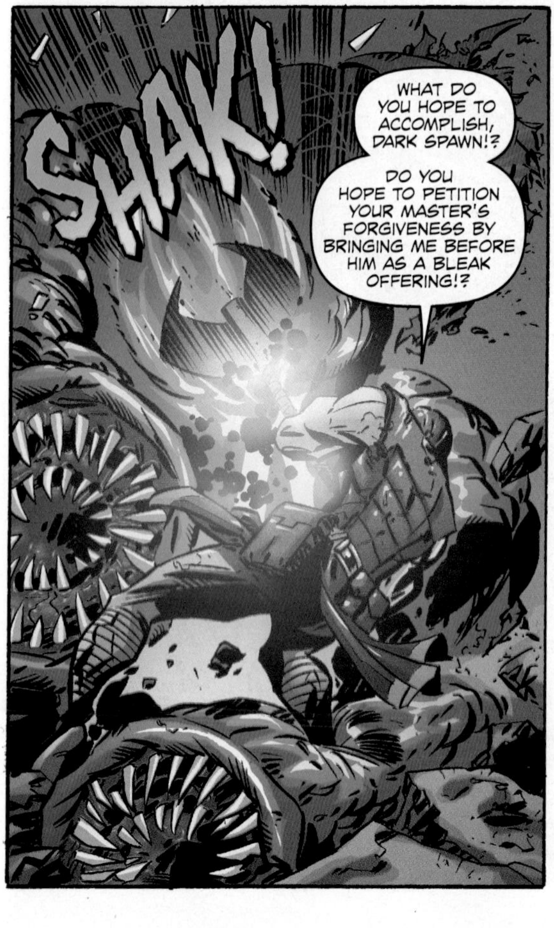
SHAK!
WHAT DO YOU HOPE TO ACCOMPLISH, DARK SPAWN!?
DO YOU HOPE TO PETITION YOUR MASTER'S FORGIVENESS BY BRINGING ME BEFORE HIM AS A BLEAK OFFERING!?

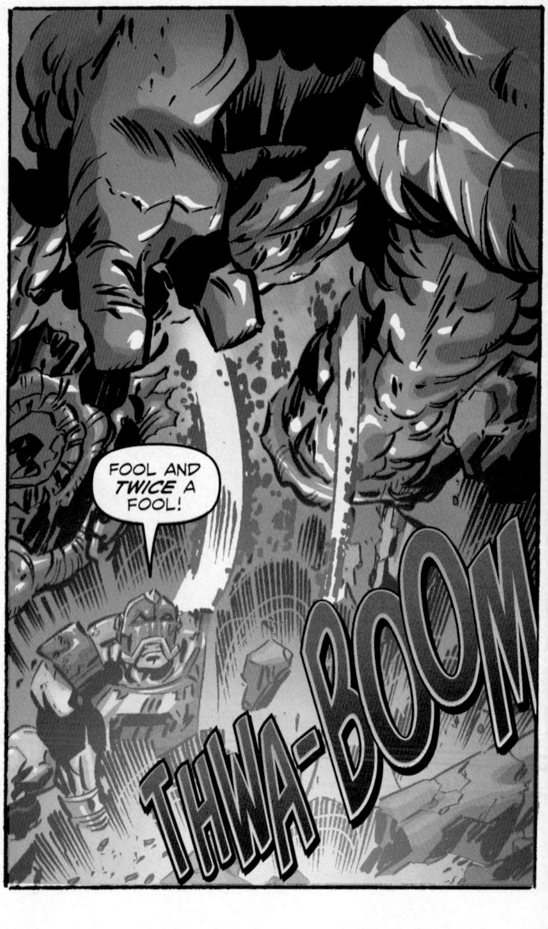
FOOL AND *TWICE* A FOOL!
THWA-BOOM

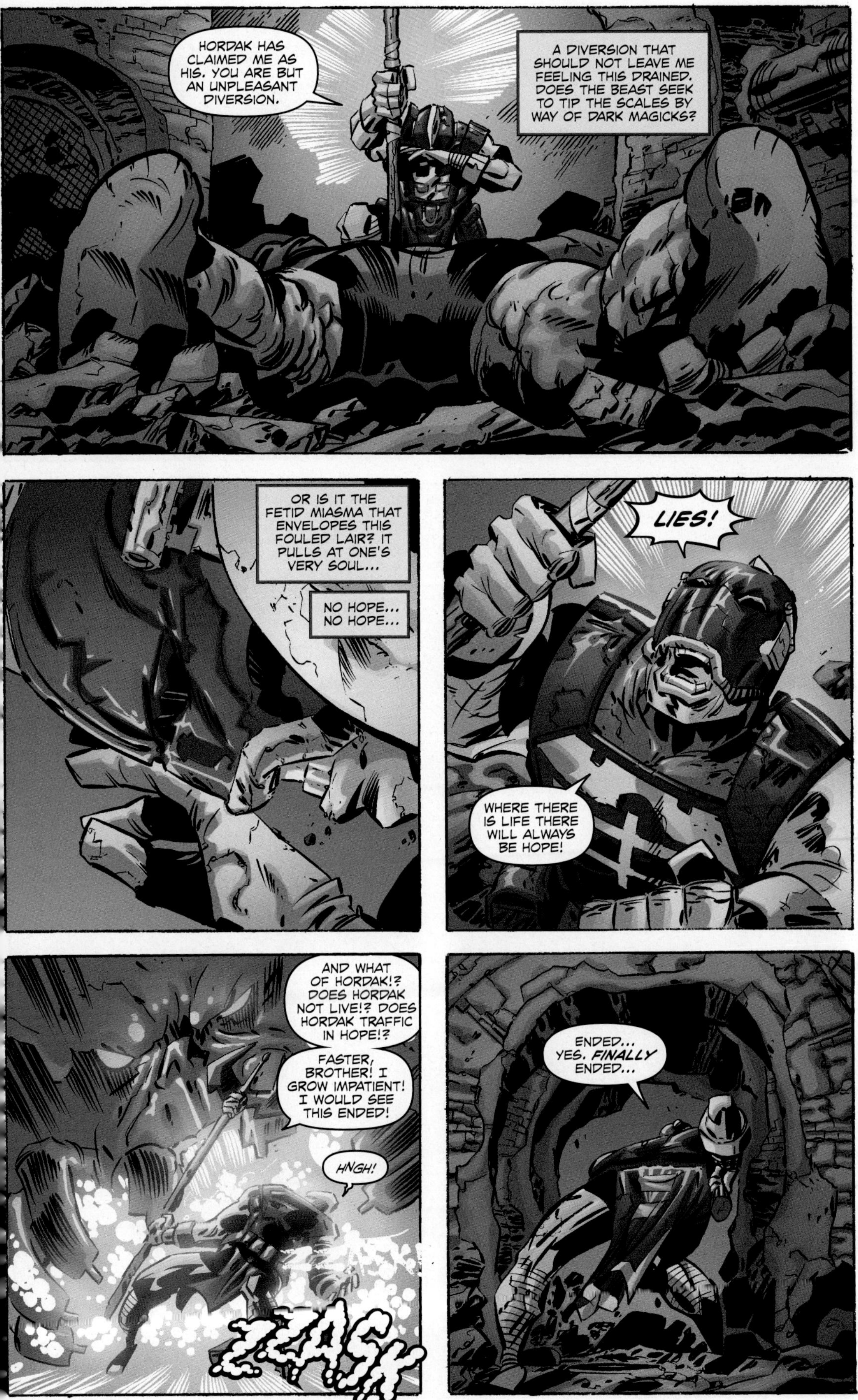
HORDAK HAS CLAIMED ME AS HIS. YOU ARE BUT AN UNPLEASANT DIVERSION.
A DIVERSION THAT SHOULD NOT LEAVE ME FEELING THIS DRAINED. DOES THE BEAST SEEK TO TIP THE SCALES BY WAY OF DARK MAGICKS?
OR IS IT THE FETID MIASMA THAT ENVELOPES THIS FOULED LAIR? IT PULLS AT ONE'S VERY SOUL...
NO HOPE... NO HOPE...
LIES!
WHERE THERE IS LIFE THERE WILL ALWAYS BE HOPE!
AND WHAT OF HORDAK!? DOES HORDAK NOT LIVE!? DOES HORDAK TRAFFIC IN HOPE!?
FASTER, BROTHER! I GROW IMPATIENT! I WOULD SEE THIS ENDED!
HNGH!
ZZASK
ENDED... YES. FINALLY ENDED...

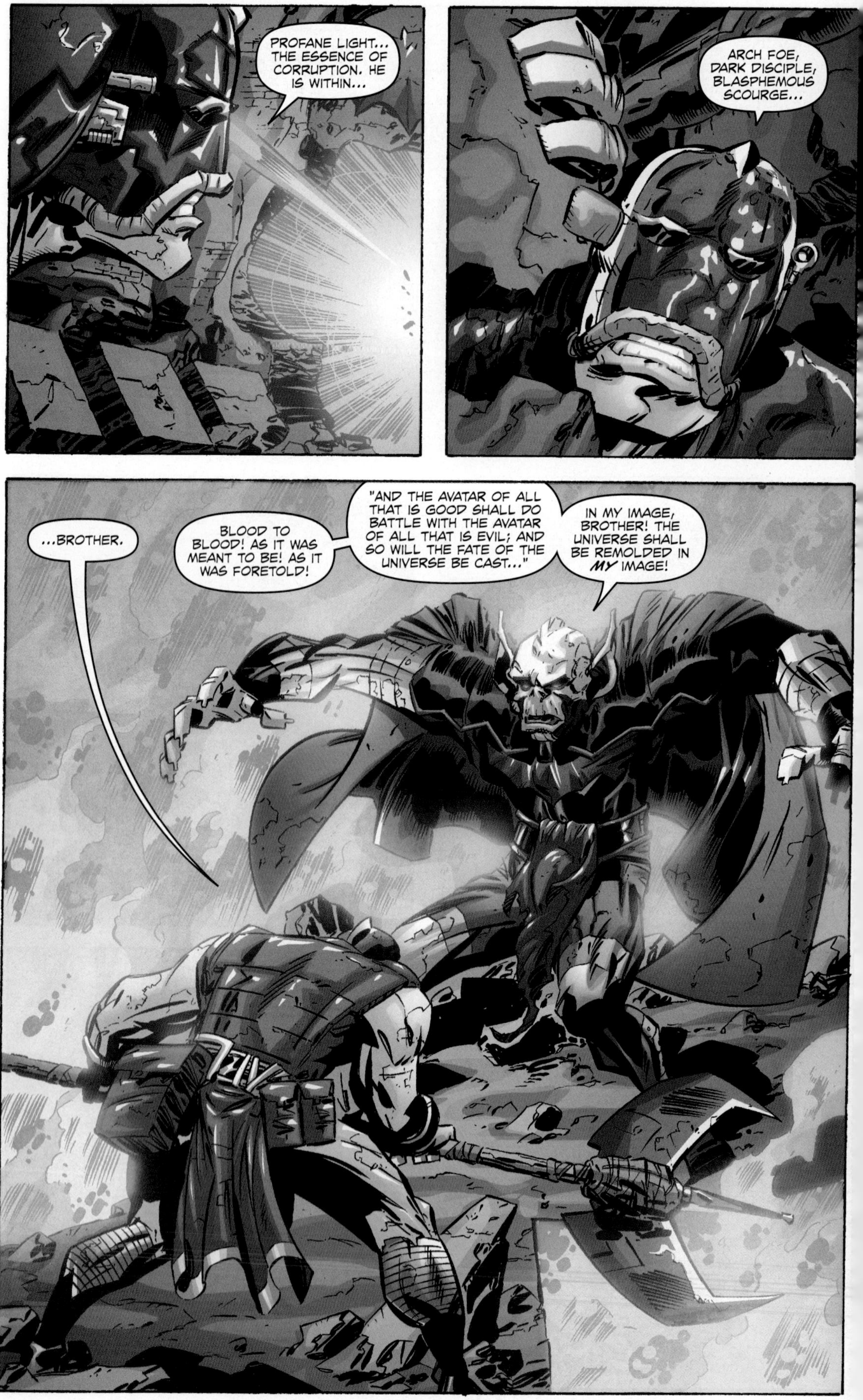
PROFANE LIGHT... THE ESSENCE OF CORRUPTION. HE IS WITHIN...
ARCH FOE, DARK DISCIPLE, BLASPHEMOUS SCOURGE...
...BROTHER.
BLOOD TO BLOOD! AS IT WAS MEANT TO BE! AS IT WAS FORETOLD!
"AND THE AVATAR OF ALL THAT IS GOOD SHALL DO BATTLE WITH THE AVATAR OF ALL THAT IS EVIL; AND SO WILL THE FATE OF THE UNIVERSE BE CAST..."
IN MY IMAGE, BROTHER! THE UNIVERSE SHALL BE REMOLDED IN MY IMAGE!

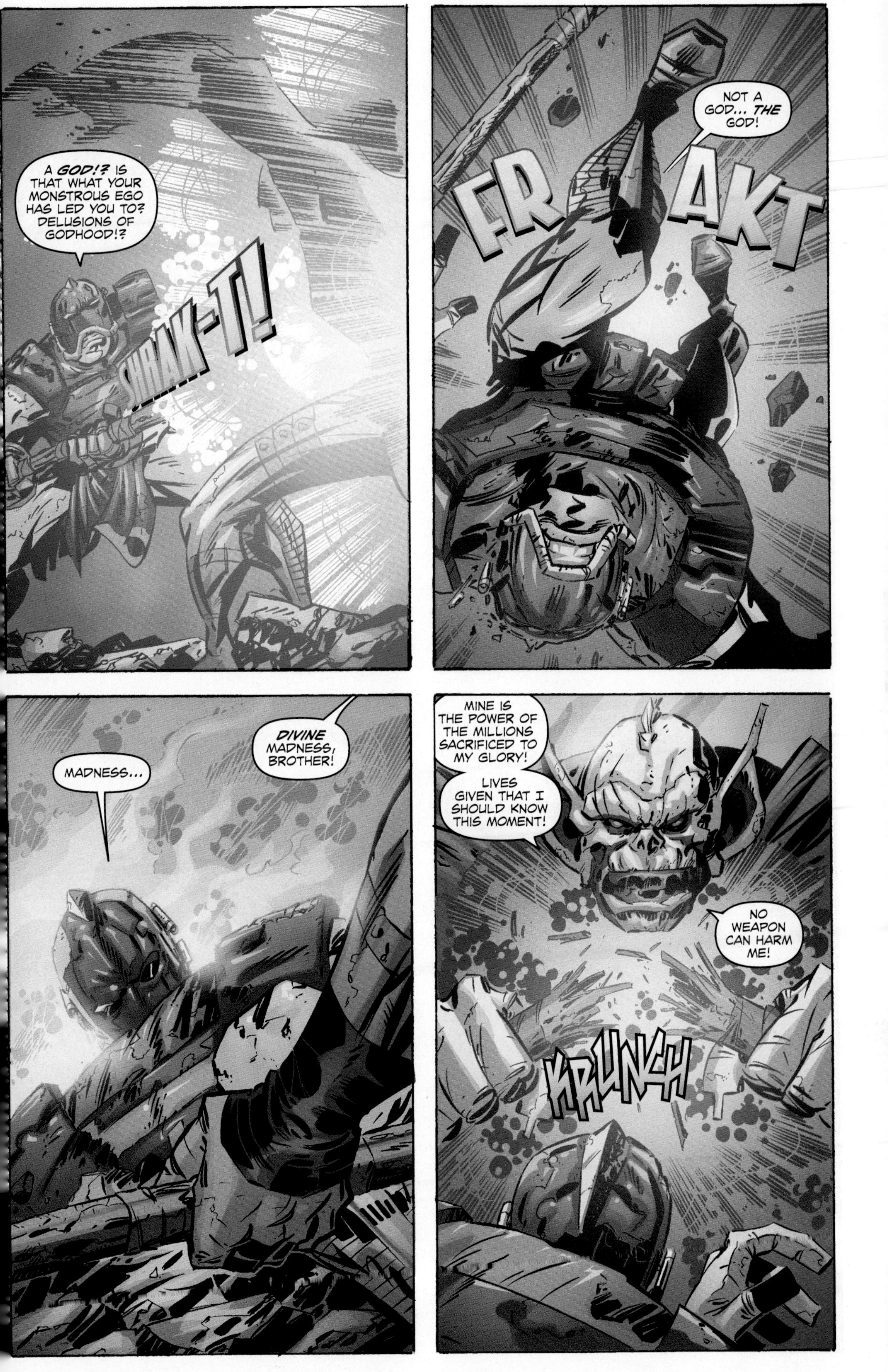
A GOD!? IS THAT WHAT YOUR MONSTROUS EGO HAS LED YOU TO? DELUSIONS OF GODHOOD!?
SHRAK-T!!
NOT A GOD... THE GOD!
FR AKT
MADNESS...
DIVINE MADNESS, BROTHER!
MINE IS THE POWER OF THE MILLIONS SACRIFICED TO MY GLORY!
LIVES GIVEN THAT I SHOULD KNOW THIS MOMENT!
NO WEAPON CAN HARM ME!
KRUNCH

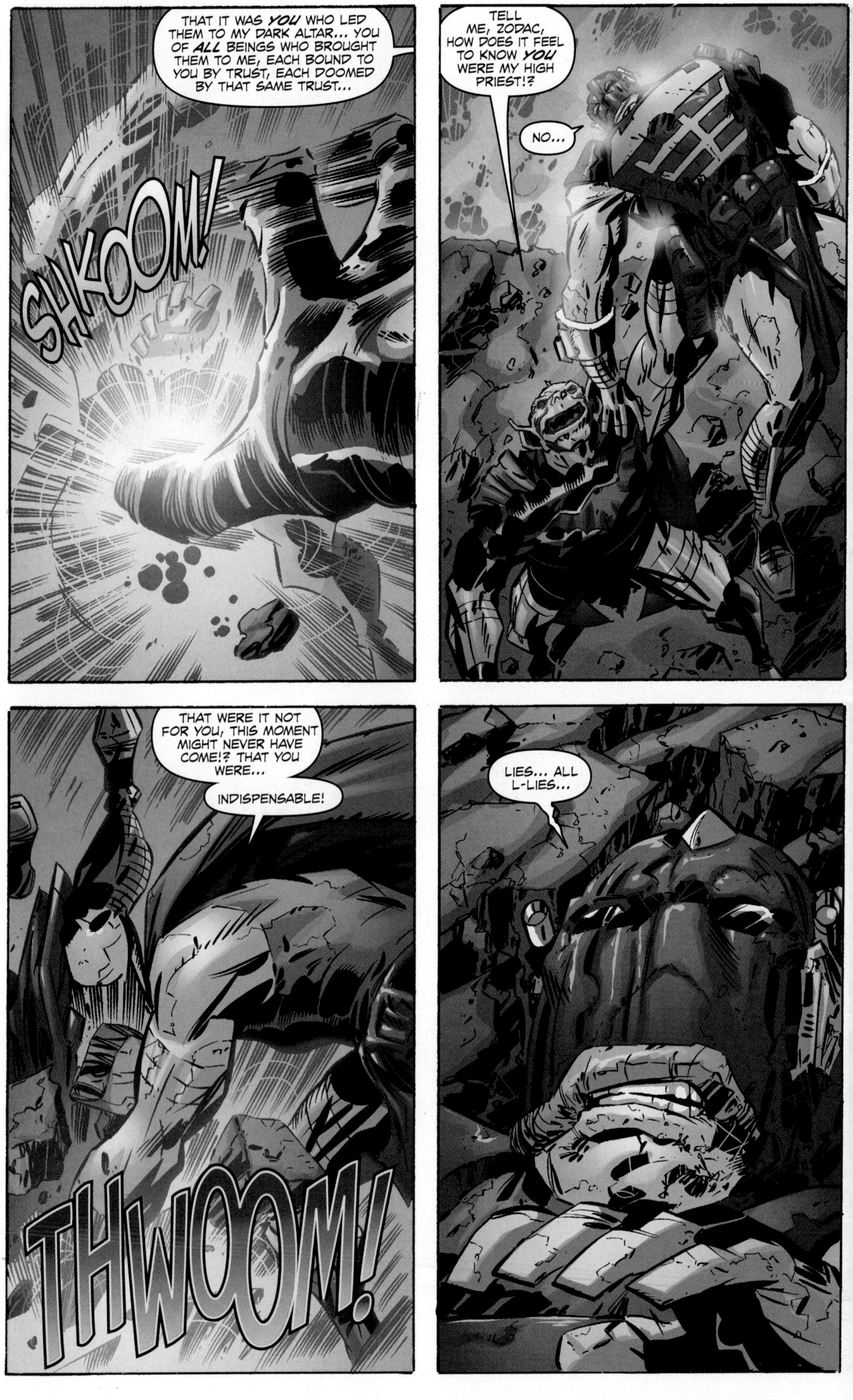
THAT IT WAS YOU WHO LED THEM TO MY DARK ALTAR... YOU OF ALL BEINGS WHO BROUGHT THEM TO ME, EACH BOUND TO YOU BY TRUST, EACH DOOMED BY THAT SAME TRUST...
SHKOOM!
TELL ME, ZODAC, HOW DOES IT FEEL TO KNOW YOU WERE MY HIGH PRIEST!?
NO...
THAT WERE IT NOT FOR YOU, THIS MOMENT MIGHT NEVER HAVE COME!? THAT YOU WERE...
INDISPENSABLE!
THWOOM!
LIES... ALL L-LIES...

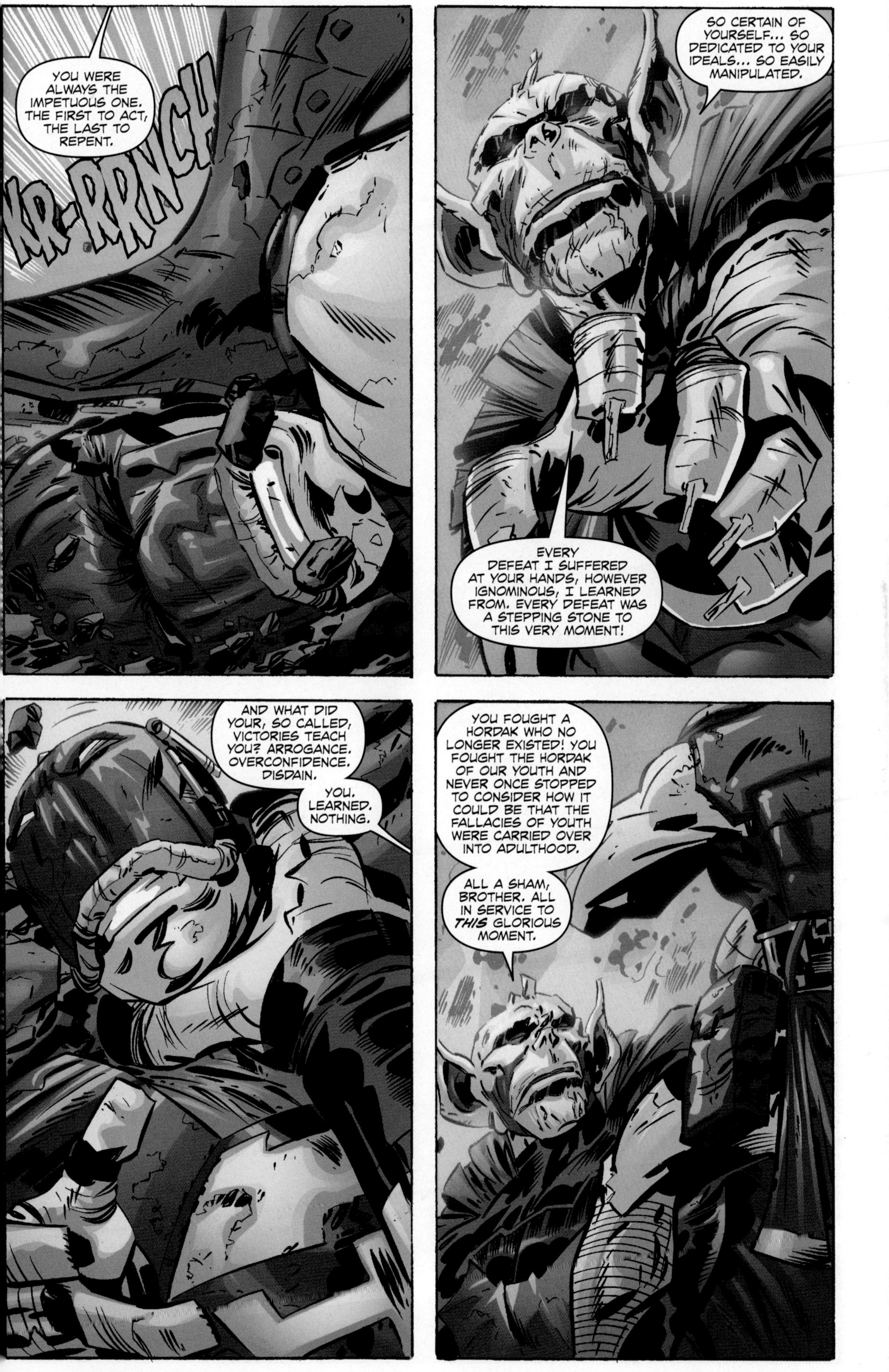
YOU WERE ALWAYS THE IMPETUOUS ONE. THE FIRST TO ACT, THE LAST TO REPENT.
KR-RRNCH
SO CERTAIN OF YOURSELF... SO DEDICATED TO YOUR IDEALS... SO EASILY MANIPULATED.
EVERY DEFEAT I SUFFERED AT YOUR HANDS, HOWEVER IGNOMINOUS, I LEARNED FROM. EVERY DEFEAT WAS A STEPPING STONE TO THIS VERY MOMENT!
AND WHAT DID YOUR, SO CALLED, VICTORIES TEACH YOU? ARROGANCE. OVERCONFIDENCE. DISDAIN.
YOU. LEARNED. NOTHING.
YOU FOUGHT A HORDAK WHO NO LONGER EXISTED! YOU FOUGHT THE HORDAK OF OUR YOUTH AND NEVER ONCE STOPPED TO CONSIDER HOW IT COULD BE THAT THE FALLACIES OF YOUTH WERE CARRIED OVER INTO ADULTHOOD.
ALL A SHAM, BROTHER. ALL IN SERVICE TO *THIS* GLORIOUS MOMENT.

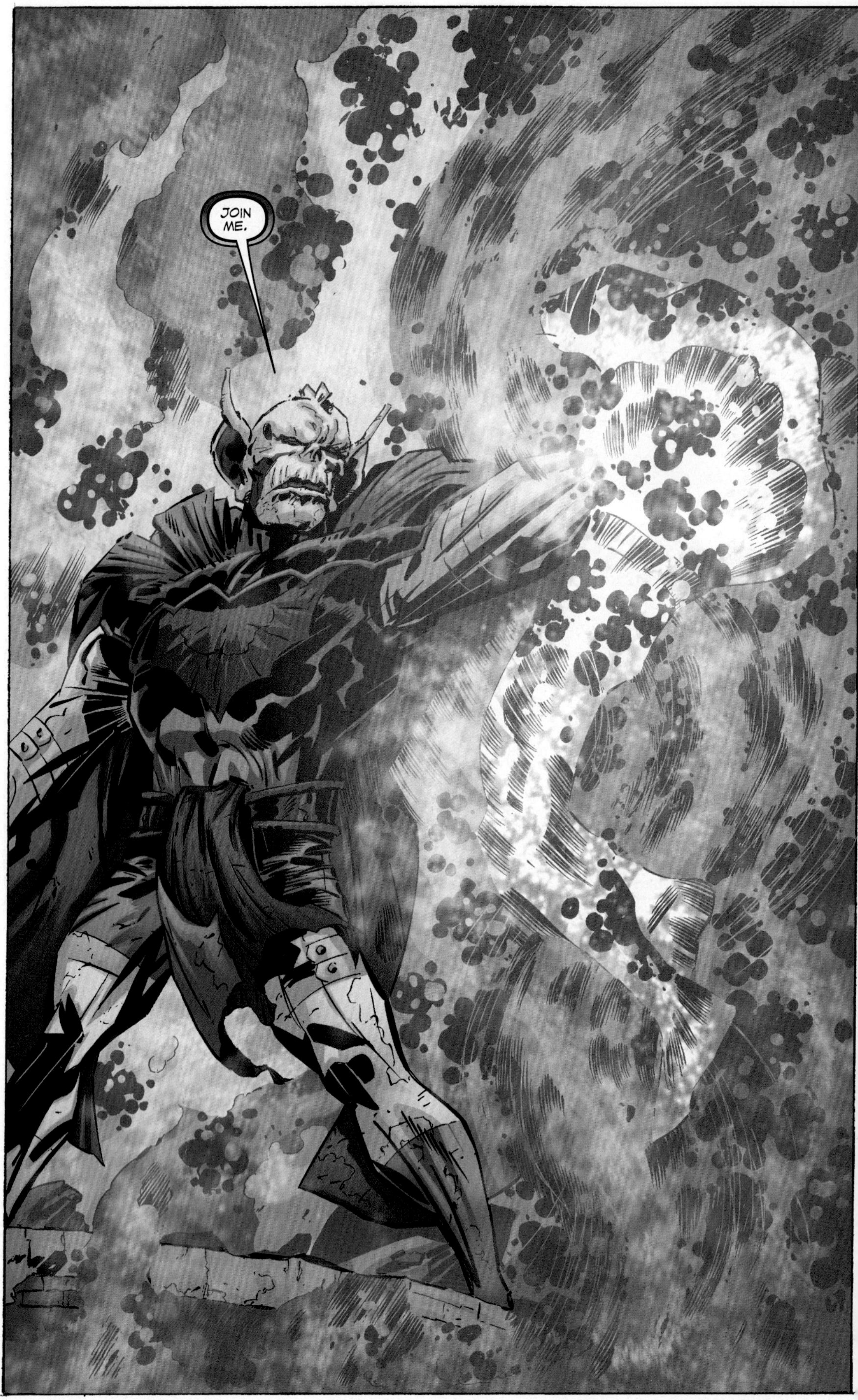
JOIN ME.

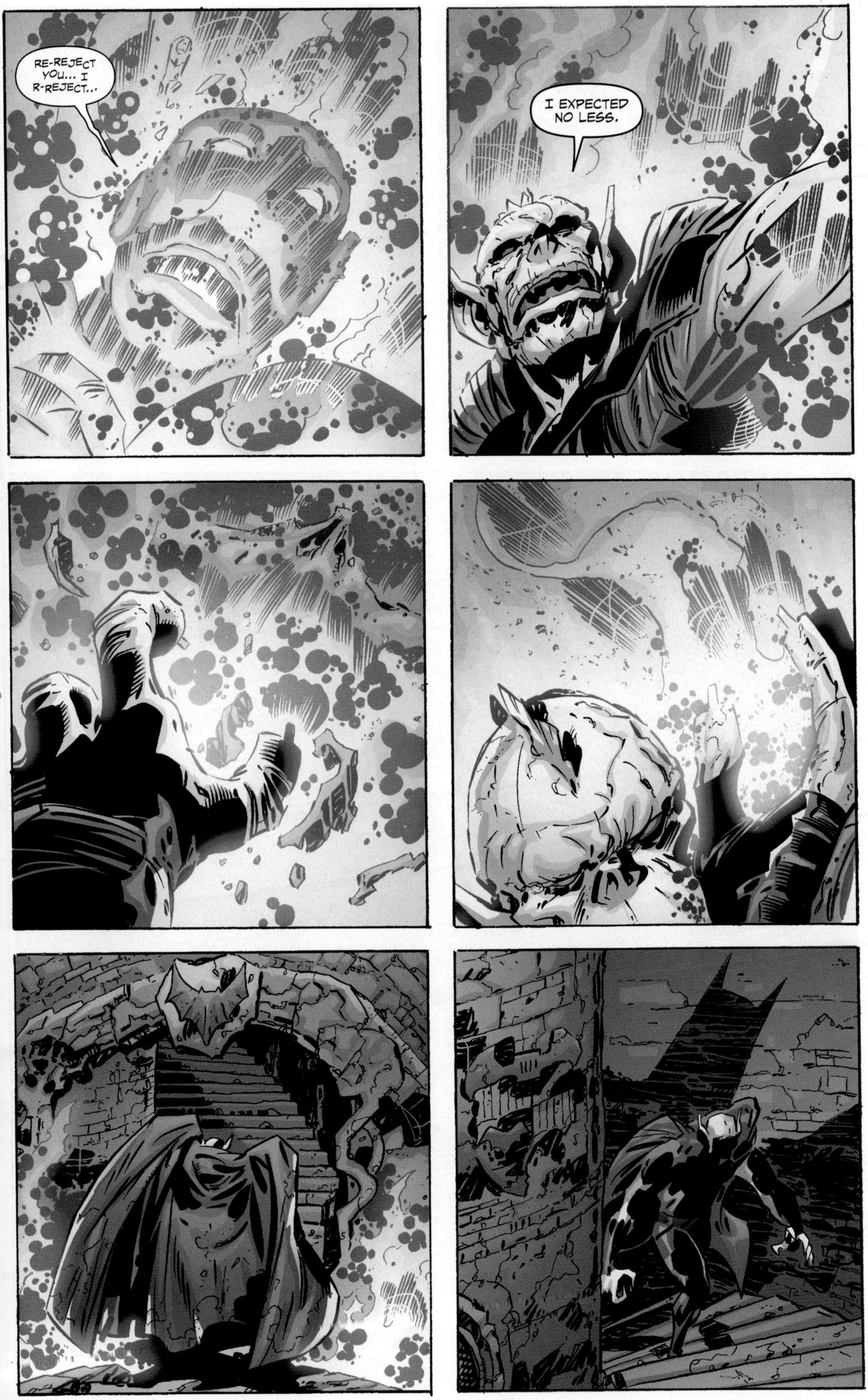
RE-REJECT YOU... I R-REJECT...
I EXPECTED NO LESS.

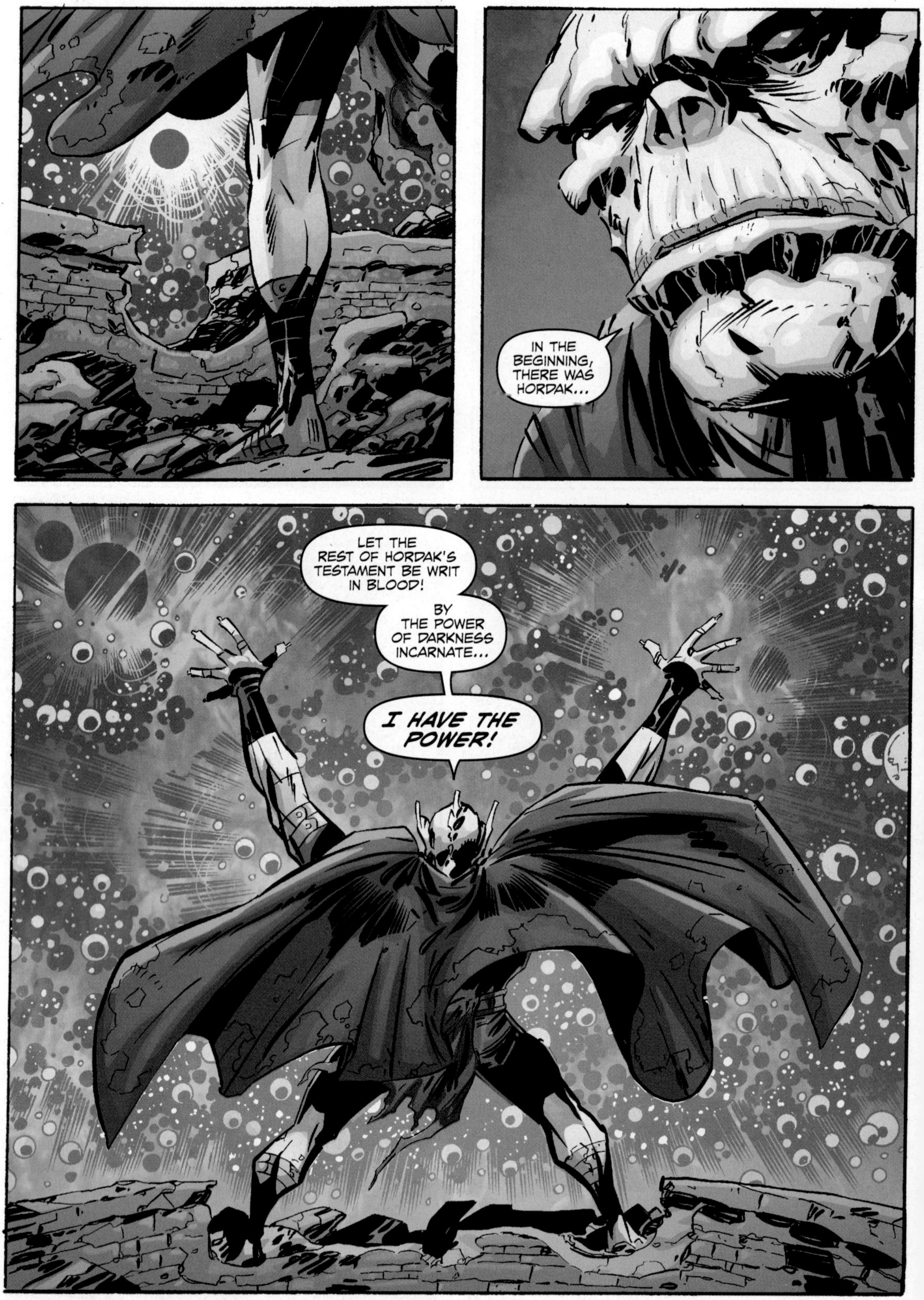
IN THE BEGINNING, THERE WAS HORDAK...
LET THE REST OF HORDAK'S TESTAMENT BE WRIT IN BLOOD!
BY THE POWER OF DARKNESS INCARNATE...
I HAVE THE POWER!

RANDOR COVER SKETCHES BY ERIC NGUYEN

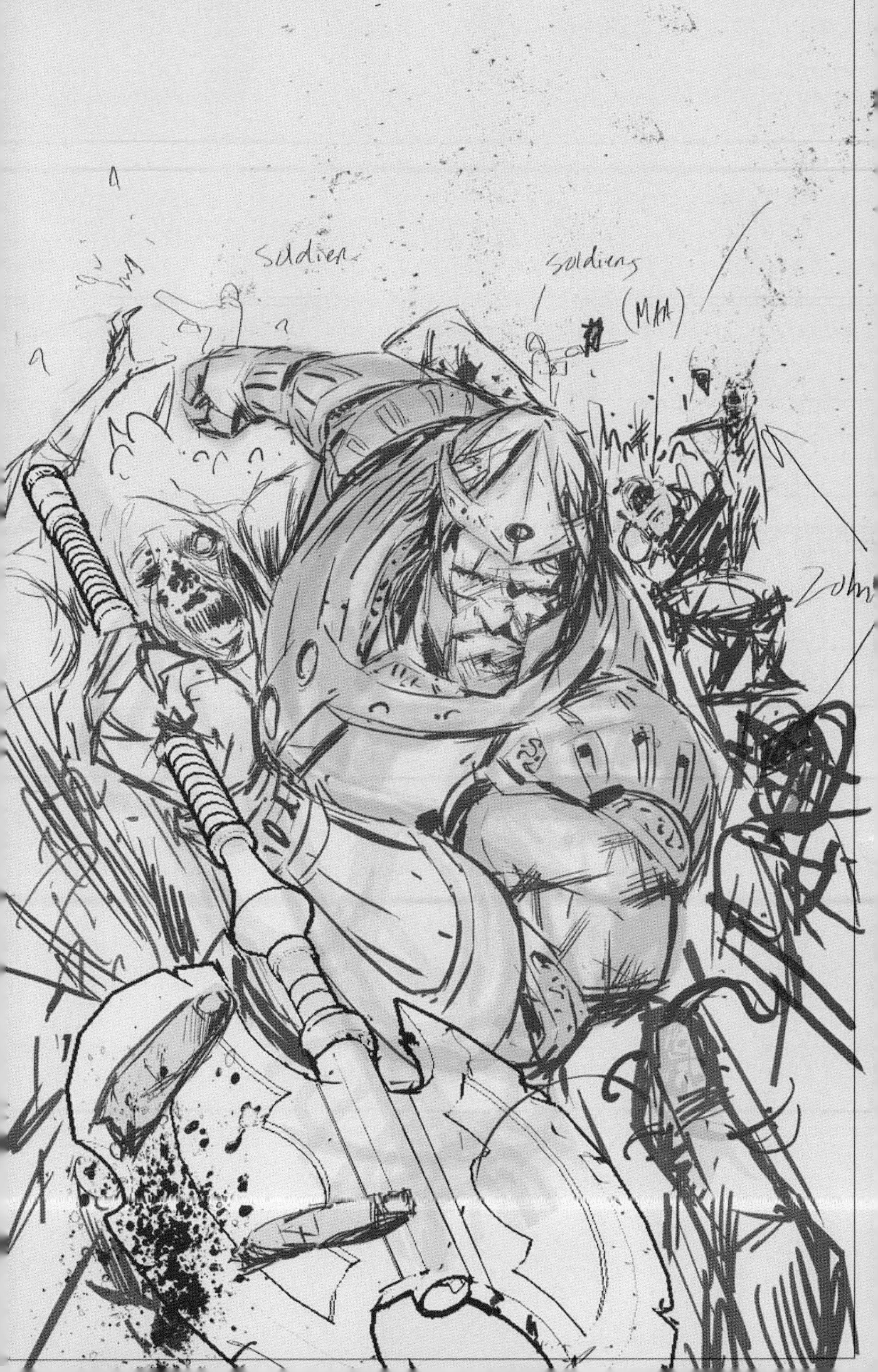
soldier
soldiers
(MAA)

RANDOR COVER SKETCHES BY ERIC NGUYEN

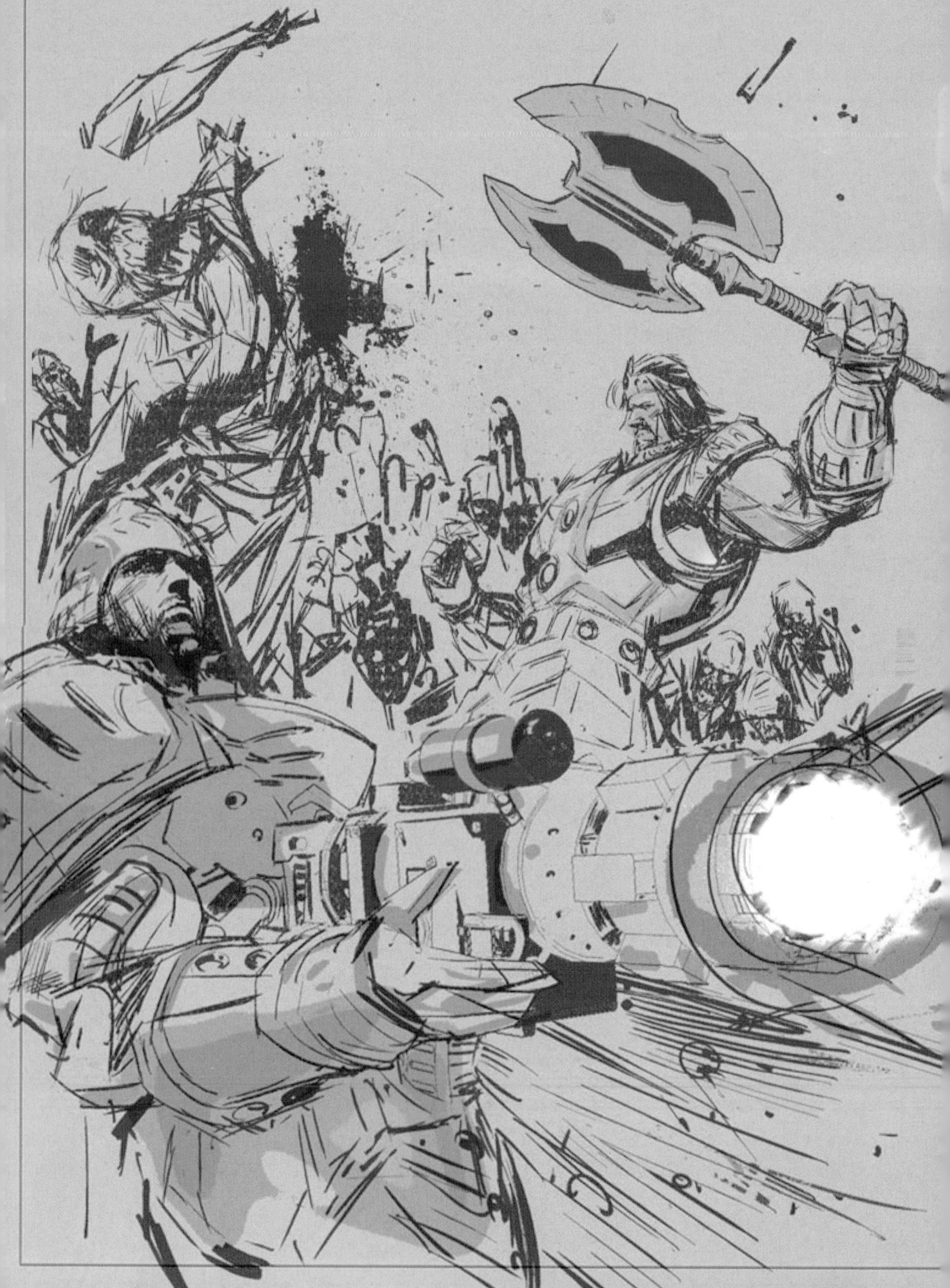